Jeanette Winterson's Narratives of Desire

New Horizons in Contemporary Writing

In the wake of unprecedented technological and social change, contemporary literature has evolved a dazzling array of new forms that traditional modes and terms of literary criticism have struggled to keep up with. *New Horizons in Contemporary Writing* presents cutting-edge research scholarship that provides new insights into this unique period of creative and critical transformation.

Series Editors:

Martin Eve and Bryan Cheyette

Editorial Board: Siân Adiseshiah (University of Lincoln, UK), Sara Blair (University of Michigan, USA), Peter Boxall (University of Sussex, UK), Robert Eaglestone (Royal Holloway, University of London, UK), Rita Felski (University of Virginia, USA), Rachael Gilmour (Queen Mary, University of London, UK), Caroline Levine (University of Wisconsin–Madison, USA), Roger Luckhurst (Birkbeck, University of London, UK), Adam Kelly (York University, UK), Antony Rowland (Manchester Metropolitan University, UK), John Schad (Lancaster University, UK), Pamela Thurschwell (University of Sussex, UK), Ted Underwood (University of Illinois at Urbana-Champaign, USA).

Volumes in the series:

Transatlantic Fictions of 9/11 and the War on Terror, Susana Araújo
Life Lines: Writing Transcultural Adoption, John McLeod
South African Literature's Russian Soul, Jeanne-Marie Jackson
The Politics of Jewishness in Contemporary World Literature, Isabelle Hesse
Writing After Postcolonialism: Francophone North African Literature in Transition, Jane Hiddleston
David Mitchell's Post-Secular World, Rose Harris-Birtill
New Media and the Transformation of Postmodern American Literature, Casey Michael Henry
Postcolonialism After World Literature, Lorna Burns
Jonathan Lethem and the Galaxy of Writing, Joseph Brooker
The Contemporary Post-Apocalyptic Novel, Diletta De Cristofaro
David Foster Wallace's Toxic Sexuality, Edward Jackson

Forthcoming volumes:

Northern Irish Writing After the Troubles, Caroline Magennis
Thomas Pynchon and the Digital Humanities, Erik Ketzam
Music, Religion, and Society in the Writings of Ian McEwan: Creaturely Forms in Contemporary Literature, Dominic O'Key
Encyclopaedism and Totality in Contemporary Fiction, Kiron Ward

Jeanette Winterson's Narratives of Desire

Rethinking Fetishism

Shareena Z. Hamzah-Osbourne

BLOOMSBURY ACADEMIC
LONDON • NEW YORK • OXFORD • NEW DELHI • SYDNEY

BLOOMSBURY ACADEMIC
Bloomsbury Publishing Plc
50 Bedford Square, London, WC1B 3DP, UK
1385 Broadway, New York, NY 10018, USA
29 Earlsfort Terrace, Dublin 2, Ireland

BLOOMSBURY, BLOOMSBURY ACADEMIC and the Diana logo are trademarks of
Bloomsbury Publishing Plc

First published in Great Britain 2021
This paperback edition published 2023

Copyright © Shareena Z. Hamzah-Osbourne, 2021

Shareena Z. Hamzah-Osbourne has asserted her right under the Copyright,
Designs and Patents Act, 1988, to be identified as Author of this work.

For legal purposes the Acknowledgements on p. vi constitute an extension
of this copyright page.

Cover design: Namkwan Cho
Cover images © Getty Images / Shutterstock.com

All rights reserved. No part of this publication may be reproduced or transmitted
in any form or by any means, electronic or mechanical, including photocopying,
recording, or any information storage or retrieval system, without prior
permission in writing from the publishers.

Bloomsbury Publishing Plc does not have any control over, or responsibility for, any
third-party websites referred to or in this book. All internet addresses given in this
book were correct at the time of going to press. The author and publisher regret any
inconvenience caused if addresses have changed or sites have ceased to exist,
but can accept no responsibility for any such changes.

A catalogue record for this book is available from the British Library.

A catalog record for this book is available from the Library of Congress.

ISBN: HB: 978-1-3501-7803-8
PB: 978-1-3502-2900-6
ePDF: 978-1-3501-7804-5
eBook: 978-1-3501-7805-2

Series: New Horizons in Contemporary Writing

Typeset by Deanta Global Publishing Services, Chennai, India

To find out more about our authors and books visit www.bloomsbury.com and
sign up for our newsletters.

Contents

Acknowledgements — vi

Introduction — 1

Part I Bodily fetishism — 29
  1 Fetishistic desire: Versatile bodies — 33
  2 Fetishistic touch: Space and time — 47
  3 Fetishistic imagination: Body and memory — 64

Part II Food fetishism — 79
  4 Fluid fruits — 83
  5 Meat as power — 90
  6 The boundaries of food — 100
  7 The sexual politics of food — 110

Part III Sexual fetishism — 121
  8 The extended boundaries: Pleasure and pain — 127
  9 The fetishistic phallus: Elongated objects — 152
  10 Soft fetishes: Membranes and senses — 160
Conclusion — 168

Appendix — 179
Notes — 181
Bibliography — 203
Index — 212

Acknowledgements

I thank all at Bloomsbury Academic and the series editors for *New Horizons in Contemporary Literature*, Bryan Cheyette and Martin Paul Eve, for their interest in publishing this book. I would also like to thank Lucy Brown for all her hard work and Ben Doyle, who encouraged me from the very start. My thanks also go to the reviewers who provided useful feedback.

I particularly wish to extend my gratitude to Jeanette Winterson for permitting the use of the interview material and for writing all the books that made me want to read them and then write about them.

This project leads on from my doctoral research at Swansea University, so thanks also go to all my colleagues there in the English Literature & Creative Writing department for their kindness and support: Professor Kirsti Bohata and Professor Daniel Williams for the office space in CREW room; my supervisors Dr Steve Vine, Dr Sarah Gamble and Dr Brigid Haines; and also to my examiners Prof Caroline Franklin and Dr Sonya Andermahr. Too many to mention, but thanks also to Dr Rob Penhallurick.

Finally, thanks to Dr Adrian Osbourne for his support, motivation and the discussions we have had all these years. My intellectual journey would be less beautiful without him.

Introduction

This book seeks to investigate the striking depictions of obsession, loss and substitution in Jeanette Winterson's fiction, which reveal what I term an 'alternative fetishism' running throughout her work. Language is the driver of fetishization in Winterson's texts as it performs the functions of masking, working through and healing the trauma of loss that infuses her writing. As her fictional version of Mary Shelley contends in *Frankissstein*, 'without language, or before language, the mind cannot comfort itself. And yet it is the language of our thoughts that tortures us more than any excess or deprivation of nature.'[1] The processes of fixation and replacement portrayed in her books indicate an alternative conceptualization of fetishism as a beneficial practice, at variance with prevailing psychoanalytical theories that tend to regard the practice as negative and injurious. The mechanisms and functions of this alternative fetishism are produced and expressed through Winterson's distinctive use of the language of obsession and repetition; this study identifies and discusses the body, food and sex as prominent fetish objects in her works to illustrate the centrality of fetishistic practice to daily life.

Winterson is an award-winning contemporary British writer and an influential figure in English-language literature, who has been described as 'one of the most gifted writers working today'.[2] Her writing strives to unlock the potency of words and to create an energetic literary space in which language has agency. She proposes that 'if we admit that language has power over us, not only through what it says but also through what it is, we will be tolerant of literary experiment just as we are tolerant of scientific experiment'.[3] Winterson considers language to be a 'fabulous tool that human beings have refined over so many centuries into this extremely sensitive instrument', and she has never confined herself to writing in any one genre; remarkably, thus far, she has written over twenty books, including autobiographical fiction, historiographic metafiction, sci-fi, non-fiction and children's novels.[4] As she says, 'I like to set myself challenges.'[5] Further proof of her endeavours to stretch herself as a writer came in 2015, when publishers Hogarth Shakespeare asked her to pick any one of Shakespeare's plays to adapt as a novel. Winterson chose *The Winter's Tale*, 'one of Shakespeare's most problematic plays', due to its unsettling mix of psychological drama and comedy.[6] Throughout her writing, Winterson's adoration of linguistic production has become a fetishistic act, an obsession with perfecting a literary language that produces multiple meanings, expresses diverse values and presents distinctive interpretations of the drives behind human behaviour.

The waves of fetishism

'Fetishism' is the key term in this study because, among other associations, it indicates a higher order of significance than 'obsession'. Fetishism brings with it the fact that the original – now lost – object of desire has been replaced with a substitute, which is not necessarily the case with obsession. This substitution allows anyone to fetishize and offers the possibility of it being a beneficial practice. In addition, Winterson's treatment of desire in her novels is often magical and ritualistic. Therefore, the religious and supernatural aspects of fetishism make it the most productive way to evaluate Winterson's work. The fetishism in her novels is alternative due to its fundamental fluidity and utility; it operates beyond deeply entrenched Freudian concepts, as well as more recent and expansive investigations, to produce a daily practice that is not necessarily negative or pathological. At all times, language is the primary medium of the production and transmission of fetishism in Winterson's writing, providing the powerful specificity of the fetish objects – the body, food and sex – in her reconceptualization of orthodox and normative notions of fetishism.

What I term here 'first-wave fetishism' signifies the psychoanalytical discourse generated by Sigmund Freud. In Freud's view, fetishism was a pathological, psychologically damaging operation, practised solely by men. He believed the fetish object was a penis substitute, created in response to the castration anxiety that occurs when a boy realizes his mother does not have a penis. Jacques Lacan's work advanced first-wave fetishism, but his theorizing still struggles to escape the rigid gender roles delineated by Freud (as discussed further). Rather, the matrifocal repositioning of psychoanalysis performed by Melanie Klein forms a bridge to what I call 'second-wave fetishism', a term that denotes the more recent studies that have posited women as active practitioners, rather than just passive objects, of fetishism. For Klein, fetishism is defined through her elaboration of Freudian sexuality theories, particularly the mother–child relationship in the early stage of a child's mental development. She observed that a boy, 'when he finds himself impelled to abandon the oral and anal positions for the genital, passes on to the aim of penetration', while in girls, 'the receptive aim is carried over from the oral to the genital position'.[7] This suggests that both males and females are able to fetishize, especially in the sense that the 'early connection between the epistemophilic impulse and sadism is very important for the whole mental development'.[8] Thus, fetishism is part of each individual's development, regardless of their gender or sexuality. Although much of Klein's work predates Lacan, her divergent perspective on the drives behind female psychosexual behaviour prepared the ground more fruitfully for second-wave fetishism, which reached a critical peak with Lorraine Gamman and Merja Makinen's *Female Fetishism: A New Look* in 1994. There followed increased scholarly activity around female and lesbian fetishism from writers such as Elizabeth Grosz and Teresa de Lauretis. Whereas Freud argued that fetishism arises from a boy's disavowed fear of castration following the discovery his mother does not have a penis, the notion of lesbian fetishism proposed by Grosz is predicated on the daughter's anxiety about her own, supposedly, castrated state. De Lauretis, discussing the lesbian perverse, suggests that lesbian desire fetishizes the female body itself, or something closely related to it, by metonymy. Second-wave fetishism tends to focus primarily on feminist analyses of fetishism, with a particular interest in female perversion, lesbian desire and cross dressing. A drawback of most second-wave fetishism is its inversion of male and female roles; while successfully subverting and overturning the phallocentrism and misogyny of first-wave fetishism, the insistence on a woman's ability to fetishize 'as much as the next man' means it still ultimately relies on the same gender binary that underpins first-wave fetishism.

In this study I propose a third wave of fetishism studies, an 'alternative fetishism', which continues the challenge to patriarchal notions of fetishism started by the second wave but rejects an exclusively gynocentric approach in order to consider fetishism in practitioners of fluid genders and sexualities. Alternative fetishism operates without reliance on any fixed identity for subjects and objects and is capable of great flexibility, depending on the situation people encounter. My intention is to show the non-pathological side of fetishism; in this reformulation, the negative and positive psychic processes of disavowal and avowal are brought together to reveal that alternative fetishism is not an operation of suppression and repression, but a radical act of expression. Language, as the primary means of conveying fetishism, creates and empowers the fetish objects ubiquitous in Winterson's texts: the body, food and sex.

The idea that fetishism arises from symbolic substitutions as a strategy of defence persists, but alternative fetishism replaces feelings of loss and fear with acceptance and integration that benefit the subject. The nature and vision of the alternative fetishism depicted in Winterson's writing revolves around a wide range of cultural, psychological and sexual factors experienced by individuals in society, when issues such as trauma and loss are met by acts of substitution and dissidence. Winterson's texts reimagine and recreate untold narratives of repression in past histories and stories through an alternative literary approach that mixes normative and unorthodox notions of gender, sexuality and identity, contrasting the experiences of the individual with those of the wider community. This book argues that the lens of alternative fetishism offers a new critical perspective on the connections in Winterson's work between, on the one hand, the performed gender and lived sexuality of the individual, and on the other, the political, ethical and cultural forces at work in society. Focusing the analysis of alternative fetishism on the body, food and sex allows for detailed investigations into the wide-reaching issues of culture, politics and ethics in her work and offers new critical pathways to explore. Winterson's texts are anti-hierarchical by their acknowledgement of the positive and negative facets of human behaviour in all its heterogeneity; hence, this book argues that Winterson repositions gender, sexuality and identity norms through her fluid, fragmentary and fetishistic approaches to the body, food and sex.

Fetishism and theory

Fetishism has been defined as 'an attachment to an object that is much stronger than an inclination or a liking', and most discussions of it relate back to Freud's *Three Essays on the Theory of Sexuality* (1905).[9] Freud's conceptual framework for fetishism viewed it as a pathological action and ignored the possibility of female practitioners. The term, and its original meaning, first entered Western cultures following the sixteenth-century encounters between European explorers and the African nations they visited. It was used to describe the extreme adoration of certain objects thought, by the indigenous African populations, to hold powers; subsequently, the meaning and use of fetishism was adopted into Western discourse, initially adhering to religion.

The associations of fetishism changed following the industrial revolution, and subsequent Marxist and psychoanalytical interpretations of fetishism provided new applications of the concept, which have a continuing impact today in the fields of critical theory and cultural studies. Marxist theories of commodity fetishism see the social relations of production as being between a commodity and the economic value assigned to it by the market, arguing that an extrinsic level of worth is created that exceeds the item's intrinsic value. Marxist theory suggests that this process excludes human relations of production, causing people to fetishize the product and its seemingly magical source of power. In his recent study, Massimo Fusillo suggests that 'fetishism appears as a device that can subvert relations between animate and inanimate, between material and imaginary, and project onto things a dense net of expectations, symbols, and affective values'.[10] This understanding of fetishism operates with all commodities, including the mundane items of everyday life, which this book argues is reflected by the notion that Winterson's alternative fetishism is a daily practice. Although Freud believed that fetishism was a pathological action that required treatment and cure, he also suggested that a certain degree of fetishism is normal and habitual.[11] For example, he considered it unexceptional if one part of the body became an object of sexual desire. However, the normal becomes pathological when the body-part is turned into a solely sexual object. Freud also argued that males are the practitioners of fetishism, leading on from his theory of castration anxiety. When a male child realizes his mother lacks a penis, he fears losing his own as he mistakenly thinks she has been castrated; this creates, according to Freud, the idea in the boy that he needs to take steps to prevent the loss of his penis. A female child, since she never had a one, develops attitudes of envy because she both wants to have a penis and to be one. Consequently, she creates substitutes as phallic signifiers, symbolic of sexual demand and desire. Thus, Freud believed that only men can be seen as practitioners of fetishism, and his work has exerted considerable influence on later scholars in the field.

However, over the decades, many other Freudian and post-Freudian thinkers have advanced the study of fetishism, and it has been a subject of much discussion by more recent theorists of female sexuality, such as Hélène Cixous, Luce Irigaray, Julia Kristeva, Grosz and de Lauretis, who have developed their theories out of conventional concepts of sexuality. According to Naomi Schor, the view that women are able to become practitioners of fetishism was always discernible in Freud's writings:

> A careful reading of Freud's writing on female sexual development strongly suggests that many little and big girls are engaged in a rebellion against the 'fact' of castration every bit as energetically as the fetishist's. Indeed, if one takes as one of the hallmarks of fetishism the split in the ego (*Ichspaltung*) to which the fetish bears testimony, then it becomes possible to speak [. . .] of female fetishism.[12]

Other psychoanalysts, sexologists and anthropologists have further challenged Freud's ideas of fetishism, especially with regard to his views on female sexuality. Lacan developed the concept of an imaginary, which is moulded from the pre-Oedipal concept, and mirror stage, wherein the child first perceives herself/himself and desires to be part of the phallus for the mother. The mirror stage starts around the age of six months, and then slowly the child begins to recognize herself/himself and the other in the reflection of the surrounding movements. Using this concept, Lacan further developed both these theories in relation to fetishism. Lacan and Wladimir Granoff explained that fetishism exists from the pre-Oedipal stage onwards, and through the stages of the symbolic, the imaginary and the real. Lacan believed that both men and women have experiences of fetishism because it is 'the representation of feminine sexuality, whether repressed or not, which conditions how it comes into play, and it is the displaced offshoots of this representation [. . .] which decide the outcomes of its tendencies'.[13] This observation opens up the possibility of a different perspective on the study of deviance in women, but Lacan's discussions of fetishism ultimately return to females as the object of the fetish, rather than the subject. In his essay, 'Guiding Remarks for a Congress on Feminine Sexuality', Lacan concluded that women are meant to submit themselves to be objects of fetishism and, while the desire to be the phallus can imbue the female subject with fetishistic elements in their thinking and behaviour, women are still in a minority when it comes to being a subject in fetishism. In his essay, 'Feminine Sexuality', Lacan argued that, for men, fetishism acts to protect what they already have, unlike women, for whom:

> [t]he relation of privation or lack-in-being symbolised by the phallus, is established by derivation from the lack-in-having engendered by any particular or global frustration of demand. [. . .] Since it has been effectively demonstrated that the imaginary motive for most male perversion is the desire to preserve the phallus which involved the subject in the mother, then the absence in women of fetishism, which represents the virtually manifest case of this desire, leads us to suspect that this desire has a different fate in the perversion which she presents. For to assume that the woman herself takes on the role of fetish, only raises the question of the difference of her position in relation to desire and to the object.[14]

In contrast, Michel Foucault's theory of sexuality develops the concept of bodies and pleasure outside of gender divides to lay emphasis on the body and the uses of pleasure beyond heterosexual constraints. Foucault challenges conventional concepts of sexuality; for him, the question is not to be either male or female but to enjoy instead the pleasure of the body, which he believes is pre-eminent, regardless of its gender. Judith Butler analyses Foucault's phrase 'bodies and pleasure', writing that

> [it] held out the possibility of unmarked bodies, bodies that were no longer thought or experienced in terms of sexual difference, and pleasures that were diffuse, possibly nameless, intense and intensifying, pleasures that took the entire body as the surface and depth of its operation.[15]

This study utilizes Foucault's notion of bodily pleasure and desire as being applicable to both men and women, and it draws upon his examination of the relationship between the body, sexuality and power, in which the phallus is seen as an object of desire for the other, without specifying a sex. In this way, Foucault's writings on sexuality oppose normative views and so can be applied usefully to a discussion of alternative fetishism. The Freudian view, which identifies fetishism as a symptom of psychological disturbance and denies the possibility of its existence in women, refuses to acknowledge and engage with the agency of the individual, regardless of gender. An analysis of fetishism that proceeds from Freud to Foucault (and beyond, to the current day) indicates that fetishism manifests itself in all genders. It is not a unilinear or discrete process but is interconnected with psychological, philosophical and anthropological presentations of the self and the other. Due to the times in which Freud lived, societal forces may have limited further discussion of female fetishism, but the increased understanding of individual difference today, in areas such as gender, race and class, has intensified the importance of acknowledging the diverse desires of any given subject. The vast majority of Western societies still attempt to impose gendered norms on individuals and promulgate heterosexual practices and beliefs, but at the same time many unorthodox expressions and enactments of desire and pleasure of the self and the other are realized. In his study of human sex relations, Alfred Kinsey wrote:

> The publicly pretended code of morals, our social organization, our marriage customs, our sex laws, and our educational and religious systems are based upon an assumption that individuals are much alike sexually and that it is an equally simple matter to confine their behaviour to the single pattern which the mores dictate.[16]

The inability of a 'single pattern' to explain the complexities of modern human behaviour makes clear the need for a more versatile and sensitive tool to analyse acts of deviation and dissidence, and the alternative fetishism found in Winterson's writing provides a non-pathological, non-neurotic way to assess the thoughts and actions of individuals. The various qualities of the fetish objects of the body, food and sex in Winterson's texts function as significant narrative factors that serve as metaphorical and symbolic elements of human life. These fetish objects contain motivating features that continuously establish the background of the action and affect the fictional realities Winterson creates through her distinctive use of language. Her diction expresses a peculiar value and is capable of communicating the deep emotions of the protagonists and other characters in her novels. My readings of Winterson's work argue that bodily fetishism, food fetishism and sexual fetishism may have different mechanisms, but they have in common the process of disavowal and avowal – the displacement of desire onto a substitute, such as sexual attraction transmuting into gastronomy. This brings forward the discussion of Winterson's use of figurative language, which shows the relationships between the body, desires, pleasures and fetishism, and how she uses metaphor and symbolism in her novels. Winterson deploys fantasy and imaginative techniques to examine sexuality, desire and pleasure, and this study promotes the approach of alternative fetishism to argue that Winterson's works have been 're-moulding the reality we assume to be objective' to reveal the provisional, fluid and mutable nature of the self and the other in society.[17]

More recent critical work has further investigated the effects of fetishism: Nikki Sullivan writes that, 'fetishism, insofar as it is – or has been constructed as – perverse, has the capacity to challenge or to queer sexual and social norms'.[18] Paul Gebhard suggests a more sophisticated structuring of sexual fetishism through his notion of a 'continuum of intensities' (which will be discussed in more detail in Chapter 8).[19] Building on Gebhard's work, Gamman and Makinen put forward their updated and comprehensive study of fetishism from the perspective of women as active practitioners.[20] Their analysis of the factors behind fetishism indicates that orthodox boundaries can be exceeded by actions that are not just sexually focused and that the outcomes can be beneficial for the participants. This has opened up a view of fetishism as something to desire and to be desired for, and, most importantly, as a practice that is not inevitably regarded as morally or pathologically deviant. Gamman and Makinen make the case for a tripartite categorization of fetishism into commodity fetishism, anthropological fetishism and sexual fetishism; thus, they use the term to explicate the complex marriage of a wide range of inner desires and outer environments.[21] However, Gamman and Makinen's argument still relies heavily on the male/female binary to position women as practitioners of fetishism, which, although it inverts Freudian analysis, continues its gender dichotomy. De Lauretis suggests that fetishistic desire contains 'the quality of all desire'; alternative fetishism reconceptualizes such desires as fluid and interchangeable, regardless of gender, sexuality and identity.[22] The alternative fetishism in Winterson's work stems from a plural, gender-fluid approach to human nature and behaviour and rewards the application of a wide array of psychoanalytical and anthropological viewpoints to illustrate individual subjectivity.

Winterson's writing, through its mix of psychological, philosophical and anthropological concerns, demonstrates the ability of fetishism to contest and destabilize heteronormativity and the social order. Hence, this book proposes that interrogating the alternative fetishism perceptible in her novels yields a valuable means of developing advanced critical insights. Building on this, the analysis of alternative fetishism in this study is not limited to a critique of neurosis or a focus solely on the sexual – alternative fetishism has a wider and deeper significance as a fluid form of obsession that leads an individual to undertake a diverse range of actions that can be directed towards a thing or a person, as either the object or subject. The body, food and sex are consistently presented as fetish objects in Winterson's novels and, although they are fetishized in different ways, a unifying feature is their representation of diverse gender, sexuality and identity in the everyday lives of her characters. This study analyses bodily fetishism, food fetishism and sexual fetishism in Winterson's work to explore how her writing blends first-wave and second-wave approaches to fetishism to produce her own distinct and alternative version. Fetishistic images exist in the mind before the motivations are transferred externally to the body; therefore, the alternative fetishism manifest in Winterson's fiction originates from psychic processes mediated through the system of language, before being inscribed on the body through physical, cultural and political interactions.

Language and obsession

Winterson's own words indicate the importance she assigns to language: 'we want a living language, a language capable of expressing all that it is called upon to express in a vastly changing world.'[23] She also believes that 'language is movement' and words do 'not only mean inevitable development or deterioration'.[24] This mobility is a mechanism of fetishism that operates through her obsessive use of substitutes – the fetish objects of the body, food and sex – to convey the many layers of meanings and perspectives found in her texts. For example, in Part I, Winterson's representations of the body, through the plurality of her discourse, whether it is of gastronomy, anatomy, typography or cartography, creates complex layers of representation of perverse desires and pleasures, which are fluid between subject and object. Food in her writing can function equally as a symbol of the patriarchal and the anti-patriarchal order, depending on the situation, and this is discussed in Part II. Sexual preferences and choices in Winterson's texts, including fetishistic behaviour, are mobile and fluid and do not belong to any specific gender or sexuality; this is discussed in Part III.

Winterson believes that 'all good writers aspire towards such precision and movement, and the experiments that writers must make are for the sake of new frequencies of language which in turn allow new frequencies of emotion'.[25] She grew up with a very small collection of books, so, for her, 'books need to be deeply read as well as widely read'.[26] She says she was raised 'not knowing that language was for everyday purposes. I grew up with the Word and the Word was God', and she still fetishizes language as 'something holy'.[27] For teenagers, rebellion against parental authority is common; in Winterson's case, this included reading. Her mother said, 'the trouble with books is that you don't know what's in them until it is too late'.[28] So, in order to acquire knowledge of a wider range of literature, she had to 'smuggle books in and out of the house', and book collecting became 'an obsession, an occupation, a disease, an addiction, a fascination, an absurdity, a fate. It is not a hobby'.[29] Her first exposure to reading was mainly the religious material of her mother's evangelical church, though she was allowed to read narratives of myth and legend, such as 'the stories of Arthur, of Lancelot and Guinevere, of Merlin, of Camelot and the Grail'.[30] When she was older, she had to illicitly bring books into her home and hide them, also reading them secretly, often in the outside toilet. This was where she first read the books of 'sin', as her mother termed them, including Freud and D. H. Lawrence. For Winterson, Lawrence enjoys a 'freebooting dark-god status', and her writing has been influenced by his focus on the sex relations between people.[31] While Winterson's works can still be read through well-established psychoanalytical viewpoints on the body and sexuality, the fetishism in her texts blends first-wave and second-wave positions to present a distinctly alternative view on gender, sexuality and identity.

Winterson says, 'I wake and sleep language. It has always been so.'[32] She grew up with a mother who was obsessed with religion and who had submitted her body and soul to God and the church: 'My parents owned six books between them. Two of those were bibles and the third was a concordance to the Old and New Testaments.'[33] She had to find a way to feel emotionally and physically secure, and literature provided a refuge where she could expand her horizons: 'Art shows us how to be more than we are'.[34] She considers reading to be a noble act that enables a person to discover new things. Thus, for her, reading 'isn't a hiding place. It is a finding place'.[35] Books, to Winterson, are meant to be read deeply, and she did just that, spending 'three years doing what modern governments more and more want to stop students doing; reading widely and thinking for themselves'.[36] At times, she invokes religious terms to describe her bibliophilia:

> [m]y book hunts and book passions [are] something pretty close to hoarding the hair of martyrs and the sweat of saints. My books are a private altar. They are a source of strength and a place of worship. I see no reason to refuse to bend the knee.[37]

Winterson is a writer who is obsessed with recreating and refreshing language, seeing art forms as a 'foreign language', and declaring that 'we have to recognise that the language of art, all art, is not our mother-tongue'.[38] Her language often seems deceptively effortless and uncomplicated, but it is beautifully ordered and controlled in its rhythm, and sequences of ambiguous images are intertwined with pervasive humour. Even though many writers address similar themes of love, sex and history, Winterson's uses of language are distinctively mysterious and erotic. Themes such as love, loss and desire, which are presented throughout her work by the fetish objects of the body, food and sex, are used to represent the different beliefs and practices of each individual in society, with Winterson coaxing her readers into seeing things from alternative perspectives. Her texts are enormously poetic through her development of style, which she discusses in relation to T. S. Eliot: 'Style; sensibility and technique distinctively brought together, frees the writer from the weight of her own personality.'[39] Winterson believes that 'it is style that makes nonsense of conventional boundaries between fiction and fact. Style that refuses history as a documentary and recognises that history is as much in the reconstruction as in the moment.'[40]

Winterson's texts reflect the thinking of Roland Barthes, who wrote that a certain kind of literary production represents 'perversion: the text, its reading, are split. [In] the text of pleasure, the opposing forces are no longer repressed but in a state of becoming: nothing is antagonistic, everything is plural'.[41] In Barthesian terms, the pleasure of texts like Winterson's arise from the moment when the body pursues its own ideas independent of the individual's consciousness.[42] The language in her works is poetic and exact, even though it energetically and rapturously seeks renewal. She is obsessed with words: 'check that the book is made of language, living and not inert, for a true writer will create a separate reality and her atoms and her gases are words'.[43] Winterson accords with what

Barthes dubs 'a sentence-thinker': a writer who is capable of expressing her thoughts, her passion and her imagination by harnessing in each sentence the cumulative power of the right words.[44] Sentences composed of such craft and deliberation become paragraphs and, ultimately, books, which are founded on the strongest literary base. The result for Winterson is the production of her simultaneously seductive, threatening and rewarding fiction. Winterson can be viewed as one of those 'very few writers' whom, Barthes argues, can 'combat both a normative ideological repression and libidinal repression (the kind, of course, which the intellectual brings to bear upon himself: upon his own language)'.[45] Even though her fiction is infused with lyrical and poetic narration, she declares she is not a poet.[46] Rather, she creates her own style which is 'flexible enough to stretch around new and difficult ideas and fixed enough within a poetic tradition'.[47] Her robust experiments with different linguistic approaches expand her use of language to create flexibility of meaning in her literary fiction 'with truly charming inventiveness'.[48] One of her distinctive methods is a triple-layering of the narrative: 'what I do use are stories within stories within stories. I am not particularly interested in folk tales, but I do have them about my person, and like Autolycus (*The Winter's Tale*), I find that they are assumed to be worth more than they are.'[49]

Some of the literary criticism she has received has had an effect on her personal life, as well as her work, so she insists on a separation between art and life: 'the language of my passion and the language of my art are not the same thing.'[50] For her, one's sexuality can even be situational, which is why it keeps moving continuously, as is evident in most of her characters; this will be explored further in Part III. Her fluid and changeable characters bring to mind Butler's notion that identity categories are 'performative' and constantly in the process of being remade.[51] Winterson defended her work and clarified her beliefs as a writer in *Art Objects*: 'Strong texts work along the borders of our minds and alter what already exists. They could not do this if they merely reflected what already exists.'[52] Winterson's intention is to speak to 'male and female, young and old' so that they can understand that art and language in her writing refigure gender, sexuality and identity.[53] In my correspondence with her, Winterson has stated that she writes 'for anyone who is interested in books, in thinking, in expanding their imagination, female or male, and sexual orientation etc.'[54] Her version of art, in other words, aims to be comprehensive and inclusive, as it refuses to be shackled by the limitations of sexual orientation, gender concerns and other socially contingent conditions. Winterson is a writer who is passionately devoted to voicing the different in the self and the other through her art and language and that is what matters most to her: 'the passion that I feel for language is not a passion I could feel for anything or anyone else.'⁵⁵ She further comments that her 'work is rooted in silence. It grows out of deep beds of contemplation, where words, which are living things, can form and re-form into new wholes.'⁵⁶ This book elaborates on her intertwining of art and language by arguing that it is in and through language – the tool of her art – that her true reconceptualizations of gender, sexuality and identity, through the fetish objects of the body, food and sex, are to be found. Ultimately, any effort to compartmentalize gender, sexuality and identity in Winterson's fiction is futile because such positions become open ended, transparent, fluid and ever expanding. Thus, an attempt to box Winterson into neat categories works against the challenges present in her writing.

Winterson's extreme obsession with the word is transformed into positive acts that represent the multiplicity of social values relating to the cultural, sexual and psychological aspects of everyday life. Her texts illustrate the fetishism behind exploration and experience as she is obsessed with sharing and telling, through her particular representations of morally ambiguous viewpoints and practices of the individual. Winterson's texts obsessively create a living language that leads to multiple perceptions of internal and external desires in human imagination and fantasy. The relationships between the body, food and sex are significant as they are packed with emotional value, relayed through the use of metaphor and symbolism that has, itself, become fetishistic in her work. These fetish objects are used by Winterson to illustrate the fluidity of different ideologies, morals and beliefs found in theory and in common practice. First-wave and second-wave views of fetishism are deconstructed through these objects as they embrace both negative and positive connotations of fetishism in everyday life. Winterson is an ambitious literary writer; one who is passionately devoted to art and language as a medium with which to communicate the plight of the underdogs of society.

Winterson's rejection of any simplistic classification and her refusal to be categorized as a particular type of author is compatible with Barthes's idea of the 'atopic' writer, who rejects a fixed voice or perspective for the plurality that becomes possible if limits and borders are disregarded.⁵⁷ In her interview with Sonya Andermahr, Winterson states, 'I hate the label [of a lesbian writer]. Nothing is more boring than wrapping your whole self around your sexuality. I am not interested in that.'⁵⁸ Prior to this interview, she argued in *Art Objects* for the autonomy and agency of literature, urging readers and critics to judge her works, her language, and the way she uses language on its own terms: 'A work of fiction, a poem, that is literature, that is art, can only be itself, it can never substitute for anything. Nor can anything else substitute for it.'⁵⁹ In my correspondence with Winterson, she has further stressed this rejection of categorizing an individual or what they produce, stating that a label 'is a way of reducing or confining a person or their work, and mostly unhelpful'.[60] In effect, Winterson creates a love affair with language; she writes: 'spoken language alters and poetry, if it is to be living, must move with those changes in language but also stretch them, refine them, so that the thoughts and sensibilities of a people, as reflected in their speech, are kept taut'.[61]

Winterson's body of writing

While Winterson has written in various genres, her books regularly revisit certain themes, such as love, desire, loss and sex, while extending and troubling the boundaries between the self and the other. Her approaches to gender, sexuality and identity are not only fluid but also precise and subversive. In her work, the body, food and sex are significant objects due to their multiple pathways into understanding the emotional, physical, psychical and cultural lives of her characters. Through the obsessive and fetishistic treatment of these objects, her texts, from *Oranges Are Not the Only Fruit* (1985; hereafter *Oranges*) to *Frankissstein* (2019), contain deeply engaging anthropological, psychological and philosophical portrayals of her characters' genders, sexualities and identities, produced by a specificity of language that gives her readers 'the extraordinary view'.[62] For her, 'the language of literature is not an approximate language. It is the most precise language that human beings have yet developed.'[63] This study argues that Winterson's writing manifests the language of fetishism because it repeatedly applies an obsessive and emotional energy of imagination to concepts that have a valued presence in everyday life.

Winterson's literary career began with the celebrated and controversial novel, *Oranges*, which fictionalized her own upbringing. It was quickly followed by *Boating for Beginners* (1985), a comic satire on the mass marketing of religion, which was again influenced by her youth. Subsequent novels have shown a continued mining of her childhood experiences, suggesting that Winterson has never quite let go of 'her own history'.[64] Material for her inspiration comes from such differing sources as, inter alia, Shakespeare, modernist authors and the idiosyncratic religious education of her youth. Despite the emotional and physical turmoil she suffered from the dominating influence of her mother's evangelical Christianity (as fictionalized in *Oranges*), Winterson still believes that 'the Bible is a great resource for any writer and was for me. [. . .] And church was a community that taught me the power of collective action, and the capacity of individuals to change – and to experience life at a level beyond the daily impoverishment of circumstances.'[65] Winterson is a literary writer, to whom writing is 'a play on form', and her novels seek to unify real-life experiences with the spectacles of history, religion, fairy tales and folk tales:

> It's a particular experiment that I am pursuing. I don't say that it's the only experiment by any means, I don't say it's the experiment for everybody, but this is my contribution, this is what I can do, and so I'm doing it to the best of my ability. For me the challenge is to fuse the densities, the exactness, the precision of poetry with the scope and the emotional possibility of the larger canvas of a novel, where you can use character and situation and place.[66]

From *Oranges* to *Frankissstein*, Winterson contests what is 'natural' or 'normal' in the eyes of society, and her works seek answers to the issues that arise when societal norms are challenged by ambiguous gender, sexuality and identity. Winterson's novels cleverly interweave history with fantasy, from *Oranges* through to her later novels such as *The Passion* (1987), which won the John Llewellyn Rhys Prize, *Sexing the Cherry* (1989), which won the E. M. Forster Award, *Lighthousekeeping* (2004) and *The Daylight Gate* (2012). *The Passion* is set during the Napoleonic Wars, *Sexing the Cherry* features mid-seventeenth-century England, *Lighthousekeeping* is partially set in the Victorian period, and the narrative of *The Daylight Gate* revolves around the Pendle witchcraft trials of 1612. Winterson writes about past events but amalgamates them with the present and the future in her attempt to give a voice to the underdogs forgotten by history and society. Her stories dwell in what she calls 'invented space' as, for her, 'inside books there is perfect space and it is that space which allows the reader to escape from the problems of gravity'.[67] In the process, she not only gives a voice to the otherwise voiceless members of society but also repeatedly creates new histories and stories. Winterson's technique of telling and retelling a story through her fiction has become a significant mode of communication to convey the fluidity of gender, sexuality and identity within her playful invention of art. Through her works, Winterson explores the entire spectrum of sexuality in the self and others, affirming the display of both feminine and masculine desire in physical, emotional, cultural and sexual ways. Winterson loves to play the alchemist with genre; for example, in 1992, she shocked and disappointed her feminist fans and critics with her nameless and ungendered narrator in the novel *Written on the Body*. This provoked much critical debate of issues around the fluidity of sexuality, gender and identity and showed that desires and pleasures know no boundaries in her fiction.

Since *Written on the Body*, Winterson has gone on to write books across many genres: *Art & Lies* (1994) contains three entwined monologues by its characters in a playful reinvention of time, space and the language of art. Next came *Art Objects* (1995), a non-fiction book that expounds her views on art and literature. The close connection between Winterson's fiction and non-fiction led Susana Onega to describe *Art & Lies* as 'the fictional counterpart of *Art Objects*'.[68] This was followed by *Gut Symmetries* (1997), an experimental novel in its mixture of genre. Its narrative is formed by three entwined monologues from characters who are on 'a journey through the thinking gut', complicated by love, hate, science and art.[69] A collection of short stories, *The World and Other Places* (1998), came next, and then Winterson entered the new millennium with *The PowerBook* (2000), a time-hopping tale of pleasure, passion and gender fluidity in cyberspace. *Lighthousekeeping* revolves around 'loss, imagination and the search for love and belonging', and *Weight* (2005) reimagines the Atlas legend, while *The Stone Gods* (2007) marks a return to the science fiction genre.[70] In 2011, Winterson acknowledged her complicated upbringing in the memoir *Why Be Happy When You Could Be Normal?*, which addressed the events in her life that were fictionalized in *Oranges*. Winterson's texts affirm the freedom literature offers to create spaces to tell the stories not found in history books, and in 2012 she explored the dark side of her psyche to write a horror novel, *The Daylight Gate*. The notorious Pendle witch trials of 1612 provide the historical backdrop to this tale of supernatural forces contending with religious, political and sexual persecution. In 2015, the invented space continued in *The Gap of Time*, a re-imagining of Shakespeare's *The Winter's Tale*, written in her 'contemporary psychoanalytical style', as she 'reveals [the] backstories and inner traumas' of the characters.[71]

Winterson describes her novels as 'great pretend games', and she uses history as a mirror of the present, suggesting what happened then could also be happening now.[72] This approach can be traced in her exuberant reinventions of the past in, for instance, *Sexing the Cherry*, *The Daylight Gate* and *The Gap of Time*. In this context, she argues that only art is capable of challenging our sense of self: 'Art opens the heart [. . .] true art, when it happens to us, challenges the "I" that we are.'[73] In *Frankissstein*, the human body is subjected to radical changes in a contemporary world of cutting-edge technology and artificial intelligence (AI). The characters, including a transgender doctor, a Welsh sex-bot entrepreneur and an AI professor, collectively push at the boundaries of what it means to be human. Gender reassignment, sexual relations with robots and the transfer of the mind to digital form are all depicted. Each of these new ways of living are met with resistance and intolerance by others in the book. Winterson reserves for herself the 'right of spell', to deliver her versions of fiction that enable her to attract a wide and disparate audience, regardless of their identity, gender or sexuality.[74]

As Eliot observed, a writer has to continue to develop emotionally, '[b]ut very few know when there is expression of *significant* emotion, emotion which has its life in the poem and not in the history of the poet. The emotion of art is impersonal.'[75] Yet, Winterson often uses her personal experiences as a base for the invented reality in her fiction, and her writing fuses the 'emotion' of the work with her own 'history' to create a certain level of impersonality, which allows her books to be enjoyed by a wide readership. Winterson states her admiration of Eliot and Virginia Woolf in *Art Objects*, and their influence is clear in the way she creates new meanings of language to convey her ideas of diverse desire and pleasure, which, in turn, drive her distinctive method of retelling stories as a means of generating emphasis. Lucasta Miller writes that

> Winterson feels an affinity with the metaphysical poets and their use of language and image. All the writers she loves tend to share her desire to break the mould. She admires T. S. Eliot because of his interest in new forms, and his obsession with the relation between past, present and future. Virginia Woolf appeals because 'she opens up new possibilities for language'.[76]

This is very clear in Winterson's works: from her first novel, *Oranges*, to her most recent, *Frankissstein*, she expresses 'unspoken emotion with powerful but never overwritten lyricism'.[77] As Winterson stresses in *Art Objects*, 'complex emotion often follows some major event in our lives; sex, falling in love, birth, death', and 'in each of these potencies are strong taboos'.[78] It is in such significant, yet commonplace, contexts that we should examine the challenges to normative boundaries articulated through her particular language of desire and pleasure. Symbolism and metaphor are her preferred means of presenting diverse genders, sexualities and identities that stem from, and respond to, cultural, social and political issues. Winterson's novels have contributed in a major way to such debates by destabilizing orthodox thinking to provide an alternative view of gender, sexuality and identity in the present day. She says: 'I think I started writing before I could read because I wanted to write sermons, because I was driven to preach to people and convert them which possibly I still am, except that now I do it for art's sake'.[79] Her novels directly and obliquely reflect current issues, including the right to sexual, biological, political and cultural choices. The importance of these subjects in her work is discussed in this book through the use of the body, food and sex as fetish objects to offer a new critical insight to Winterson's writing.

Due to the particular way Winterson reconceptualizes gender, sexuality and identity through depictions of diverse desire and pleasure, she is seen as a controversial figure in the field of literature. Since her first novel, her works, her life and, in particular, her perceived self-consciousness have attracted critics across the media. Winterson has been labelled a lesbian, a feminist, a lesbian-feminist, a neomodernist and a postmodernist writer. But in terms of her depictions of gender, sexuality and identity, her readers and critics have often restricted their responses to her work by attempting to place her as a writer who belongs to a particular category. Identifying the limits of such pigeonholing is vital to enable a new critical approach to Winterson's oeuvre, since her sexual orientation as a lesbian is well known and can overpower the reading of her work. Ultimately, it is not a question of whether Jeanette Winterson is a neomodernist, postmodernist, lesbian or feminist author (even if she can be associated with any of these categories); instead, it is the richness of her texts that have enabled critics to see in her writing the theoretical angle they have chosen to utilize, occasionally narrowing down the exploration and collocation of other interpretations. To expand the interpretative possibilities for Winterson's work, I suggest that it also rewards readings that consider post-postmodernist concepts, particularly New Sincerity. According to Alexei Yurchak:

> [this] post-postmodern phenomenon [. . .] is acutely self-aware and self-ironic. However, it is a particular brand of irony which is sympathetic and warm, and allows its authors to remain committed to the ideals that they discuss, while also being somewhat ironic about this commitment.[80]

Winterson uses the play of fancy with an ironical approach to dip in and out of her past as she remoulds the present and future into a highly textured mental and emotional landscape. Eliot suggested that a good writer produces 'a finely perfected medium in which special, or very varied, feelings are at liberty to enter into new combinations'.[81] Winterson's thinking in this area aligns with the linguistic preciseness Eliot demanded of poetry, a precision that opens up interpretive and signifying possibilities rather than closing them down. For Winterson, the right words need to be chosen for their connotations, their polysemy and their dynamism:

> That every word [should] be charged. Charge: to load, to put something into, to fill completely, to cause to accumulate electricity, to lay a task upon, to enjoin, to command, to deliver an official injunction or exhortation. To accuse. To place a

bearing upon, to exact or demand from, to ask the price. To attack at a rush; the load of power. A device born on a shield. The object of care.⁸²

Gender, sexuality and identity

For Winterson, normative rules of given gender and sexuality are to be bent and broken, to show the different choices and preferences available in society. Her texts utilize fetishistic elements in their treatment of the subject to overcome any negative conception of fetishism in general. As Lisa Moore claims:

> For Winterson, the 'rules' don't work for anyone (even heterosexual men), and never have. She offers neither a critique of heterosexual culture nor a salvific account of lesbianism, largely because she refuses to accept that conventional distinction in the first place.⁸³

Winterson acknowledges the feminist struggle for equality in a masculine world and has proudly declared that 'if not because of feminism, I would not sit here to the next day'.⁸⁴ She writes, in correspondence with the author: 'I am a feminist – as is any sane woman. Feminism isn't a label, it is a political position, and I believe that writers need to be actively involved in the world, and yes, to make a difference where we can.'⁸⁵ However, even if she considers as reductive the idea that female authors are only able to write about their life experiences, she believes that writers of all genders possess creativity and imagination, and her work goes beyond the binary oppositions of female/male and feminism/patriarchy. Winterson says she likes to be different and oppose such constraints, and her works are capable of enhancing the reader's imagination and stretching their thinking beyond conventional limitations, thereby altering perceptions of the self and the other. Accordingly, her work deals with the subject of fluid sexualities and the reconceptualizing of psychic, physical, biological, cultural and social norms in a dissident way. This is often seen in Winterson's fiction by the recurring trope of the quest: a voyage of literal and metaphoric discovery in which love and passion, mystery and fantasy, are sought and encountered. These journeys enable those who are classified as different to redefine their status in respect to the social norms of their society, as the conventional boundaries of gender, sexuality and identity are challenged and crossed.

In Winterson's reconceptualization of gender, sexuality and identity, a re-evaluation of first-wave and second-wave fetishism produces her own, alternative, type of fetishism. The Freudian notion of fetishism operates through disavowal, anxiety and melancholy in the desiring subject and is labelled as pathological disturbance. It is usually associated only with sexual acts and is perceived negatively; thus, it is necessary to reiterate the modes and forms of fetishism used in this study. The new concept of fetishism deployed here is not merely limited to attempts at sexual gratification; it turns the processes of substitution and loss into acts of replacement and reclamation. This is specifically achieved in Winterson's novels through the fetish objects of the body, food and sex, and their cultural relationships that revolve around physicality, sexuality and the psyche. The alternative fetishism in Winterson's texts, therefore, encompasses not only well-established associations of a sexual nature but also includes the more recent expansion of what comes under the purview of fetishism: for example, the body and food are presented as fetish objects by the multiple meanings of Winterson's figurative language. Gamman and Makinen suggest that the slippery nature of language invites confusion when discussing fetishism, whereas this book argues that such linguistic slippage is crucial in analysing the alternative fetishism in Winterson's works.[86] Her representation of diverse desire and pleasure stems from a distinctive combination of metaphor, metonymy and synecdoche; for example, Winterson utilizes synecdoche to depict the deconstructed body as sometimes more and sometimes less than the sum of its parts. The deconstructed body is a fetish object in Winterson's writing as it is non-gender specific; it is fluid and mobile depending on the situations faced, and parts of the body are often given a prominence and an autonomy which undermine notions of a unified whole.

Fetishism, as Lacan and Granoff argue, 'is by definition a displacement of meaning through the synecdoche, the displacement through the object of the desire onto something else through a process of disavowals'.[87] While Lacan's work made an early and important contribution in advancing Freud's model of fetishism with regard to female participation, this study seeks to argue that Winterson's work, by its amalgamation of form and content, reveals an alternative fetishism that furthers the understanding and acceptance of differences in gender, sexuality and identity of the self and the other in everyday life. Hence, her approaches to fiction, which debate moral values, religious beliefs and political practices, convey the fluidity of thought in each individual and reveal threatening, inventive and seductive stances on human nature and behaviour, indicating that the self and the other can be better understood through the acceptance of difference in society. Reading Winterson's texts through this conceptual lens leads to greater understanding of desire in her works, and by examining the diverse bodies, sexualities and identities in her novels, this book demonstrates how the different in society can be too readily coded as perverse and abnormal.

As discussed, fetishism has long been acknowledged as a male phenomenon, and women are less often recognized as practitioners; nevertheless, in the novels discussed in this book, the practices of fetishism are not the sole preserve of any one gender. As Gamman and Makinen have successfully shown through their comprehensive study on female fetishism, women are entirely capable of fetishizing and that there is a space for women to be 'practitioners and question psychoanalysis's denial of women's fetishism'.[88] The female practitioner has generally been effaced in studies of fetishism because female bodies, as argued by Jon Stratton, are fetishized and desirable objects for males.[89] Thus, the female body functions in the context of cultural judgements as an object of fetishism, not as a subject who is capable of fetishizing. Stratton further suggests that the female body exemplifies the 'phallic economy of cultural fetishism' because the mainstream media, especially advertising and films, promote female bodies as a spectacle to be surveyed.[90] Female bodies are seen as objects of desire inviting the male gaze to satisfy an androcentric fascination with the self and the other. However, Winterson's texts show that, regardless of gender, fetishism is present in all individuals as a substitute that is always already eroticising some symbolic reference to the other in everyday life.

Winterson has a distinctive style of capturing the various facets of sensuousness and sensual engagements. As she claims, 'the pleasure of a book is, or should be, sensuous as well as aesthetic, visceral as well as intellectual'.[91] This statement, along with the new model of fetishism perceptible in her texts, reflects the post-postmodernist elements of Winterson's work, such as the notion that in these increasingly secular times, authors might be the remaining bearers of unironic beliefs. According to Jeffrey Nealon,

> writers have become the last believers – not in any positive content or anything as predictable as 'meaning', but writers are the last believers in language's ability to be the primary driver in the interruption and reshaping of subjectivity (which is also to say, the resisting and disrupting of so-called normative subjectivity).[92]

Winterson's texts do not present gender, sexuality and identity as singularly constructed by physical, biological, cultural or social forces. Rather, they amalgamate all these potentialities and interrogate their operation through the uses of various fetish objects. As a result, Winterson deconstructs and remaps the body, gender, sexuality and identity as fragmentary and multiplying. Hence, the metamorphosis of normative views into diverse desire and pleasure of the bodily self and the other is one way of reimaging pleasure and desire.

The work of Freud, Foucault and Butler on the links between sexual identity, discursive practice, desire and gender performance as reiterated rituals have been extremely influential in challenging the common assumption that gender, sexuality and identity are determined by the sexed body. These theorists' contributions to the debate on the body are part of a broader attempt to dissolve the given gender and the binary division of sexes. Freud believed sexuality was an essential and innate characteristic, whereas later theorists have proposed a socially constructed and determined aetiology. Foucault provocatively posits sexuality as socially inscribed on the body, and Butler argues that gender does not necessarily proceed from biological sex. In this context, Butler, like many other feminist critics, has often focused her views on the limits for feminism in Foucault's conceptions of the body. For example, she observes that Foucault said that 'the rallying point for the counterattack against the deployment of sexuality ought not to be sex-desire, but bodies and pleasures'.[93] In other words, sexuality, gender and identity as proposed by Butler and other similar feminist theorists and thinkers are understood to be culturally dependent, even though these theorists may not always agree with each other on all points.

A number of feminist critics share reservations about the potential for feminist approaches to sexuality and the body in Freud's and Foucault's work; however, Freud and Foucault remain crucial to our understanding of the discursive production of the body, sexuality and gender – in particular, the production and proliferation of outlawed fetishism through the mechanisms of juridical prohibition. Winterson's invented realities contain aspects of all the above theorists' distinct positions on the subjects. That is to say, her characters perform both subversive and conventional expressions of gender, sexuality and identity. Her writing insists on presenting a mixed idea of diverse desire and pleasure of the bodily self and the other, which is an act of alternative fetishization. Therefore, Winterson's works consists of first-wave, second-wave and alternative fetishism.

The works of Butler and Elizabeth Grosz on concepts of the body also offer an important theoretical approach in this study. Gender theory opens up possibilities for change in the mode of production and construction of gender, sexuality and identity:

> Construction is neither a subject nor its act, but a process of reiteration by which both 'subject' and 'acts' come to appear at all. There is no power that acts, but only a reiterated acting that is power in its persistence and instability.[94]

Winterson's shifting approach to gender, sexuality and identity needs to be read through the multiple lenses of psychoanalytical, cultural and gender theory, as her work embraces extraordinary complexities of the meanings and perceptions of the self and others in their internal and external desires and pleasures. In this context, while Freud's concepts of the body and sexuality are mainly internally rather than externally influenced and focus on desire and sex, Foucault's theorizing of the body and pleasure result from the material effects of power on the bodily self and the other. Butler argues that Foucault 'proposes an ontology of accidental attributes that exposes the postulation of identity as a culturally restricted principle of order and hierarchy, a regulatory fiction'.[95] This is debated and developed by Butler; her expanded notion of gender, and understanding of identity and sexuality, is 'performatively produced and compelled by regulatory practices of gender coherence', which contrasts with Winterson's versions of gender, sexuality and identity as being free-floating and dependent on the situations encountered in life.[96] However, this study makes use of Butler's perceptions of gender and sexuality, particularly her proposition that identity should not be separated from the discussion of gender as 'it would be wrong to think that the discussion of "identity" ought to proceed prior to a discussion of gender identity'.[97] For this reason, the following chapters draw upon Butler's notions of performativity in respect to gender, sexuality and identity, which 'is not a singular act, but a repetition and a ritual, which achieves its effects through its naturalization in the context of a body, understood, in part, as a culturally sustained temporal duration'.[98] This aligns with the reading of Winterson's texts as offering fluid, mobile and fragmented enactments of gender, sexuality and identity and leads towards an analysis of the fetishism they manifest.

Winterson's particular approach to gender and sexuality adheres to neither essentialist nor constructionist beliefs; rather, she brings forth her own ideas of gender and sexuality through supposed contradictions. In Winterson's works, the other is recognized, regardless of gender and sexuality, and is marked as other or different due to their diverse choices and/or preferences. Consequently, it is important to identify this recognition of diversity in Winterson's works through the lens of alternative fetishism, from which the fetish object provokes emotional responses. Such questions of psychological enquiries and moral values, which encompass concepts of modernism and postmodernism, also point the way to post-postmodernist assessments of her fiction; Nealon argues that

> for thousands of years before (in fact, for virtually all of its existence), literature was equipment for living in myriad ways, not just as a provider and/or frustrator

of 'meaning'. Hopefully, a more robust sense of the literary can make it crucial, or at least useful, equipment again for post-postmodern living.[99]

In light of post-postmodernist efforts to reclaim the utility of literature, the relationship between Winterson's anti-hierarchical texts and fetishism indicates that the fetish objects of the body, food and sex can be linked to constructive ways of considering gender, sexuality and identity. Winterson's characters embody diverse desires and pleasures as a way to redraw the boundaries of libidinal life, and so this study also addresses the political convergence of heterosexual, homosexual, bisexual and lesbian perspectives on gender, sexuality and identity.

Section outlines

This book consists of three main parts, each discussing in turn one of the main fetish objects present in Winterson's works: the body, food and sex. Each chapter explores and reveals a multiplicity of meanings around gender and sexuality in Winterson's writing, as internal desires and external actions are revealed by the alternative fetishism performed in the text through language. Winterson's treatment of various bodies is discussed in detail in the chapters comprising Part I: 'Bodily fetishism'. This section illustrates how Winterson reconceptualizes gender, sexuality and identity in her work by fluidly combining first-wave and second-wave fetishism. The alternative fetishism in Winterson's works transcribes the body and its parts, commingling them with the mind and psyche. This resists dualism and shows the domains of subjectivity and objectivity to be overlapping and compatible. Through acts of extreme physical and psychical obsession, worship and madness are often transformed into mourning and melancholy for the subject (self) and bodies (others). Bodies act as significant fetish objects in her representation of diverse desire: 'the body can and does function to represent, to symbolize, social and collective fantasies and obsessions.'[100] The theoretical formulations on fetishism used in this section derive from the work of Freud, Lacan and Foucault. These ideas were challenged and extended by feminist theorists such as Elizabeth Grosz, Teresa de Lauretis, Judith Butler, Sarah Kofman and Mary Russo. These theories help understand how Winterson's texts employ an alternative fetishism that presents a distinctive approach to gender, sexuality and identity. The discussion also shows how Winterson's works embrace fetishistic desire by promoting fluid and changeable fetishism. 'Bodily Fetishism' focuses on *Oranges*, *The Passion*, *Written on the*

Body, *The PowerBook* and *Frankissstein* to show how her presentations of the body and its parts and desire reveal a bodily fetishism that is produced from the defamiliarization of orthodox, normative and contemporary views of fetishism.

This section comprises three interrelated chapters, each examining a range of Winterson's texts from a particular angle, linked by the main object of the body and embodied existence. Chapter 1 is 'Fetishistic desire: Versatile bodies', which discusses the diverse desires of various bodies and minds. This is followed by Chapter 2, 'Fetishistic touch: Space and time', which focuses on the reconceptualization of space and time in Winterson's work to reveal the connections between corporeality, spatiality and temporality. Finally, Chapter 3, 'Fetishistic imagination: Body and memory', discusses the substitutions caused by loss, in which a replacement for the lost object is created through language and imagination. Throughout, this section discusses the impact of Winterson's refiguration of the body, which contests mind/body dualism to reveal an alternative fetishism that reflects the diverse desires of the individual.

The body is not one in Winterson's literary fiction; instead, the body is changeable and fluid, described in various forms by sensuous and sensual language. For example, in *Written on the Body*, the Unnamed Narrator describes and worships Louise's body through the language of topography during their relationship. After their relationship ends, this extreme obsession threatens melancholy and madness for the Unnamed Narrator; however, a reading through the model of alternative fetishism reveals that the substitution of Louise's body with medical textbooks, replacements for the lost object, allows the Unnamed Narrator to divert their narcissistic stage by the pursuit of scientific knowledge. Thus, at this particular situation, such an act of diversion and replacement turns into an alternative stage for the Unnamed Narrator as a strategy of defence and psychological acceptance.

The analysis of the deconstructed body leads on to Part II: 'Food fetishism', which investigates the use of food and its consumption in Winterson's texts to illustrate the connection between the politics of food, fluid gender and diverse desire. Winterson is obsessed with healthy ways of eating for the body because 'the pleasure of real food is one of the true pleasures of life'.[101] In her works, food is a mirror of the self and the other, one that is capable of endless meaning and interpretation; it is not gendered, but rather a cultural attribute that is fluidly performative.[102] Through analysis of her fetishistic use of language, this section shows how food functions as a substitute object of alternative fetishism and how its preparation and consumption have many different meanings for Winterson's characters in relation to politics, power and psychology. The discussions also illustrate how food is a way for Winterson to represent the fluid gender identities and sexuality of her characters.

The main novels analysed in 'Food fetishism' are *Sexing the Cherry*, *The Passion*, *Written on the Body* and *Boating for Beginners* to elucidate the links Winterson makes between food, fetishism and the fluidity of desire and pleasure. Various other texts by Winterson are also mentioned in brief, to further augment the argument that she deploys an alternative fetishism of food across her entire body of work as an object of replacement and diversion. Food functions as a fetishistic substitute for a lost object and shows that Winterson manages to exploit the erotic potential of food stuffs to represent the notion of diverse desire of the self and the others. It can be argued that Winterson's use of food terminology in her texts is influenced by her upbringing. Not only does she use the lexicon of food in her works to present her perspective of gender and sexuality, she also seems to be obsessed with food and its consumption: 'I learnt about the politics of food through eating it.'[103] Winterson he has written many articles about food and her experiences during her childhood, when she 'got curious about where everything had come from and how it was grown and harvested'.[104] She says her 'attitude to food is simple: A) Life is too short to eat badly. B) What you eat is the most political thing you do every day'.[105] Because of these concerns, she opened a coffee shop-cum-greengrocer's in Spitalfields in 2005, and she says 'the quality of food' that she sold was paramount to her.[106] Thus, in her own life Winterson matches the views of Elspeth Probyn, who says: 'food is a hugely powerful system of values, regulations and beliefs', and Arjun Appadurai, who proposes that 'food may generally possess a special semiotic force because of certain universal properties'.[107] Theoretical concepts used in this discussion include Foucault's approaches to the pleasures and desires of the body, Butler's work on gender, Gamman and Makinen's discussion of female fetishism, Jeremy MacClancy's analyses of the relationship between food and culture, Probyn's thinking on food and sex in society, Counihan's arguments about the language of food and manipulation and Carol J. Adams's writings on politics and meat.

This section is composed of four chapters, each focusing in detail on a particular text, although other works by Winterson are discussed where relevant: Chapter 4 – 'Fluid fruits' and *Sexing the Cherry*; Chapter 5 – 'Meat as power' and *The Passion*; Chapter 6 – 'The boundaries of food' and *Written on the Body*; and Chapter 7 – 'The sexual politics of food' and *Boating for Beginners*. The language in Winterson's works often utilizes metaphors associated with feeding and eating because such acts have distinct and emotive power in describing culture, behaviour, the psyche and the physical body. As a result, food is closely entwined with the production of gender, sexuality and identity. In Winterson's texts, it can be seen that food assumes the symbolic function of communicating the diverse desire of the body. Through food terminology, Winterson revaluates the notion of fetishism, which often acts as a substitute for the inner and outer desires that revolve around the self and the other. Hence, food in Winterson's invented reality signifies the disavowal and substitution of normative desires for something more peculiar when looking into the desires of the body. That is, the use of food terminology functions as a metaphor for the temporary or permanent replacement of an actual object and as an act of disavowal for diverse desire in daily practice. Gamman and Makinen's statement that 'reading about food [. . .] is almost comparable with reading about sex' leads us to the topic of the next section, which discusses how Winterson's fetishism of language helps create an alternative discourse on sexual fetishism in her novels.[108]

In Part III: 'Sexual fetishism', Winterson's works are explored through the lens of alternative fetishism to argue that the mixing of pathological, negative practices of sexual fetishism with positive, consensual acts shows a freedom of choice in society. Consequently, this section identifies Winterson's notions of diverse sexual pleasures and desires as processes of shifting and re-imagining between normative and unorthodox views of gender, sexuality and identity, which provide alternative views of fetishism in the subject. I provide an overview of the sexual fetishism found in Winterson's texts and discuss three key terms: 'perversity', 'deviance' and 'dissidence' to argue that Winterson's discourse of gender and sexuality appreciates sexual differences and challenges taboo perceptions and conventional notions of sexual pleasure and desire. I suggest Winterson's fiction speaks to all sexualities and challenges the notion of heteropatriarchy, while sexual deviance and dissidence can be considered normal due to the situations faced and the influences of external and internal forces.

Chapter 8 is titled 'The extended boundaries: Pleasure and pain', and it discusses the sadomasochism in Winterson's texts and how this relates to alternative fetishism. Chapter 9, 'The fetishistic phallus: Elongated objects', assesses the substitute phalluses in Winterson's work through psychoanalytical theories to see how the substitution of sexual objects is manifested. Chapter 10 titled 'Soft fetishes: Membranes and senses' illustrates how and why certain body parts become integral to the alternative fetishism in Winterson's novels. The critical framework for 'Sexual fetishism' builds on first-wave and second-wave fetishism theory, including the work of Freud, Foucault, Gebhard, Schor and Grosz. This section focuses on *The Passion*, *Sexing the Cherry*, *Written on the Body* and *The Daylight Gate* to show the representation of sexual fetishism in her works. I argue that a particularly Wintersonian model of sexual fetishism emerges in her work from the complex sexual struggles between conventional external expectations and the body's idiosyncratic internal desires. Winterson maintains a certain ambiguity in the language she uses to describe the plural nature of gender and sexuality, as evidenced by the Unnamed Narrator of *Written on the Body*. Similarly, in her representation of sexual repression, she extends this ambiguity and fluidity as if to admonish against a reductive codification of a person's sexual orientation or sexual behaviour in relation to their sexual choices. This section analyses the diverse desires and pleasures of various bodies and their parts, which act as objects and subjects of fetishism for the self and the other. The concepts of perversion, deviance and dissidence are deployed to interrogate the role of the body and its parts, revealing that the sexual preferences and actions of Winterson's characters stem from the will to survive and are influenced by both internal and external factors. For example, in *The Passion*, when Villanelle is dressed like a soldier, the Queen of Spades immediately comprehends the significance of the fetishistic acts performed by Villanelle, conceived for the pleasure and benefit of the Queen of Spades. Villanelle enjoys performing masculine and feminine roles – chameleonic behaviour that also satisfies her lover. For instance, when Villanelle wears men's clothes in her sexual encounters with the Queen of Spades it is called 'fancy dress' and triggers both their internal desire – the source of a fetish – and compels their bodies to act in certain ways.[109]

The book concludes with a summation of Winterson's contribution to contemporary discussions of fetishism, gender and sexuality and the value that can be derived from this study for scholars and students of her work. There are also suggestions for future applications of alternative fetishism to other authors and fields in the humanities.

Part I

Bodily fetishism

The body is the supreme object of knowledge in Jeanette Winterson's fiction. Written on it, in 'a secret code only visible in certain lights', are stories and histories to be discovered and appreciated, regardless of its gender, sexuality and identity.[1] This section illustrates how Winterson's texts reconceptualize the body through an alternative fetishism that rethinks corporeal materiality by transcribing the body and its parts in ways that resist mind/body dualism and blur subjectivity and objectivity. In Winterson's novels, acts of extreme obsession often lead to worship and madness and are transformed into mourning and melancholy of the subject (self) and bodies (others). Winterson's fetishistic discourse presents the diverse desires and pleasures directed towards, and enacted upon, bodies; as Elizabeth Grosz says, 'the body can and does function to represent, to symbolize, social and collective fantasies and obsessions'.[2] In Winterson's fiction, 'the life of the body is scrutinised with the introspective intensity which puritans used to invest in the life of the soul', according to Ina Schabert.[3] This section shows how Winterson's scrutiny of the body challenges its boundary norms through her depictions of the diverse desires and pleasures of the bodily self and the other. She is obsessed not only with the beauty of the body but also the body of difference: the monstrous and the divine, the decaying and the enduring, alike. Bodies are worshipped in Winterson's novels regardless of their shape or condition, as both a manifestation of extreme obsession and of worship turning into madness and melancholy for the lost object. A broad theoretical understanding of fetishism enables a more productive engagement with the specificities of Winterson's work, and this chapter discusses the work of Sigmund Freud, Jacques Lacan, Friedrich Nietzsche and Michel Foucault, along with more recent feminist perspectives from Elizabeth Grosz, Teresa de Lauretis, Julia Kristeva and Judith Butler. Winterson's work repays analyses made with respect to their literary and cultural theorizing, as her novels engage with, respond to and adapt such views on gender, sexuality and identity. Her texts refashion normative material into alternative situations through sensuous and sensual language, revealing the fluid and diverse pleasures of the body and its parts. Grosz addresses very adroitly the oppositions and contradictions that are, literally, embodied:

> The body is a most peculiar 'thing', for it is never quite reducible to being merely a thing; nor does it ever quite manage to rise above the status of thing. Thus it is both a thing and a nonthing, an object, but an object which somehow contains or coexists with an interiority, an object able to take itself and others as subjects, a unique kind of object not reducible to other objects. Human bodies, indeed all animate bodies, stretch and extend the notion of physicality that dominates the physical sciences, for animate bodies are objects necessarily different from other objects; they are materialities that are uncontainable in physicalist terms alone. If bodies are objects or things, they are like no others, for they are the centers of perspective, insight, reflection, desire, agency.[4]

Winterson's fetishistic approach to language depicts the 'tensions and harmonies between word and meaning that gradually can be resolved into form'.[5] The bodies discussed in this chapter regularly fall outside binary classifications of male or female; rather, they are fluid and the desires they evoke and enact depend on the cultural and physical environment. Grosz states that 'for Foucault the body is the field on which the play of powers, knowledges, and resistances is worked out, for Nietzsche the body is the agent and active cause of knowledge'.[6] In Winterson's writing, the body is both field of play and active agent; the bodily self and the other venture on circular journeys through time and space, in search of diverse pleasures and desires. Hence, the discussion here also shows how Winterson's works treat the body and its parts as spaces to discover and conquer, which embrace fetishistic desire. The body is portrayed as an object of obsession, seduction, memorialization and idolization that enables narcissistic investment and the expression of innate drives, often to the benefit of the subject.

This chapter looks at several of Winterson's novels, including *Written on the Body*, *The Passion*, *Oranges*, *Sexing the Cherry*, *The PowerBook* and *Frankissstein*, to illustrate the alternative mode of fetishism with which she depicts the body. The idea of subjective unity is challenged in her texts by fluid gender performances, free-floating sexuality and the deconstructed body. In addition, many seemingly divergent subjects are linked back to the body by the plurality of Winterson's discourse: gastronomy, typography, anatomy and cartography all add complex layers of symbolic and metaphoric representation to the desires and pleasures of the physical body. Winterson's fetishistic approach to language is the means by which all other fetishes are revealed and traced, and desire provides the linguistic, emotional and psychosexual energy; as de Lauretis argues:

> desire itself, with its movement between subject and object, between the self and an other, is founded on difference – the difference and separateness of one from the other. And what signifies desire is a sign which both elides and remarks that separation in describing *both the object and its absence*. This sign, I am arguing, is a fetish.[7]

The body and its parts, therefore, provide the physical signifiers of difference and the borders that separate the self and the other required for fetishism. Obsession over an absent object is a recurring theme in Winterson's works, and she often portrays acts of worship of the body that are transformed by loss into mourning and melancholy. To Freud, melancholy results from an aggrieved or unacknowledged loss. However, in Winterson's writing, such losses invariably create the desire for a replacement. The embrace of this substitute converts disavowal into avowal, overlaying the negative emotions linked to the loss of the original object with beneficial ones.

1

Fetishistic desire

Versatile bodies

The body is a prominent image and a central narrative component in all of Winterson's works, and I now explore and assess how the versatility of the body responds to the diverse desires and drives of her characters in all the varying and volatile situations they encounter. Winterson's writing questions gender and sexuality norms and opposes gender stereotypes, leaving the essential nature of love as a focal point of desire between the self and the other. In her novels, conventional and gendered perceptions of the body are disturbed, while desire prompts the reassessment of gender, sexuality and identity. Winterson's fiction uses the materiality of the body to communicate and translate the language of fluid desires and pleasures into visible and acceptable forms, which can be seen as non-pathological acts of fetishism. The body's relationship with the mind is a crucial component of the alternative bodily fetishism in Winterson's texts, and the correspondence between the two is complex and changeable. Grosz believes that 'the body functions, not simply as a biological entity but as a psychical, lived relation' and conversely that 'the psyche is a projection of the body's form'.[1] This mutually productive and constitutive relationship within an individual is further complicated by the subject's body image, which does not consider the self in isolation but as necessarily involved with 'the relations between the body, the surrounding space, other objects and bodies'.[2] Hence, the desires and pleasures that lead to bodily fetishism arrive at an individual through a shifting matrix of origins, viewpoints and references. Bodies of difference and diverse desires in Winterson's fiction are presented in a variety of ways according to the effect and influence of internal and external energies and how they resist social, cultural and political norms.

In *Written on the Body*, Winterson uses metaphors of corporeal inscription to question and rewrite conventional views of the body, while the narrative forms a confession of how the quest for love can deleteriously affect it. Initially, Louise's body is admired externally by the Unnamed Narrator's physical, psychological and emotional perceptions.[3] In the second part of the novel, when illness has set into Louise's body, the Unnamed Narrator imagines seeing into its interior, analysing its parts and organs, to meet the gaze of the decaying body with the language of medical knowledge. Consequently, Louise becomes transparent when perceived through such extreme obsession and desire for the other body. Heather Nunn argues that the ripping apart of the body in *Written on the Body*, and the focus on body parts, such as sinew, scars and bones, 'challeng[es] the fetishization of the female body by worshipping all of its elements'.[4] However, I propose that this living autopsy in fact reveals the alternative fetishism in Winterson's writing. The conventional fetishization of women may be disrupted by the Unnamed Narrator's forensic dissection of Louise's body, but this reduction to parts also leads to a non-pathological outcome as it ultimately enables the Unnamed Narrator to work through their emotional obsession to the point where they can (at least attempt to) reconnect with Louise. That is to say, through the Unnamed Narrator's desire for Louise's deconstructed body and her individual body parts, Winterson's notions of fetishism defy conventional ideas to become beneficial practices.

Written on the Body presents the fetishistic body here through the deconstruction of its unity and beauty, defying normative notions of attraction. However, the Unnamed Narrator's extreme obsession with Louise has to work through madness and melancholy before it can become beneficial. The Unnamed Narrator determines to trace the working of Louise's body and its parts through different terminologies, one of which argues that the body is unstable, thus questioning the traditional view that the female body must be beautiful to be desired. Instead, no matter what the condition of the body, it should be admired even if it is decayed or monstrous. Bodies in Winterson's novels are worshipped whether they are healthy or sick, and their diverse desires and pleasures stand revealed through language. Winterson's language of worshipping the body shows how a person can cross the boundaries of normality of desire and pleasure in order to fulfil one's inner and external needs. *Written on the Body* is narrated in the first person throughout, allowing readers intimate access to the Unnamed Narrator's thoughts and feelings and thereby creating an accessible path to survey the expressions of love and loss. The language often contains colloquial speech that imbues the narration with a conversational tone, certainly towards the start of the novel. For instance, the Unnamed Narrator refers to a previous lover as 'The clap-giver'.[5] This type of narration encourages the reader to understand the Unnamed Narrator's diverse desires as non-pathological.

The tone of the language changes in the second half of the book, in which a bodily obsession is revealed. This is shown by the anatomical language used for chapter headings, such as 'The Cells, Tissues, Systems and Cavities of the Body'.[6] The specificity of this medical terminology articulates the depth of the Unnamed Narrator's desires for, and obsession with, Louise's body. The Unnamed Narrator initially views Louise's body holistically, as a complete physical unit, but following her cancer diagnosis they move on to look at her body's internal operations and its separate parts. Following the break-up of their relationship, the Unnamed Narrator uses medical books as substitutes for the lost object of Louise's body, determined to trace the working of its parts to divert their melancholy. The unstable body questions any traditional view of the female body as coherent, whole and beautiful, but in this particular situation, these acts of diversion and replacement produce a non-pathological process that benefits the psyche of the Unnamed Narrator. As it is in most of Winterson's work, the fetishism in *Written on the Body* is interchangeable and fluid and goes beyond the previous theorizing of first-wave and second-wave fetishism – it is not so much about bodies and loss as the transformation and re-inscription of the desire and pleasure of the fluidly gendered body. This offers a site of resistance and dissidence to patriarchal hegemony as the Unnamed Narrator experiences the fluidity of desire and pleasure, rather than repressing the internal and external desires of the bodily self. The body subjected to fetishism in Winterson's fiction is not only separated but also expanded, moving beyond notions of surface perfection to something deeper, even in monstrous or diseased bodies. Thus, obsession with the beauty of the other is not a romantic or clichéd gesture but an act of alternative fetishism that can provide relief to the subject in the face of absence – absence that is effaced and overwritten by the inscription of language.

A fetishistic treatment of the body has been in Winterson's fiction from the start of her career, with the publication of *Oranges* in 1985. Concerns and themes found in this book, such as an obsessive focus on the correlation between body and mind, can be detected in all her subsequent novels. In *Oranges*, the obsessions of Jeanette and her mother, Mrs Winterson, transform into mourning and melancholia of the bodily self and the other, and tip into madness. Mrs Winterson's religious obsession results in abuse to her body and her psyche as she devotes both to the church, at the expense of her own mental and physical well-being. In terms of desire and fetishism, the novel positions Jeanette's fascination with Melanie against Mrs Winterson's passion for God. Winterson dismantles the conventional perception of diverse desire through these two characters, producing an alternative fetishization from their transferal of obsession. Mrs Winterson dedicates her body and soul to the worship of God and forces Jeanette to do likewise. The result is confusion between Jeanette's love of God and her religion, and her love and desire for another person; for instance, she enters dangerously sacrilegious ground when she tells Melanie, 'I love you almost as much as I love the Lord'.[7] As Mrs Winterson says, Jeanette 'had flouted God's law and had tried to do it sexually'.[8] Due to her evangelical background and the relative values she has learnt in school, she tries to be honest with her orthodox mother, hoping she will understand her inner feelings and help her resolve her confusion. She tells her mother about her feelings for Melanie and how she 'needed that kind of friend'.[9] The devout Mrs Winterson is horrified by Jeanette's same-sex passions and tells her that 'romantic love for another woman was a sin'.[10] Mrs Winterson denounces her to the church, which acts as the legal and governing body in their lives. She blames her daughter for having 'made her ill, made the house ill, brought evil into the church'.[11] Mrs Winterson's obsession precludes her from thinking compassionately, which eventually leads to the loss of her daughter's love.

The novel positions Jeanette's love for Melanie, which eventually leads to self-determination and freedom, against Mrs Winterson's passion for God, which makes her ignore her own health and overlook her family's needs. For example, she stays awake most of the night to pray to her God and read the Bible, which, more than coincidentally, means she only shares a bed with her husband for an hour before he gets up for work: 'he was never quite good enough' for her.[12] Worshipping God and devoting her body and soul to her religion is a pleasure for her that replaces physical and emotional intimacy, and she talks as if she was physically with God: 'I am busy with the Lord in Wigan.'[13] However, the bodily self is denied, by both Mrs Winterson and her daughter, due to their external obsessions, and in the long run their bodies give way to physical and emotional deterioration. The versatility of the body as instigator and object of sacrifice is presented here through the contrast of tangible and intangible loves these two characters fetishize. As in all of Winterson's works, every obsession comes with a consequence to the self and the other.

Fetishism, according to Kant, refers to 'the illusion that one can possess the art of bringing about a supernatural effect through wholly natural means'.[14] Mrs Winterson's foremost fetishistic belief is that everything happens because of God and so all occurrences are, in her world view, the entirely natural result of divine action. Jeanette suffers from her mother's excessive religious devotion, such as not always having enough food: 'I haven't time to make you chips', Mrs Winterson tells her at one stage, even though she spends 'most of her time' cooking 'things for the faithful'.¹⁵ Her extreme behaviour turns her into a neglectful mother as her obsession with God leads her to become increasingly superstitious. For example, when Jeanette becomes deaf, her mother does not initially notice and then thinks it must be because she is 'full of the spirit' and in a 'state of rapture', rather than the more down to earth reason of infected adenoids.¹⁶ Mrs Winterson's devotion to God blinds her judgement but Jeanette herself is also prey to such fervent thinking. For instance, when Melanie looks ill from the stress of Pastor Finch's fire-and-brimstone sermon on 'unnatural passion', Jeanette thinks it 'must be the spirit'.¹⁷ Flooded with excessive delusion, such extreme obsessions eventually become acts of madness for both Mrs Winterson and Jeannette, ending in self-destruction and melancholia for them. Mrs Winterson has violent outbursts, such as smashing 'every plate in the kitchenette', while Jeanette lingers on 'in a kind of numbness', 'unable to forgive' herself or her mother for the loss of her loved object, Melanie.¹⁸ Jeanette's emotional state remains ambivalent and unresolved, setting her firmly on the path to alternative emotional and sexual behaviour. However, Mrs Winterson's obsession with religion is still her coping strategy, the substitute object for her absent maternal feelings for Jeanette and sexual feelings for her husband. For Jeanette, the bodily experiences she enjoyed with Melanie offer the substitute for the religious obsession of her younger years, and the search for religious salvation becomes a quest for personal redemption.

Religious mania is also a feature of *The Passion*, but in this novel the devotion to God is more allegorical as Napoleon stands as a human manifestation of immense might, with power over life and death. Self-destruction happens to Henri, Villanelle and Napoleon, who each have their fetishistic worship and devotion for a replacement object. Henri initially devotes himself to Napoleon, before becoming obsessed with Villanelle, even though he ultimately turns away from her. For Henri, suffering and masochism are drives, pleasures even, that align body and mind in penitence. He worships Napoleon from childhood and cannot wait to join his army as it seeks to conquer Europe. Napoleon is seen as a semi-divine figure and Henri's local priest understands the influence his aura has on suggestible people like Henri: 'the priest looked towards the track that led away and held my arm too tight. "He'll call you," he whispered, "like God called Samuel and you'll go."'¹⁹ This religious approval makes Henri believe even more fervently in Napoleon and worship him as the object of his fetish. This obsession entraps Henri and joining the army has many undesirable repercussions for him, ultimately transforming him into a murderer, although this life choice is also how he meets Villanelle.

Henri, and many others in France, see Napoleon as God because he is male and appears to be omnipotent. However, Winterson's narrative challenges the absolute control of patriarchal hegemony by giving some voice and agency to those without power. For example, women are capable of moments of solidarity that show a community separate to, and sometimes more unified than, the men's. On New Year's Eve when Henri exits the church, the difference is clear: 'Most of the men are in groups of five or six, still by the church, but the women are joining hands and making a great circle that blocks the road and fills the space from one side of the street to the other.'[20] Thus, Winterson reveals how women can oppose male hegemony if collective, physical action is taken and how the powerless can contend with the powerful if they unite. This action can be viewed against Luce Irigaray's thoughts on 'the modification of women's status', in which 'women's movements challenge the forms and nature of political life, the contemporary play of power and power relations'.[21] Irigaray argues that such movements must challenge the established forms of power and not merely seek a redistribution of power, as this would leave women within the same political structures of the phallocratic order. It may be only for a night and in response to a festival atmosphere, but the difference between the circle of women, controlling the street, and the clusters of men, clinging near to the church, offers a microcosm of what can be achieved by the female community and their bodily resources.

It is not only through mass gatherings that women display their power, but such expressions also happen individually. For example, when Villanelle, Henri and Patrick run away from the army, it helps them all that she 'was skilful with the compass and map; she said it was one of the advantages of sleeping with Generals'.[22] Clearly, her female body gives her the ability to survive and allows her access to different worlds, demonstrating her own position of power and enabling her survival. Sex becomes another tool at Villanelle's disposal: 'I was getting to know the warder and I had an idea that I could buy him out for money and sex.'[23] According to Foucault, 'pleasure and power do not cancel or turn back against one another. They seek out, overlap, and reinforce one another. They are linked together by complex mechanisms and devices of excitation and incitement.'[24] Thus, women like Villanelle use their bodies and their sexual prowess to control situations, utilizing their capacity to fulfil desires and pleasures to attain a goal. The sex slaves in the novel are another example of how often the ability for women to survive depends on their bodies: 'the *vivandiéres* are runaways, strays, younger daughters of too-large families, servant girls who'd got tired of giving it away to drunken masters, and fat old dames who couldn't ply their trade anywhere else.'[25] Winterson's characters float not only in gender, sexuality and identity but also in situations in order to survive.

Napoleon's obsession for power leads to the death of millions, many of whom were, like Henri, young men who worshipped him:

> [Napoleon's] desire burned for longer than ours because it was never likely that he would pay for it with his life. He kept his valuable, fabulous thing behind the secret panel until the last moment, but we, who had so little except our lives, were gambling with all we had from the start.
>
> He saw what we felt.
> He reflected on our losses.
> He had tents and food when we were dying.
> He was trying to found a dynasty. We were fighting for our lives.[26]

Napoleon's obsession dictates not only his actions but also the fate of those around him. The bodies of his armies are like neglected baggage, so the body is a separate entity from the person. Napoleon treats his people's bodies as if they were worthless objects, things that had no feeling or emotion. For example, Napoleon treats men as numerical items, and his abuses can be seen as discrimination against the other, such as the soldiers and prostitutes. All his actions are the result of his extreme obsession with power, and they are targeted at fulfilling the pleasures of his bodily self. To the emperor, individuals lack distinction, and the 20,000 soldiers who are likely to die in the attempt to invade England by sea are seen as easily expendable: 'Bonaparte thought them good odds, he was used to losing that number in battle.'[27] Thus, even though Napoleon dehumanizes his soldiers, they worship him as a man with great power and knowledge. Napoleon is able to exploit the bodies of others (the soldiers and the women in the camp) due to his apparent omniscience and omnipotence. These bodies are fetish objects for Napoleon in his quest for world domination, the means and the end of his power. Grosz's summary of Foucault's thinking on the body is apposite:

> [T]he body is the object, target, and instrument of power, the field of greatest investment for power's operations, a stake in the struggle for power's control over a materiality that is dangerous to it, precisely because it is unpredictable and able to be used in potentially infinite ways, according to infinitely variable cultural dictates.[28]

The subjects of Napoleon's exploitation have little resistance to their subjugation; they are powerless before Napoleon, despite wanting to free themselves: 'We should have turned on him, should have laughed in his face, and should have shaken the dead-men-seaweed-hair in his face. But his face is always pleading with us to prove him right.'[29] Napoleon's will to conquer, from the unfortunate other to whole nations, sways those under his command. He believes in the teleological purpose of language and power, and thus a form of religion arises around him that manipulates others, as shown by the priest comparing his voice to God's. His perennial desire for power appears, at first, to cast him as an idol to be admired, but his obsession with domination prevents him from achieving that goal. Instead, his obsession with mastery leads him to insanity and grief for his lost empire.

Bodily fetishism is also central to *Frankissstein*, a novel in which bodies are altered, augmented and ultimately discarded in the quest for improvement and immortality. In a post-postmodern vein, in which the subject seeks to intervene and fashion, rather than merely experience, the world they live in, the choice of sexual individuation is key for Ry Shelley, who has undergone surgery for their gender nonconformity.[30] They see Victor Stein as a superior being, physically, sexually and psychologically: 'I'm watching him as he talks, I love watching him. He has that sex-mix of soul-saving and erudition. His body is lean and keen.'[31] Victor's body is an extremely conventional, clichéd even, example of masculinity, down to his 'straight jaw, blue eyes'.[32] Ry is less straight, having been born female but suffering with gender dysphoria from an early age: 'My build is slender. Narrow hips, long legs. When I had top surgery there wasn't much to remove, and the hormones had already altered my chest.'[33] Ry decides not to have lower surgery and so lives in an interstitial location on the gender spectrum: 'I am what I am, but what I am is not one thing, not one gender. I live with doubleness.'[34] Victor is attracted to Ry but this is contingent on their body still having a vagina (see Chapter 9 for further discussion), a troublingly heteronormative standpoint that reduces Ry to an assemblage of body parts.

Both Ry and Victor, albeit in different ways, believe that the body can be – *must* be – altered in the name of progress and evolution. For Ry, the lived experience of gender realignment has allowed them to become physically what they perceive themself to be mentally and emotionally. Victor, while he is still embodied, emulates the hubris of Mary Shelley's mad doctor, although, unlike in *Frankenstein*, Winterson's Victor wishes to give new life, in the form of bodiless digital consciousness, to himself. What he seeks to achieve is 'shapeshifting. The disembodied future. Eternal life. The all-powerful gods not subject to the decay of nature.'[35] Ry remains firmly rooted in their androgynous bodily existence, which is understandable having been through great changes already to align their interior and exterior being. By contrast, Victor has lived a consistent, normative life, in terms of his gender, sexuality and identity, up until the novel's conclusion. At this point he undergoes his transition to a digital consciousness, which raises the difference between transgender people, who wish to physically change their bodies, and post-humanists, who aim to leave all bodies, all genders behind. Victor's obsession with Ry's doubleness (even as it is weighted towards the feminine) is the temporary substitute for his long-term obsession with a bodiless future. At the centre of Victor's attraction to Ry is a presence/absence binary that foreshadows his own dematerialization: 'I love the confidence of your skin over the hesitation of your body, the appearing/disappearing of you, changing according to the light. Now male, now not quite, now quite clearly a woman who will slip inside a boy's body.'[36] In fact, I would argue that Ry's transness is exactly what Victor needs to experience, even if only vicariously, to provide him with the final motivation to transition to post-human. Victor's relationship with Ry gives him the needed insight into a mode of forming attachments that is not based on 'reproduction. Not economic necessity. Not scarcity. Not patriarchy. Not gender. Not fear. It could be wonderful!'[37] The central paradox at the heart of Winterson's collocation of transgender and transhuman issues is that Ry, who has undergone significant change, desires physical stability and bodily stasis, whereas Victor, who has made no alteration to himself (there is the slightest suggestion of a face-lift, but Ry does not pursue this further), wants to leave the body entirely behind.

Across all the genres Winterson has written in – autobiographical fiction with *Oranges*, historical fiction with *The Passion*, science fiction with *The PowerBook*, and so forth – an imaginative reconceptualization of the body has mediated the diverse desires between the self and the other. An alternative fetishism has consistently been the process by which her distinctive yet fluid depictions of love and loss, obsession and replacement, have been performed by versatile bodies. As Grosz says, 'the body is a pliable entity whose determinate form is provided not simply by biology but through the interaction of modes of psychical and physical inscription'.[38] In Winterson's fiction, this inscription is driven by the alternative fetishism her characters regularly practise.

The fluid and subversive gender, sexuality and identity of Ry, the Unnamed Narrator, and Villanelle, for instance, can also be traced to Ali/Alix in *The PowerBook*. In this novel, the body is once again deconstructed through the language of fetishistic imagination, this time in the cyber world. The body becomes fluid and mobile in terms of gender and sexuality, while diverse desires and pleasure of the bodily self and the other are explored. Within an obsessive cycle, the imagination of the central character, the e-writer Ali/Alix, wanders actively through cyberspace; Gavin Keulks believes that Ali/Alix's obsessions with her dual identity, her sexuality and her hunt for freedom are evidence of 'the dual crises of the postmodern self', which are crises of autonomy and agency.[39] For Ali/Alix, the fact that she is ordered to write stories and that the narratives are directed by her clients shows her own lack of autonomy and agency in her work. As Ali/Alix becomes trapped in her imaginative story, the body and its parts are worshipped as objects and subjects of desire, and her fictive self falls lustfully for her client's character: 'Suddenly, very badly, I wanted to see her body.'[40] As in all Winterson's novels, love and loss are among the main themes, along with the recurring, and complicating, presence of the love triangle. However, in *The PowerBook*, Winterson uses a medieval love story, filtered through the lens of cyber technology and the contemporary reality of the novel, as a base for most of Ali/Alix's e-narrative. Thus, in *The PowerBook*, the body and its parts act as a vehicle to challenge boundary norms across time, space, genre, gender and sexuality.

In the first story, Ali/Alix is born a girl, but her 'mother dressed her as a boy' and due to this she absorbs certain stereotypical masculine traits, such as the determination to provide financial support to 'bring any wealth to the family'.[41] Ali/Alix is ubiquitous in her stories, but always changing, whether in terms of place, gender, sexuality or identity. She talks incessantly about freedom: 'Freedom for a night. Just for one night the freedom to be somebody else.'[42] All Ali/Alix's characters are obsessed with challenging boundaries and conventions to fulfil their desires. For example, whereas a flower conventionally symbolizes female genitalia in literature, in *The PowerBook*, a tulip is made to substitute for a penis; thus, Winterson deconstructs culturally dominant uses of symbolism to offer an alternative possibility. Ali/Alix's flowery phallus is the focus of obsession from the Princess (for whom she is writing the story 'in reality'). In this scenario, the Princess is to learn about sexual pleasure before getting married, and Ali/Alix has been chosen to assist. She has been carrying a tulip and some bulbs in her trousers to pass as a man and as a means of smuggling these treasures, and these are what the Princess mistakes for penis and testicles. Thus, the Princess worships the tulip as an object of pleasure and a means of fulfilling her and Ali/Alix's desire. This reflects the notion of lesbian fetishism as Ali/Alix accepts her lack of a penis according to the disavowal of 'I don't have it but I can/will have it'.[43] As Grosz argues, 'the displacement of value from the penis to another part of the body or onto an inanimate object' is crucial for the performance of female fetishism, and it is the beneficial aspects of the practice for Ali/Alix and the Princess that make this more specifically an example of alternative fetishism.

As mentioned earlier, an extreme obsession can lead into madness and then melancholy; Ali/Alix still has doubts about their sexual relationship and questions her own contentment: 'I was happy in a sad sort of way, because I knew this was never going to work.'[44] In this way, fetishism is already on the way to melancholy. Initially, being an e-writer is just a job for Ali/Alix, but it transforms into an obsession as she appears in all her stories, changing gender, sexuality and identity in different places and time: 'Who was I last night? Who was she?'[45] Her excessive fetishistic desire tips into madness through the pursuit of desire for others, at the cost of her own identity. Consumed by creating gender-bending, cross-dressing versions of herself, it is her boundaries and desires that are continually exceeded. As Andermahr says of the novel, 'all of the stories are about either illicit or obsessive love and its (usually fatal) consequences', and as a result of the alternative fetishism that Winterson presents in her writing, the multiplying objects and possibilities of desire sometimes lead to an exhausting quest for the subject.[46]

Women and unfortunate others in Winterson's texts often react with dissidence in order to meet basic needs, such as food and shelter, and to gain a space to be physically, psychologically and emotionally free. In *Sexing the Cherry*, Dog-Woman displays typically masculine traits in terms of her physique and mentality, but she maintains certain feminine characteristics, such as her maternal instincts with Jordan. Her body and behaviour transgress the boundaries of gender, and she represents both a father figure and a mother figure. Nevertheless, armed with masculine strength and feminine sensitivity, she uses her physical power to destroy those who abuse their position in society, such as hypocritical preachers. When Dog-Woman attacks and murders Preacher Scroggs and Neighbour Firebrace at the brothel, she literally deconstructs the bodies of the other; a thumb, a leg, and, ultimately, both their heads are chopped off by her axe as the bodies become sites of violent rupture and enforced lack.[47] Although Dog-Woman does not attack their genitals, the dismembering and beheading still suggests castration, reflecting the gender reversals implicit in these men's deaths at the end of a masculine woman.

Dog-Woman is an example of a disobedient woman who opposes the idea of the passive female body and is prepared to challenge patriarchal norms, as she cannot restrain herself and she acts monstrously in the brothel to those who misuse their power and abuse those beneath them. Conversely, Dog-Woman's son, Jordan, experiments with transvestitism to experience being a woman and to venture into the feminine world. Through language, Jordan's fetishism derives from the specific value conferred upon his cross-dressing, which allows him to figuratively become the phallus, the signifier of the desire of the other that is being a woman. Jordan's acts of cross-dressing mean he is mobilized by that act which, within the structure of signification in his world, is a symbolic signifier of the other. Through this cultural experience, Jordan discovers how women communicate to each other and to their male counterparts. He masks his male body in women's clothes and learns a feminine codification of language. Butler's contestation of Lacan's 'The Signification of the Phallus' offers a useful theoretical approach to help analyse Jordan's actions. Butler argues, '"being" the Phallus and "having" the Phallus denote divergent sexual position, or non-positions (impossible positions, really), within language.'[48] In this view, Jordan's acting as a woman means he goes from having the phallus to, at least temporarily, being the phallus. He occupies a 'divergent sexual position' due to his gender-switching, a 'non-position' due to the underlying contrast of his ever-present male body, and an 'impossible position' from his inability to perform the role permanently, or to any depth. The crucial function Lacan ascribed to language in relation to the signification of the phallus, highlighted by Butler, is reflected in the importance attached to Jordan's ability to enter the female world, in which, from the language of 'having', he adopts the language of 'being'. This results in his knowledge that women behave and communicate in different ways, depending on the situation. Therefore, the phallus is fluid as an object and a subject of the self and the other. The phallus in Winterson's texts can be seen as either a dominant or subordinate signifier. Jordan's disguise as a woman is readily accepted by the men he encounters because of his young body and the softness of his heart: 'I watched [the women] collapsing into laughter, sharing the joke, while the men, all unknowing, felt themselves master of the situation and went off to brag in barrooms and to preach from pulpits.'[49] This stereotype of male and female behaviour shows the way in which 'the body, once it is constituted as such, is transcribed and marked by culture', but it is these transcriptions and marks that are, at least temporarily, covered by cross-dressing.[50]

Jordan is constantly seeking to know about the world and searches for romantic love but finds only loss. He leaves the maternal protection of Dog-Woman and searches for Fortunata, the dancing Princess, who will never return his love. However, Jordan replaces this loss by diverting his desire for Fortunata into the further performance of transvestism, thereby turning his own being into his fetish object. Sexual acts by Jordan are absent from the novel; instead we hear his sympathy and empathy for women and his dismay at the way they are treated by men. Therefore, Jordan's actions and voice are vital in *Sexing the Cherry* to show how unfair society is towards its more unfortunate elements, especially women. However, if Winterson uses her characters to show us the inequality in society, she also depicts resistance. Jordan observes how women's language is different, as 'though they were communicating without words' and that 'women have a private language'.[51] Through these cultural experiences, he learns how the female community survives in the face of patriarchal exploitation.

Winterson's texts suggest that fluidity and changeability are principal ways for us to experience the world and Jordan's experiments with cross-dressing mirror those by Villanelle in *The Passion*, as they both embody the cultural performance of internal and external desires. This cross-dressing suggests that deviant, perverse and dissident desires are engendered, as the body contains both masculine and feminine traits. Jordan's dressing as a woman and displaying attributes of a (conventionally understood) female passivity derives from an internal need to understand his own self and the other. His experiences in the feminine world cause him to take pity on the female other, which suggests that gender and sexuality are to a large degree performative and contingent on the situation, rather than essential. Thus, Jordan's cross-dressing is an ability to undo the normative binaries of the relationship between male and female, and it provides a space for fluid gender, sexuality and identity. Cross-dressing shows the illusory power of the value of clothes of the opposite sex and suggests the relation between the individual (subject) and clothing (object) can produce an excess emotional value regarding the object. The subject believes, through an act of emotional and mental fetishization, that they can replace their desire to be the other with an invested performance.

Like Jordan, Villanelle traverses gender boundaries through her bodily experiences in *The Passion*. Villanelle's physical appearance at birth shocks her mother and the midwife because there 'never was a girl whose feet were webbed in the entire history of the boatmen'.[52] This physical abnormality had previously been the preserve of the men of the boatmen society, and so her destabilized gender identity and sexual preferences are, in part, due to her nature. Her father teaches her never to take off her boots in case someone should notice that she is physically different but, as mentioned earlier, Villanelle takes advantage of her fluid gender, sexuality and identity. She enjoys performing acts of transvestism as they convert her deprivation into a mode of behaviour that allows her to perform in society. Winterson's fetishistic description of both Jordan and Villanelle reveals that the notion of masquerade belongs to any gender and sexuality. Villanelle performs her masculine role by dressing as a young man when she is working in the gambling den, in a job usually reserved for men. She enjoys both males and females sexually; she is married to an abusive man and has an affair with a married woman and Henri. Winterson creates characters who are searching for their self but who also show a willingness to explore multiple fragmented fictions of identity through fetishist acts with their own body, such as cross-dressing. Such actions challenge the boundaries of gender, which Butler defines as, 'the repeated stylization of the body, a set of repeated acts within a highly rigid regulatory frame that congeal over time to produce the appearance of substance'.[53] Many individuals in Winterson's texts, including Jordan and Villanelle, transgress this regulatory frame and prevent the congealment of gendered acts by practices such as cross-dressing, thus physically undermining gender norms through the versatility of the body.

As this chapter has illustrated, many of Winterson's characters exercise their bodily desires and pleasures according to a combination of internal and external factors. Gender, sexuality and identity are fluid formations, rather than fixed identities, that can respond according to the specifics of a situation. Hence, bodies are destabilized and deconstructed in Winterson's novels by her language of diverse desire. As Grosz says, 'The body can be regarded as a kind of *hinge* or threshold: it is placed between a psychic or lived interiority and a more sociopolitical exteriority that produces interiority through the *inscription* of the body's outer surface.'[54] The versatile bodies in Winterson's fiction are subjects and objects of an alternative fetishism that provides a process of replacement and substitution that can benefit the practitioner mentally, emotionally and physically. The next chapter focuses on the body in relation to space and time, including how intangible passions, such as the desiring gaze, can be transformed across space and time from invisible desire into physical contact.

2

Fetishistic touch

Space and time

There is a strong connection in Winterson's novels between fetishism, bodies and the spatio-temporal, particularly through the acts of looking and touching. Her texts regularly portray the body and its parts as spaces to be discovered and conquered, while time is constructed and mutable. Underpinning this, as ever, is language, which acts as a substitute for the obscured meanings of ambiguous desires in Winterson's works and creates forms of obsession that give space for emotional, psychical and physical exploration and expression. As Grosz suggests, bodies and the conceptions of space and time are significant in understanding the positions, knowledges and experiences of women in society, and scholarly studies of Winterson have addressed the importance of space and time in her work.[1] However, research in this area has tended to focus on categorizing her as a modernist/postmodernist lesbian writer, rather than sufficiently addressing how time and space relate to the fluidity of desire in her remapping of gender and sexuality.

Grosz further argues that 'if bodies are to be reconceived, not only must their *matter and form* be rethought, but so too must their environment and *spatio-temporal location*'.[2] In Winterson's reconceptualization of the body, there is no idea of 'permanence', as she has indirectly noted: 'The space that art creates is space outside of a relentless self, a meditation that gives both release and energy.'[3] Olu Jenzen argues that Winterson's texts 'endorse a notion of temporality that tries to reach beyond regulated, linear and (re-)productive time, but has also a romantic vision of a utopian temporality, governed by passion and desire'.[4] This claim opens up new readings of Winterson's works because time and space are characteristic and recurring themes in all her novels and vitally contribute to her representations of transgressive gender, sexuality and identity. Time and space cannot be separated in Winterson's fiction as they occupy the same space-time. As Grosz explains:

space is no more 'tangible' or perceptible than time, for it is only objects in space and time which can be considered tangible and amenable to perception. Space is no more concrete than time, nor is it easier to present. The subject is no more clearly positioned in space than in time; indeed, the immediacy of the 'hereness' of corporeal existence is exactly parallel to the 'newness' of the subject experience.[5]

Grosz also raises Irigaray's claim that time is conceived as masculine and space associated with femininity; such an interpretation is challenged by Winterson's writing in which temporality and spatiality resist such gendering by their fluid and changeable deployment.[6] Resultingly, alternative fetishism is a disruptive and transgressive gesture as her characters travel in time and journey through space in their quests for the diverse desires of the self and the other. In this connection, there is a particular use of images, symbols and repetition in Winterson's works to show her approach to time and space; as Winterson herself says:

> All of my books are preoccupied with time – it starts right back in *Oranges* in the Deuteronomy section. In *Sexing the Cherry* I use time vertically, not just horizontally, and in *Gut Symmetries* I wanted to explore the dimensionality of time. How do we understand time? What happens to the past? Does the future already exist? These are questions the book deals with, not because I hope to answer them, but as a way of adding to the puzzle.[7]

As mentioned elsewhere in this book, Winterson's work is an amalgamation of literature, psychology and philosophy, bringing together different themes and genres, including history, fairy tales and science fiction, all of them dealing with aspects of spatio-temporal representation. Her writing challenges orthodox ideology by deconstructing normative perceptions of the body as simply an object and language as merely a means of communication. Winterson's fiction is rich with extraordinary temporal shifts in multiple historical and magical worlds, and her interest in spatial and temporal metaphors has remained remarkably consistent from *Oranges* to *Frankissstein*. It is important to acknowledge that these metaphors represent her resistance to conventional notions of space and time as she reconceptualizes gender, sexuality and identity through acts of alternative fetishism. From these, historical, conventional and contemporary notions of the subject and bodies are deconstructed and destabilized. This alternative perspective is particularly made manifest in her writing when time moves backwards and forwards repeatedly through different situations and locations. The repeated switching between the past and the present, making an alternative to challenge the normative, is itself a fetishistic action in literary form as the constant shifting of the narration between the past and the present displaces the lost object of linear chronology that is suggested by its absence.

Winterson's metaphoric use of space and time in relation to the deconstructed body dismantles normative desire to illustrate an alternative way of alternative fetishization in daily life – one that reject any stereotypes of gender and sexuality. There is a strong connection between the concept of fetishism and the spatio-temporal in Winterson's works, particularly through the act of touching and its relation to time past, present and future. The fetishistic behaviour of looking and touching in Winterson's texts is incorporated into stages of obsession that give space for the emotions to explore and express themselves. The first stage is that of being obsessed with just looking to satisfy the subject's inner desire for an object. The second stage is being obsessed with the need to touch the desired object in order to fulfil that need. This can happen either in reality, through physical touch, or in fantasy, through the fetishistic imagination.

In *Written on the Body*, the Unnamed Narrator fetishes Louise's body. Winterson gives importance to the minutiae of desire, allowing her readers to fathom the complexity involved in meeting the needs of the bodily self and the other. The act of looking is, so often, simultaneously an act of imagining, and so it is when the Unnamed Narrator first sees Louis: 'If I were painting Louise I'd paint her hair as a swarm of butterflies.'[8] Later, it leads to touching, which gives the Unnamed Narrator immense, shocking pleasure: 'She touched me and I yelped.'[9] Due to extreme longing, every contact with Louise is an intense experience, teeming with pleasure, for the Unnamed Narrator: 'We lay down on the floor, our backs to the day. I needed no more light than was in her touch, her fingers brushing my skin, bringing up the nerve ends.'[10] The Unnamed Narrator and Louise enjoy each other, allowing desire to transport them out of time, rendering the quotidian world inconsequential. Yet, the Unnamed Narrator's desire for Louise is so extraordinary that everyday items such as cutlery and plates turn into seductive objects for the Unnamed Narrator when Louise touches them, the space between the self and the other temporarily closed by the substitute object of her attention.

Winterson's fiction shows the impossibility of stasis, although memory persists: 'nothing is gone, everything can be recovered, not as it was, but in its changing form.'[11] She illustrates that all thwarted desires can be temporarily or permanently fulfilled by a substitute object in an alternative mode of fetishization. The Unnamed Narrator sees Louise even when she is absent, as they imagine her constantly. When they have to spend some time apart, the Unnamed Narrator says, 'I spent the three days trying again to rationalise us, to make a harbour in the raging sea where I could bob about and admire the view. There was no view, only Louise's face. I thought of her as intense and beyond common sense.'[12] The physical need for Louise consumes the Unnamed Narrator's psychological space and time, and she remains present in the Unnamed Narrator's psychic space when absent from their physical touch thanks to fetishistic imagination. Both characters lose their individual identities within their mutual, dissident desire, and the Unnamed Narrator voices the feeling of the two wanting to be inside each other, imagining it as a combination of exploration and imprisonment:

> 'Explore me,' you said and I collected my ropes, flasks and maps, expecting to be back home soon. I dropped into the mass of you and I cannot find the way out. Sometimes I think I'm free, coughed up like Jonah from the whale, but then I turn a corner and recognise myself again. Myself in your skin, myself lodged in your bones, myself floating.[13]

The body is not merely a body for the Unnamed Narrator – it is a map, a space with its own geography, a country to be discovered and understood over time. Grosz, discussing Deleuze and Guattari, argues that the body is both surface and interior; as surface, 'the body needs to be interpreted, read, in order to grasp its underlying meaning'; and as interior, 'the body is a surface to be inscribed, written on, which can be segmented, dissolved into flows'.[14] The surface and the interior of Louise's body are subjects of diverse desire of the self and the other, and the Unnamed Narrator's explorations lead to gazing and touching to create fetishistic space within an imaginary world. The Unnamed Narrator is constantly looking for lost objects of desire in the fragmentary nature of the body in reality and in the imaginary, searching for pathways to replacement; as Grosz comments, reality takes a backseat to conceptualization when it comes to one's formation of body image: 'This imaginary anatomy is an effect of the internalization of the specular image, and reflects social and familial beliefs about the body more than it does the body's organic nature.'[15] The Unnamed Narrator thinks they have found what they are seeking, but instead, by only imagining getting into the other body, they are still looking in the floating space of their own mind. As Lacan states, it is only in the imaginary that the other can be an image of another person.[16] The Unnamed Narrator's extreme obsession with Louise's skin, bones and the body in general produces a multitude of fetish objects. The body is not simply a body but a country full of treasures for lovers to track and discover:

> Louise, in the single bed, between these garish sheets, I will find a map as likely as any treasure hunt. I will explore you and mine you and you will redraw

me according to your will. We shall cross one another's boundaries and make ourselves one nation.¹⁷

Thus, the Unnamed Narrator needs to keep producing maps to locate and recover the treasures buried in their and Louise's lives. Through this discovery, an intense love for the other body emerges. This deep feeling, that the action of worshipping began consciously and unconsciously, turns into obsession. For the Unnamed Narrator, this exploration of the other body, even when deconstructed and in parts, with the imaginary provides the true knowledge of another person; it does not stem from cognitive perception but from a more instinctive grasp of the other's body: 'the recognition of another person that is deeper than consciousness, lodged in the body more than held in the mind.'[18] Therefore, the body presents a holistic ground in which multiple entrances into desire exist. The Unnamed Narrator continues to watch every act of Louise's body, touching its parts to communicate their satisfaction with her body.

When Louise has cancer, the Unnamed Narrator uses language associated with archaeological exploration to describe her body, which is imagined akin to a pyramid:

> Let me penetrate you. I am the archaeologist of tombs. I would devote my life to marking your passageways, the entrances and exits of that impressive mausoleum, your body. How tight and secret are the funnels and wells of youth and health. A wriggling finger can hardly detect the start of an ante-chamber, much less push through to the wide aqueous halls that hide womb, gut and brain.[19]

The suggestion is Louise's internal secrets can be discovered and deciphered by one who has sufficient commitment, courage and hermeneutical ability to do so. The resort to extended metaphorical conceits indicates that Winterson's fetishistic language in relation to the body is within the Western philosophical tradition that 'must simultaneously rely on and disavow the role of the body'.[20] The Unnamed Narrator is a mapmaker creating their own route through Louise's body, where the lines and spaces intersect and the body is internally and externally inscribed. Through the actions of the Unnamed Narrator, Winterson reveals the complex relationship between love, lust, passion, loss and the body, and how these emotions affect corporeality in time and space. In this connection, the intense moments of looking and touching take place alongside acts of spying and waiting. For instance, the Unnamed Narrator spies on Louise from outside her house: 'I didn't go in straight away, I stood lurking outside with my collar turned up, hiding to get a better view.'[21] They are expected by

Louise and so should just knock the door, but in their endlessly fetishizing mind it seems that stealing a look at Louise is a preferable replacement for an actual encounter at this stage. They consciously acknowledge their actions: 'I felt like a thief with a bagful of stolen glances.'[22] Later the Unnamed Narrator tellingly uses the slang term for a detective, which also idiomatically denotes the penis, to suggest how easily looking slides into the more sexual activity of voyeurism: 'I spent the whole night prowling outside Louise's house like a private dick.'[23] They obsessively study Louise's bodily acts from a distance: 'Ordinary things. Look how she picks them up and puts them down, wipes her hands briskly on the edge of the table-cloth; she wouldn't do that in company.'[24] Even when in the same room, and not looking in through a window, the Unnamed Narrator still gazes at Louise when she is unaware or otherwise occupied, which may be more intimate but is voyeuristic nonetheless: 'how many times have I enjoyed you with my lascivious naked eye? I have seen you unclothed, bent to wash, the curve of your back, the concurve of your belly.'[25] The Unnamed Narrator's obsession with Louise makes them engage in stealthy acts that gratify an instinctual, physical and psychological pleasure – not just inspecting Louise's body externally through her bodily gestures and appearance but also internally, by fantasizing about being inside Louise. Winterson also uses the discourse of gastronomy and consumption to translate this extreme obsession into an alternative type of fetishization: 'I would gladly have traded the blood in my body for half a pint of vegetable stock. Let me be diced carrot, vermicelli, just so that you will take me in your mouth.'[26] The Unnamed Narrator would gladly be transformed into a vegetable so that they could be held, eaten and chewed by Louise, just to be close to her, to be tasted by her, to be inside her.

The Unnamed Narrator also fetishizes Louise's body by reading it as a historical text. Printed in her body, traceable through a 'certain light', they sense a 'palimpsest [. . .] so heavily worked that the letters feel like braille'.[27] Grosz argues that the body is 'a text which is as complicated and indeterminate as any literary manuscript', and the Unnamed Narrator would agree with this view.[28] Their and Louise's life stories are written and rewritten over their bodies, while at the same time always allowing space for new stories for a new writer or reader to emerge and provide new interpretations of the body. Conversely, the Unnamed Narrator's body acts as Louise's writing material, somewhere for her to mark her story: she uses her 'hands as branding irons' and 'the pads of her fingers have become printing blocks' on the Unnamed Narrator's body.[29] Louise also has 'reading hands' and 'has translated [the Unnamed Narrator] into her own book'.[30] The body is inscribed with the experience of lives, love and loss; thus, it gives the lover the opportunity to rewrite and reread the inscriptions of the body with an extreme obsession. This is because it can only be read in a certain light by someone with a specific skill – as the letters are invisible, only 'reading hands' like Louise's can follow the story. As Butler says the subversive body 'is figured as a surface and the scene of a cultural inscription'.[31]

In relation to looking, surface representations and print, the Unnamed Narrator and their lovers discuss the works of famous painters like Renoir and writers such as Henry Miller and D. H. Lawrence, all of whose work exhibits excessive fetishist behaviour with the body and its parts. This book argues that the alternative fetishism in Winterson's writing resists established notions of fetishism and refuses simple categorization by the tenets of first-wave or second-wave models of fetishism. The fetishism in *Written on the Body* moves across boundaries of orthodoxy into fluid, subversive and changeable notions of fetishism. Alternative fetishism shows that the act of fetishism can transform the subject into both a subject and an object, depending on the situation. By refusing to assign a gender to the Unnamed Narrator, Winterson illustrates that the fetishizing of the body and its parts is possible, and prevalent, in heterosexuality, homosexuality, bisexuality and all available positions along the whole continuum of sexuality. In Winterson's literary worlds, desire observes no gender boundaries or sexual orientation, and it is fluidly interchangeable and contingent, whether being expressed by the Unnamed Narrator, Jeanette in *Oranges* or Ry in *Frankissstein*.

Winterson also expands the metaphorical language around time and space by playing with normative presentations of seasonal and meteorological elements. For example, characteristics of the seasons, such as changes in the weather, ecology and daylight hour, are used as metaphors for the journey the body undertakes. Winterson utilizes the lexicon of climatology to tie the physical conditions of the natural world to the journeys and events faced by the body in fulfilling desire and seeking the pleasure longed for by the self and the other. The metaphoric use of the season and climate relates to the ways in which bodies are coded and decoded, scripted and encrypted, with the diverse desires of the self and the other. The body's desires, pleasures and loves are limned through seasonal metaphors to indicate that the variations of the seasons can be the variations of the heart and that the external factors of the weather mirror the lack of control an individual faces when it is obsessed with the body of the other.

Winterson uses the seasons to portray ambiguity and to question conventional associations and common perceptions. For instance, the month of August is in the British summertime and, thus, should be hot and sunny with long days. Most people eagerly anticipate this season and August generally sees a lot of outdoor activity, so it is commonly associated with happy times. On the other hand, the British winter is usually bitterly cold and miserably wet. However, Winterson's texts often destabilize the conventional view of the seasons, as the sun-filled days of summer do not always provide happiness. Instead, this time of the year can prove to be hot, humid and uncomfortable for her characters who, conversely, often enjoy the rain and cold of winter. Such seasonal elements play a significant role in *Written on the Body* as they portray the Unnamed Narrator's emotional state, sexual needs and physical and psychological conditions. For example, the first page of the novel opens on a dry, stressful note: 'It hasn't rained for three months. [. . .] The grapes have withered on the vine.'[32] However, the ability to share the abnormally warm summer with Louise reduces its emotional, physical and psychological stress on the body. During this period, the Unnamed Narrator experiences the most intimate times with Louise they have ever known, the heatwave representing their bodies on fire with passion. The demand and desire seduced their bodies just like the hot sun streaming down onto their skin: 'It was a hot August Sunday. [. . .] You laughed and waved, your body bright beneath the clear green water, its shape fitting your shape, holding you, faithful to you. [. . .] You put your arms around my burning back.'[33] The seasons are the space and time in which the bodily self and the other venture and explore. The months come and go in tandem with the characters' emotional and psychological ebbs and flows; sometimes the body is stable and fulfilled, at other times it feels broken and worthless.

However, the Unnamed Narrator faces a low point in their relationship in another August: 'August. We were arguing. You want love to be like this every day don't you? 92 degrees even in the shade. This intensity, this heat, the sun like a disc-saw through your body.'[34] At this moment, the Unnamed Narrator cannot bear to be with Louise because of the demands being made of them. This 'intensity' is too hot, and it burns their relationship. The emotional, physical and psychological status of the Unnamed Narrator's life ebbs and flows, and the affairs of the heart change like the seasons. The Unnamed Narrator, due to their numerous failures in love, is worried and constantly questions their happiness in relationships:

> This is what I have been afraid of, what I've avoided through so many shaky liaisons. I'm addicted to the first six months. It's the midnight calls, the bursts of energy, the beloved as battery for all those fading cells.[35]

The Unnamed Narrator's earlier experiences colour their relationship with Louise, and these concerns are brought to the fore in August, once again, when they are facing a difficult moment with Louise. The Unnamed Narrator is ecstatic about their relationship, but at the back of their mind they fear Louise wants to end the affair. The Unnamed Narrator muses:

> August. The street like a hotplate cooking us. Louise had brought me to Oxford to get away from Elgin. She didn't tell me what had happened in the previous three days, she kept her secret like a war-time agent. She was smiling, calm, the perfect undercover girl. I didn't trust her. I believed she was about to break it off with me.[36]

The alternative depictions of seasonal terms metaphorically represent the Unnamed Narrator's inner and outer desires, thus becoming gestures of fetishization by a process of destabilization and stabilization. Time passes and, after the Unnamed Narrator leaves Louise, they face the worst August of their life. They fall into extreme depression, and madness ensues:

> August. Nothing to report. For the first time since leaving Louise I was depressed. The previous months had been wild with despair and cushioned by shock [. . .] In August I felt blank and sick. I had sobered up, come round to the facts of what I had done. [. . .] Body and mind know how to hide from what is too sore to handle.[37]

This stressful August, dry and hot, is contrasted with the previous June. For the Unnamed Narrator, that month had been full of intimacy, desire and the seductive pleasure of a reignited love affair with Louise. Their bodies were on fire, seduced by the innate desire that seeks love intertwined with pleasure. As bodies crammed with each other, they did not notice anything around them and there was no time to talk; instead, they communicated in the language of sensuality to express their pleasure. In other words, only their bodies spoke. Both bodies were like letters written in amatory desire, and the lovers were drawn into the pleasure and desire they always sought:

> June. The wettest June on record. We made love every day. We were happy like colts, flagrant like rabbits, dove-innocent in our pursuit of pleasure. Neither of us thought about it and we had no time to discuss it. The time we had we used. Those brief days and briefer hours were small offerings to a god who would not be appeased by burning flesh.[38]

According to Grosz, the perceptual relations of bodies – form, size, direction, location and centeredness – correlate with 'tactile and visual sensations' to form 'the basic ideas of localization and orientation; place and position are defined with reference to the apparent immediacy of a lived here-and-now'.[39] Desires that are driven by lust and drawn with temporary pleasure are not usually permanent, but the relevance of Grosz's argument here is that the immediate present is a necessity for bodies that live and move in space in relation to other bodies. The present June and the presence of Louise become absent in the future August, which is when the replacement objects, where material or linguistic, of alternative fetishism find their purpose.

Love, for the Unnamed Narrator, comes and goes or at least slowly fades, whether consciously or unconsciously. Seasonal metaphors represent the journey the body is on; they reflect the changing experiences the body faces every month and every season. However, like most journeys in life, seeking love is not a simple thing, and the Unnamed Narrator comes to know regret well across other months:

> June. The driest June on record. The earth that should have been in summer glory was thin for lack of water. The buds held promise but they didn't swell. The beating sun was a fake. The sun that should have brought life was carrying death in every relentless morning.[40]

This excerpt can be interpreted in two ways. First, the body is lacking sex, and thus love, as the Unnamed Narrator concludes in the novel that sex and love appear to be the same: 'sex can feel like love.'[41] The body feels pain and the swelling of desire from the lack of pleasure, while the ensuing depression leads the Unnamed Narrator to unworthy feelings about themself. Second, this quotation represents the decay of love and the loss of affection, pleasure and desire for the body. The longer the journey, the hotter the flame of sex and love should be. However, the same events do not mark the same seasons and the journey is not always predictable. Once again, the seasonal discourse veers from normal expectations; as the months change, spring arrives, which is usually the most beautiful season. Flowers should bloom, parks should be blanketed in greenery, and the weather should improve as winter recedes. However, against such a background, the Unnamed Narrator is dispirited:

> March. Elgin had promised to write to me. [. . .] It was bitter cold and the woods were filled with wild white daffodils. I tried to take comfort from the flowers, from the steady building of the trees. This was new life, surely some of it would rub off on me?[42]

The Unnamed Narrator trusts Elgin to ensure that Louise would be looked after and that they would be kept updated about the state of her health. Instead of enjoying the spring, the Unnamed Narrator 'counted the days like someone under house arrest'.[43] They hide their sadness and fill their physical and psychical time and space thinking Louise is going to get well, the idea of her replacing the lost object of her actual body. The Unnamed Narrator tries to ignore the desire and melancholy inside them and to act normally, wearing a mask of happiness that hides the sadness and worries dwelling inside: 'I slapped a plastic grin on my face like a server from McDonald's and pretended to be having a good time.'[44] However, the temporary mask cannot be worn forever, and soon, the worry and sadness inside the Unnamed Narrator finds its way out. This inversion of the typical connotations of spring is reminiscent of the opening of 'The Burial of the Dead' in Eliot's 'The Waste Land', which was an acknowledged influence on Winterson. The opening speaker of 'The Waste Land' describes April as 'the cruellest month', and where Eliot's speaker talks of 'Lilacs out of the dead land', Winterson's Unnamed Narrator sees daffodils in the cold woods.[45] Both portray the spring negatively, showing how their external worldview has been affected by their internal suffering.

The Unnamed Narrator continues their mundane life working in the bar, hoping all the time for some news of Louise. Finally, they take matters into their own hand and phone Louise's husband, Elgin, but there is no answer. To divert themself from the disappointment, the Unnamed Narrator both remembers and imagines exploring Louise's body as an act of disavowal of their sadness. This shows how fetishization can arise from deprivation and dispossession and instigate ownership of disavowal. The Unnamed Narrator continues with their life, wondering about Louise and feeling regret. In their attempt to be closer to Louise, they learn 'clinical language', which replaces the romantic language that has been lost along with Louise's presence, because they 'want to know what it's like' to suffer from cancer as Louise does.[46] Thus, as they wait for news about Louise, the Unnamed Narrator expresses their desire for Louise's decaying body and wants to feel what is happening inside it, as an act of mourning for the lost object:

> I would go on knowing her, more intimately than the skin, hair and voice that I carved. I would have her plasma, her spleen, her synovial fluid. I would recognise her even when her body had long since fallen away.[47]

As mentioned above, Winterson's representation of the deconstructed body illustrates the fluidity of diverse desire by destabilizing and stabilizing normative fetishism, which produces an alternative form of fetishization. Her language is often witty as it moves into alternative spaces and times, and her diction has a pleasantly familiar feeling, offering not a reduced and simplified version of the text, but one that operates on its own level of difficulty through concept, not lexis. Thus, though it is clear that the seasons and the weather represent mood swings, the feelings are not linear, and instead they go back and forth just like the body. Its curves, wrinkles and lines are seen differently through Winterson's reconceptualization of beauty/youthfulness and decay/senescence, as these binaries are deconstructed by an alternative way of fetishizing the new bodily form. This recalls the discussion above on the body as a metaphor for the novel itself; surfaces and interiors require different strategies of hermeneutics and reveal different outcomes and routes because the 'metaphor of the textualized body asserts that the body is a page or material surface, possibly even a book of interfolded leaves [. . .] ready to receive, bear, and transmit meanings, messages, or signs, much like a system of writing'.[48] As such, while Winterson continues to use her art to refigure the structure of the novel as a metaphor for the bodily self and the others, all the tools of critical reading that are applied to literature can be applied to the body. The emergence of psychological, emotional and cultural influences affect the physical performance of the body both internally and externally, and these influences also represent the structure of *Written on the Body*, which goes back and forth in thoughts and memories, even though it is a single emotional journey.

Besides the use of the seasons as temporal and spatial metaphors, domestic spaces such as the living room, bedroom and kitchen are also depicted as locations in *Written on the Body* that relate to bodies and obsession. For example, the Unnamed Narrator longs to have Louise's presence in the kitchen: 'Louise was eating breakfast when I arrived [. . .] There was a dangerously electrical quality about Louise.'[49] When she leaves the kitchen, the room no longer has significance for the Unnamed Narrator: 'Now she's gone for a bath and the kitchen's empty. Silly kitchen without Louise.'[50] Finally, the kitchen is where they see Louise at the novel's conclusion, although it is left ambiguous whether it is a real memory or a fetishistic act of imagination to replace Louise as a permanently lost object: 'From the kitchen door. Louise's face. Paler, thinner. [. . .] Am I stark mad? She's warm.'[51]

The acts of touching and gazing and how they relate to space and time can also be seen in *The Passion*. The narrators are Henri and Villanelle, while the character of Napoleon Bonaparte looms large throughout, and they all experience their own obsessions. These obsessions, whether temporary or permanent, eventually keep them captive in metaphorical prisons created by their own passionate mania for someone or something they experience in their life. The body and its parts are mainly presented through Villanelle and Henri. For example, Henri is obsessed with Villanelle's feminine body and androgynous characteristics. He looks at Villanelle's body, focusing intently, in a way over-emphasizing it:

'I touched her when I was sure she was asleep. [. . .] I think about her body, a lot; not possessing it but watching it twist in sleep.'[52] Henri's obsessive gazing at Villanelle's body and its parts is similar to the Unnamed Narrator's focus on Louise in *Written on the Body*, but while the latter novel has one specific body as the subject of fetishist obsession, the twin narratives in *The Passion* multiply the physical explorations. For Villanelle, a constant passion is her hometown of Venice. Grosz rightly argues that there is a 'constitutive and mutually defining relationship between bodies and cities. The city is one of the crucial factors in the social production of (sexed) corporeality: the built environment provides the context and coordinates for contemporary forms of body.'[53] Thus, subject and object play interconnected roles – the body's exterior is psychically constructed from the social processes of bodily inscription, as there is the relationship between the individual and the city, and then between the individual and all the others who are also bound and produced within the city's physical and conceptual limits. Venice is where Villanelle is born and then reborn. She claims the gambling den as a safe space, a shelter for her to dream and to imagine; it is there she meets her husband and embarks on a quest for the self and the other. Her husband's abuse of her body and emotions, however, compels her to leave him and go back to the gambling den.

Like the recurring words and phrases the novel presents the reader, the content of the characters' lives is just as repetitive and cyclical, going to and fro between the past, the present and the future, coming and going to the same places and spaces. This relates to Winterson's fetishistic literary discourse, which is circular and uses repetition: 'the real and the invented were parallel lines that never met. Then we discovered that space is curved, and in curved space parallel lines always meet.'[54] Consequently, Villanelle moves back and forth from her husband's home to the houses of others. It is important for Villanelle to have a space that she can claim as her own, and so she seeks sovereignty in physical, emotional and sexual pleasure. While she is constantly looking for freedom, she also seeks belongingness in the casino, where she can play with both gender and identity in a fetishistic performance of the freedom she desires. Indeed, in a certain sense, Villanelle projects such behaviour because she does not feel at ease with her husband. Her body is inscripted and encoded by those in power, such as her husband and the city-state; however, her chameleonic characteristics, her will to survive and the drives of her desires combine for her to perform in society, ultimately with success.

Winterson adeptly utilizes figurative language to deepen the representations of her characters' fluid desires and pleasures through the deconstruction of the body. She is deeply conscious of the function of time and space, using them to execute an effective narration and characterization to illustrate bodies and desire in a gesture of alternative fetishization. Villanelle's career in the gambling den reflects the realities of her own life, in which casino games that involve 'raking dice and spreading cards' can be compared to her own description of her personality: 'I have always been a gambler. It is a skill that comes naturally to me like thieving and loving.'[55] In her quest for freedom, she strives to create a space she thinks will be safe following the various experiences in her life. However, her desperation to fulfil her desires means she recklessly enters into temporary spaces, which is itself a gamble. She also shows her fluidity when it comes to gender as she gives space to her sexual practices with both male and female partners.

True to her risk-taking nature, when her husband catches up with her in Vienna, she plays cards against him to decide her fate:

> A friend of his, a sophisticated man, suggested a little wager for the two of us, a way of solving our differences. We were to play cards and if I won, I should have my freedom to come and go as I pleased and enough money to do so. If I lost, my husband should do with me as he pleased, though he was not to molest or murder me.[56]

Villanelle's fetish for freedom often forces her into making an unethical decision. It is obvious that Villanelle's innate desires eventually drive her into a desperate situation, causing her to partake in a fixed game of cards. This does not remedy her situation because she inevitably loses, and her husband wins the liberty to sell her into slavery. Villanelle is still emotionally impoverished, unable to retrieve the source of her passion, which was lost in the chaotic scramble to survive: 'They didn't give me enough time to collect my heart, only my luggage.'[57] But her heart, with all its passion and capacity for feeling, does not belong in a space of sexual slavery. Therefore, she is 'grateful to them for that; this is no place for a heart'.[58] Thus, she leaves behind her heart, toughening herself instead for what her new situation has in store for her: 'I was to join the army, to join the Generals for their pleasure. It was, Murat assured me, quite an honour.'[59] Sex with strangers is always a possibility for Villanelle as she is perpetually battling between the desire to guard her heart and the need to make use of her sexuality as a way to survive.

As Winterson's characters regularly battle with various aspects of power, they often have to contain their own bodily desires. This often results in repression and the channelling of such feelings into destructive sexual acts, most often deviant ones, due to the demands of power and the environment that requires them to act thus in order to survive. Henri's repressed hatred for Villanelle's husband stems not only from the physical abuse inflicted on him by the powerful Meat Man[60] – 'He pushed me back against the onion sacks and spat in my face' – but also from his desire for Villanelle.[61] Thus, when he later re-encounters the Meat Man, Henri not only recalls his own ill-treatment but also realizes he is facing the man who has been abusing the object of his desire all these years, which fuels his murderous response. In addition, Henri's murder of the Meat Man can also be interpreted as situational. His actions are compelled by two forces, first, from his internal demands because Villanelle is his object of fetish, and, second, from his external environment, where the chaos and brutality of the war have triggered a murderous passion in him to be equally destructive and aggressive in order to survive his desperate predicament. Ultimately, Winterson's characters are bound by a complex exchange of desires in internal and external environments that complicate an easy understanding of their deeds, virtues and vices.

Grosz notes how advances in scientific theory correlate with the philosophical means of addressing the human condition; for instance, Kantian subjectivity coexisted with Newtonian physics, while both Freudian and Einsteinian models decentred rationalism. Grosz suggests that

> the postmodern subject finds its correlative in the virtuality of cyberspace and its attendant modes of respatialization. Such conceptions are both ways of negotiating our positions as subjects within a social and cosmic order, and representations that affirm or rupture pre-existing forms of subjectivity.[62]

In *The PowerBook*, Ali/Alix is the e-writer in a cyberspace that she remakes and respatializes at will. In one of the stories Ali/Alix invents, she has a lover who is a married woman, which for all *The PowerBook*'s postmodern virtual trappings is one of Winterson's most typical plot devices. In this story, Ali/Alix's obsession with her lover's body compels her into deranged actions, and she starts spying on and stalking her lover in the hope of being able to spend another night with her.[63] Ali/Alix also takes an obsessive pleasure in watching her lover's hands and imagines them in a fetishistic manner as other; she wonders what objects her lover's hands can make and pictures them disembodied in the midst of a creative task: 'Beautiful hands – deft, light, practical, practised.'[64] Other parts of the body are also praised and Ali/Alix reminds herself of each part when she reminisces about how they made love:

> You kissed my throat. You kissed my collarbone. You put your tongue into the channel of my breasts. I open your legs onto my hip. You began to move with me – hands, tongue, and body. You took my breasts in both hands and I slid

you out of your jeans. You don't wear knickers. You keep your breasts in a black mesh cage.⁶⁵

Ali/Alix crafts the lost figure in her psychic space by remembering their good times together, and this reminiscence repeats frequently in her mind. This happens because she is unable to be with her lover and is mourning the absent object through memory. The mourning and depression at not being able to have someone or something reveal themselves in hidden aggression against the lost object, whether physical or emotional. Thus, the act of imagining is an important step in the stage of mourning or depression because, as Kristeva says, 'the psychic space of the human being is immediately taken into charge by verbal representation and consciousness'.⁶⁶ The environment or space a person inhabits will, somehow or other, influence a person's behaviour and change them. For example, in *The Passion*, after a few months, the new army recruits are 'no longer shy boys with cannon-fire in their eyes. They are rougher, tougher.'⁶⁷ Other examples include Henri becoming a murderer, the Meat Man acting violently with others and Villanelle being trapped by her obsession.

In *Frankissstein*, Winterson blurs the lines of time and space by travelling to the past and visiting the future. It seems to Winterson's Mary Shelley that temporality and spatiality are inextricably linked by physical location: on Lake Geneva, 'where time is neither so crammed nor so scarce [as London], I fancy, anything might happen, anything is possible'.⁶⁸ The novel takes artificial intelligence (AI) as a central theme, which is associated with fluid gender, sexuality and identity through the characters of Ry and Victor. The logical extension, in fact, is that AI will render gender irrelevant in a world where the human body becomes superfluous, in which case sexuality would also require reconsidering for a post-human world. *Frankissstein* questions the sexual politics of today and the near future, and offers one vision of what such technological advances may mean to an embodied society. In this way, Winterson conforms to her declaration that the 'artist is a translator', as this novel seeks to explain, among other things, how the rise of sex-bots might impact society.⁶⁹ The Frankenstein story is refashioned through the constantly reacquiring, reproducing and transforming nature of Winterson's language, and what she writes of art can be easily applied to the structure of *Frankissstein*: 'to live beyond the moment. Art helps us to do this because it fuses temporal and perpetual realities.'⁷⁰

The future of a technological world such as the one in *Frankissstein* is disturbing, as serious issues of gender equality, sexual freedom and restriction, and erasure of identity are depicted. One aspect of *Frankissstein* that is far from fictional is the dearth of women involved with the creation and execution of technological applications – what has been called the 'sea of dudes' working in AI.[71] Winterson's satirical portrayal of this through the masculine caricature of Ron Lord reveals the stereotyping of female bodies in the sex-bot industry, in which they are overwhelmingly seen as objects of cis-heterosexual pleasure that must obey the needs of their male owners: 'Very tight figure – little waist, double-G-cup – and I tell you what, her tits and her pussy are always warm.'[72] However, opportunities for progress also exist, and Ry's ability to choose their bodily experience indicate the benefits that technology can bring to the corporeal: 'you, Ry, gorgeous boy/girl, whatever you are, you had a sex change. You chose to intervene in your own evolution. You accelerated your portfolio of possibilities. [. . .] The here and now, and a harbinger of the future.'[73] Although Ry has not read any influential texts of heteronormative resistance, such as *A Room of One's Own*, Ry challenges conventions through their bodily existence.

Through the discussion above, we see that specific environments and spaces play an important role influencing the choices that Winterson's characters make in life. The deconstructed body and dismantling of normative desire through the metaphoric use of space and time illustrates an alternative way of fetishizing in daily life. Her characters visit or inhabit these diverse spaces and times, either temporarily or permanently, and this has an effect on them physically, emotionally, culturally and psychologically. Some use their experiences to fill in their psychological space, remembering their past in the present moment so that they can continue to recall both good and bad times as a guide for the future. Their past experiences never fully pass; instead, they act as counter-memories in a current mode, siphoning resources from imagination into real-life efforts to replace lost objects.

3

Fetishistic imagination

Body and memory

I discuss here how memory and the retelling of stories communicate the diverse desires of the body in Winterson's fiction. I argue how the alternative fetishization of the bodily self and the other in Winterson's writing is also informed by her approach to historicity and counter-memory. The work of Foucault, Butler and Grosz in relation to memory, language and the body usefully supports Winterson's acts of anamnesis that resist dominant narratives and prevailing accounts of history. I argue that Winterson often locates her fiction within imaginative versions of historical and contemporary settings to offer a voice to those silenced by the hegemonic narratives of history and to represent the past in the present. According to Foucault, counter-memory is an act of memory that resists dominant narratives and prevailing accounts of history. It is 'a transformation of history into a totally different form of time' and is constructed by 'a use of history that severs its connection to memory [and] its metaphysical and anthropological model'.[1] The important aspects of counter-memory are: who does the remembering, what the historical contexts were and what the memory seeks to oppose.

Counter-memory is a response to institutional and hegemonic authority when it ignores the voices of the oppressed and powerless. When these silent and silenced groups are suppressed, they have to learn to survive without being able to make their views heard. Winterson uses the language of fiction to give these unfortunate others the opportunity for a space to challenge what has been written in history and to create a new story, and these literary counter-memories function within a fetishistic framework of obsession and repetition. A particular feature of Winterson's fiction relating to memory is the close neurological link it has with hallucination, as illustrated by Henri's disorganized mental state at the end of *The Passion*. Grosz, discussing Freud's writing on memory and hallucination, offers an explanation of how this mechanism can work:

> The memory trace differs from hallucination and perception because its cathexis is contained within the mnemic system. The hallucination can pass itself off for a current perception only insofar as it is able to transfer its intensity to the conscious system.[2]

For Henri, the intensity of his hallucinations matches that of his memories and so the two become mixed in his consciousness. The combination of memory and make-believe proves irresistible to a writer like Winterson, and in her novels histories and stories are blended. Dominant historical narratives are lesser parts of her stories, as she dismantles orthodox and normative stories through counter-memories, destabilizing official accounts into fluid, adaptable and alternative reworkings. Thus, for Winterson, storytelling itself has become a gesture of fetishization because it acts as a carrier for revealing the internal and external desires of the self and the other. She presents new stories as counter-memories that shift into an alternative fetishization of the bodily self and the other, the body acting as a vehicle of communication, articulating tangible expressions of desires and pleasures; as Winterson's Mary Shelley says in *Frankissstein*, 'I sense what I cannot say, except in the form of a story.'[3] Winterson deconstructs the act of storytelling by the use of counter-memory focused on narratives of the bodily subject, which produces a memorial object as an alternative form of fetishization that satisfies, either temporarily or permanently, a subject's desires.

Winterson's texts frequently offer a smaller, physically and psychically, embodied story that acts as a counter-memory and destabilizes the larger, normative story that forms the backdrop of the novel, such as the Napoleonic Wars (*The Passion*), the Pendle Witch Trials (*The Daylight Gate*) or Brexit (*Frankissstein*). This alternative narrative breaks down the overarching story into smaller units so minority stories and voices can be heard and recorded, by Winterson's fetishistic repetition of memory through language. These memories can often be traced through the inscription of the body as well as through mental patterns, as is the case with Christopher in *The Daylight Gate*. Counter-memory is a response to institutional authority when the voices of the oppressed and powerless are ignored. These silenced and suppressed groups have had to learn to survive without their views being heard or considered, and Winterson uses the language of fiction to give these unfortunate others the opportunity for a space to challenge what has been recorded in the orthodox chronicles of history. Winterson continually assails historicity in her fiction, as shown by the paradoxical catchphrase repeated throughout *The Passion*: 'I'm telling you stories. Trust me.' As mentioned earlier, storytelling is itself an act or gesture of fetishization as it is repetitive and, at times, becomes a substitute object or subject as a form to divert sadness or unhappiness of the self and the other. Sometimes a story can change a person's beliefs; it can even transform their moral outlook and ethical actions. Memory and its operation are also central acts of obsession in Winterson's works and can lead to madness, mourning and melancholia. Memory in the form of sorrowful pleasure can occupy a central position in the psychic space of the unfortunate other. This memory focuses on the lost object, moving quickly into the verbal stage through repetitions of language and symbols. In Winterson's subversive method, 'stories' can allude to tall tales, inventions that belong to the realm of fantasy and imagination and the temporary spaces one wishes to be in, rather than simply relating the facts of a person's past. This act of rethinking the narrative is an inventive gesture of fetishization in Winterson's texts as her characters travel through both time and space, countering the memory of the past in the present and, perhaps, creating a new future.

In *The Passion*, as in her other novels, Winterson makes frequent use of repetition and figurative language to highlight both the ubiquitous and infinite nature of words in the creation of meaning and the cyclical lives of her characters. Villanelle's and Henri's dialogues often contain repeated phrases, such as 'I'm telling you stories. Trust me', which suggest that the narrative is a continuous loop in which history is repeated as though it achieves no climax or closure.[4] In the light of Winterson's dedication to the power of language and literary devices and her interest in history, it is interesting that Villanelle repeatedly uses a particular phrase, 'You play, you win, you play, you lose. You play', as if suggesting that time, and thus history, are cyclical, and one has to join in the rhythm of life to survive in the world.[5] For example, Villanelle's life begins in Venice and, despite her various adventures taking her all around the world, it is to Venice that she eventually returns – Villanelle's past memories linger in her present until they bring her back from whence she came.

At the end of the novel, Henri utters his favourite words for the last time: 'I'm telling you stories. Trust me.'[6] With these words, Winterson is telling the reader that the 'story' here can be seen as part of history – the small or untold tale which is fetishized through Henri's narrative. Henri tells his story in the present moment, but it also, paradoxically, belongs to the past. Henri's narrative does not follow a linear chronology; instead, there are many jumps in time: 'This year is gone, I told myself. This year is slipping away and it will never return. Domino's right, there's only now.'[7] The telling of stories is crucial for Winterson because it provides a means for her characters to understand their predicaments, which are most often created when their inner desires fail to fit into their outer realities.

They battle with powerful passions that are already framed by sociological and historical limitations, such as war, as well as social expectations of their given gender and sex. Winterson's characters' obsessive behaviour turns sooner or later into madness; Henri, for example, is trapped in a persistent memory:

> When I think of that night, here in this place where I will always be, my hands tremble and my muscles ache. I lose all sense of day or night. I lose all sense of day and night, I lose all sense of my work, writing this story, trying to convey what really happened. Trying not to make up too much. I can think of it by mistake, my eyes blurring the words in front of me, my pen lifting and staying lifted, I can think of it for hours and yet it is always the same moment I think of.[8]

In the grip of this madness, he is willing to do anything to win Villanelle's love. Thus, his obsession with Villanelle and Napoleon transform him from a young village boy into a killer. In relation to the concept of mourning and melancholy, it is clear that in *The Passion*, Henri's obsession with Villanelle and Napoleon makes him insane and imprisons him mentally and physically. Due to the madness and the effects of the war, he becomes a murderer and ends up in prison for life.

On a more subversive level, the 'stories' the reader is asked to trust can allude to tall tales, inventions that belong to the realm of fantasy and imagination, and the temporary space that one would want to be in, rather than just the field of history or a person's past. Nevertheless, history plays a big part in Winterson's novels, such as the Napoleonic era setting of *The Passion*, which raises the question of the accuracy of these 'stories' in their historical context. Winterson plays with time – past, present and future – but a vital point is made regarding the numerous stories that get omitted from official historical discourse. Through Villanelle, Winterson shows how powerless groups have been treated historically and how the female body can be used as a tool to survive. Thus, Winterson's dismantling of canonical history into individual accounts exposes the suppressed desires of the unfortunate others, like Villanelle, and remakes the normative historical accounts.

Villanelle's husband, exemplifying people in power, dominates her mentally and physically. She is raped and forced to serve men sexually and she cannot verbally express her unhappiness as she has to acquiesce to survive. This is an example of the enforced passivity of women in a patriarchal society; they are symbolically castrated and so the female body is a site of lack and is vulnerable to domination. However, through Winterson's linguistic acts of resistance, women such as Villanelle create the opportunity for individual freedom. In Villanelle's case, this is achieved by her cross-dressing to enter the realm of masculine signification, while the memory of previous experiences, such as her dalliances with the Queen of Spades, provide her with motivation and energy. It is clear that Villanelle's innate fascination with freedom eventually drives her to a kind of situational madness, akin to intense desperation, causing her to act in reckless ways and take risks with her life and body. However, Villanelle refuses to see her actions in a negative light: 'Gambling is not a vice, it is an expression of our humanness. We gamble. Some do it at the gambling table, some do not. You play, you win, you play, you lose. You play.'[9]

For Henri, the memory of his worship of Napoleon becomes a cloying, maddening regret. As power vacillates, so does passion, and Henri's passion for Napoleon turns from love into hatred. Henri says, 'I don't want to worship him anymore. I want to make my own mistakes. I want to die in my own time.'[10] After eight years of war and obsessing over Napoleon, Henri rescinds his allegiance to Napoleon and decides to desert. The devotion he felt for Napoleon is transferred almost instantaneously when he meets Villanelle:

> Then she said, 'They're all different.'
> 'What?'
> 'Snowflakes. Think of that.'
> I did think of that and I fell in love with her.[11]

Henri, Villanelle and Patrick leave the army camp, which turns into a physically damaging quest for survival: 'We walked for a night and a day without stopping. Our legs assumed an ungainly rhythm and we were afraid to stop in case our lungs or our legs buckled under us.'[12]

However, Henri is willing to sacrifice his body following the transference of his fetish object from Napoleon to Villanelle. It is a journey that will lead Henri towards melancholia and madness, although by the end he feels he has learned the significance of love and passion on the way; he declares in a typically Wintersonian manner: 'Love, they say, enslaves and passion is a demon and many have lost for love. I know this is true, but I know too that without love we grope the tunnels of our lives and never see the sun.'[13] As the idea of Villanelle catches hold of Henri's heart and mind, Napoleon's position falls with equal and alarming rapidity. When Napoleon ceases being the primary fetish object for Henri, his military and political power simultaneously end: 'Europe hated him. The French were tired of going to war and going to war and going to war.'[14] Exiled for the final time to St Helena, Napoleon dies a sad and unmourned death in comparison to the grandeur of his life and dynastic vision: 'he didn't last long on his rock. He put on weight and caught a cold, and he who survived the plagues of

Egypt and the zero winter died in the mild damp.'[15] In this way, the relationship between Napoleon's body and power accords to a combination of Foucauldian and Nietzschean thinking:

> For Foucault, the body is penetrated by networks and regimes of power-knowledge that actively mark and produce it as such: the body seems to be [. . .] manipulated and utilized by various systems of social and self-constitution [. . .]. For Nietzsche, by contrast, the result of the body's activity, its self-expansion and self-overcoming [. . .] involves a struggle to survive [. . .] to overcome itself on the level of the cells, tissues, organs.[16]

Napoleon's body, which was so long the source of power, becomes subjected to it entirely in his enforced exile, so perhaps it is no surprise that the self-constitution that saw him survive Egypt and Russia weakly evaporates on his prison island. In these circumstances, his will to survive cannot even overcome the damp weather, and so the body and all its parts are unable to struggle onwards with sufficient vitality.

Henri's physical liberty also comes to an end, following his murder of the Meat Man, but as far as *The Passion*'s conclusion is concerned, he is at least surviving the damp in his prison. Incarcerated in 'the rock', the prison for the insane, Henri lives in his past with his diary, his counter-memories in the form of the written word, which substitutes as a fetishistic replacement for all his lost objects. Through language, Winterson illustrates that an extreme obsession as fetishistic action is the core motivational factor in *The Passion*, as it is in her other novels. If mismanaged, as Henri observes, this obsession is a destructive force. Yet, for Winterson's characters, obsession is a crucial element in the formation of relationships, whether they are between lovers, leaders, subjects or things. In prison, Henri's psychic space is full with his memories of the experiences he has undergone over the years. For example, he imagines that his two lost objects – Napoleon and Villanelle – are visiting him. He imagines Napoleon's hands, covered with chicken grease, suggesting that Henri has not entirely forgotten his Napoleon, even though he forsook him. His thoughts of Villanelle remain inextricably linked to his prior obsession with Napoleon, and his lost objects become symbols of love and hatred of the other:

> I am still in love with her. Not a day breaks but that I think of her, and when the dogwood turns red in winter I stretch out my hands and imagine her hair. I am in love with her; not a fantasy or myth or a creature of my own making. Her. A person who is not me. I invented Bonaparte as much as he invented himself. My passion for her, even though she could never return it, showed me the difference

between inventing a lover and falling in love. The one is about you, the other about someone else.[17]

'I am still in love with her' stages a melancholic relation to the lost object; imagining touching the other body is a way to install the lost object into oneself. This counter-memory plays in Henri's psychic space not only for Villanelle but also for Napoleon and his other colleagues. This relates to Kristeva's definition of a melancholy that requires:

> a severe super-ego and an entire complex dialectic of idealisation and devalorization, both of oneself and the other; the set of these mechanisms being based upon the mechanism of identification. For it is indeed an *identification* with the loved/hated other – through incorporation, introjection, projection – that is effected by the taking into myself of an ideal, sublime, part or trait of the other. This becomes my necessary and tyrannical judge.[18]

In relation to the previous excerpt, it is finally clear to Henri that Napoleon was not the true object of his worship but a projection of Henri's depressed mind that sought a figure he could love and hate. However, Henri believes that his feelings, along with his memories, for Villanelle are genuine and that she is no construct of his mind. This is perhaps rather doubtful to the reader, but in any case, both Napoleon and Villanelle become lost objects for him. Eventually, Henri cuts off all contact with the outside world and chooses to remain imprisoned to spare his heart from further anguish:

> I keep getting letters from Villanelle. I send them back to her unopened and I never reply. Not because I don't think about her, not because I don't look for her from my window every day. I have sent her away because she hurts me too much.[19]

Moreover, now that he is in prison, a physical space of his own, and at leisure to repeatedly contemplate and counter his memory of the past, Henri is free to imagine what might have been. He uses his memory as a substitute for his loss of Villanelle and to counter his own depression. In this way, he embodies the idea of his wartime colleague Domino, who told him that there was no future: '*There's only the present, Henri.* [. . .] He didn't believe in the future, only the present, and as our future, our years, had turned so relentlessly into identical presents, I understood him more'.[20] For Henri, his old war-ridden life was full of obsessions for Napoleon and Villanelle and intense thoughts about the future. In the process, he neglected to understand the present. Only towards the end does he think of the magnificence of present life as something that he desperately wants.

Unfortunately, only the past is left in the form of his memory and his diary. He tells himself the story of his past continuously, and this act of repetition, of retelling, becomes an obsession that reproduces pleasures and satisfactions to Henri that are acts of fetishization. His story is too powerful to allow him to live in the moment because the past is never passed over lightly in Winterson's novels, especially if it contains the loss of a desired object to the subject.

In *Written on the Body*, the Unnamed Narrator is a further example of the use of counter-memory to reject an existing narrative in order to remember, beyond reasonable parameters, a lost object. Their lost object is, of course, Louise, and in order to survive and make sense of their existence, they refigure and recreate her over and over again in their mind, challenging the idea of a univocal history of their relationship. The Unnamed Narrator correlates the body and mind in remembrance of Louise through medical language; their past experiences and obsessions coalesce into an image of Louise that combines her body in health and in sickness. This is quite ironic for the Unnamed Narrator who once thought of marriage as 'a plate glass-window just begging for a brick'.[21] Their obsessive immersion in memory is an extreme form of replacing the lost object, and it is an ongoing process that is available to them at any stage of their mourning. The Unnamed Narrator is fascinated with the medical textbooks they are hoarding, which become a melancholic replacement for the lost object: 'I become obsessed with anatomy. If I could not put Louise out of my mind I would drown myself in her.'[22] Thus, the Unnamed Narrator uses another object, replacing Louise with 'clinical language'.[23] Hence, Winterson, through the Unnamed Narrator, shows that madness is also one way of alternative fetishization:

> If I could not put Louise out of my mind I would drown myself in her. Within the clinical language, through the dispassionate view of the sucking, sweating, greedy, defecating self, I found a love-poem to Louise. I would go on knowing her, more intimately than the skin, hair, and voice that I craved.[24]

The Unnamed Narrator hides their aggression against Louise; this reveals ambivalence on the part of the afflicted, the Unnamed Narrator, with respect to the lost object of the mourning, Louise. Thus, they have to act on the imaginary in their psyche, creating the space to counter the memory of her.

Winterson's novels are always fluid in terms of the gender, sexuality and identity of their characters, and this is supported by their non-linear structures. A recurring feature in her texts is the postmodern technique of multiple narrative strands, overlaying the main story by injecting a fairy tale, or some other fiction, as an alternative mode of transmission in her character's story.

This multiple-strand technique is a powerful tool in the formation of fetishism in Winterson's texts, as it allows for mirroring, repetitions and substitutions. In this way, unfulfilled desires are not repressed, but instead, expressed though the alternative narrativity of telling the story within a story. In *The PowerBook*, for instance, the normative is fluidly interchangeable with the alternative through the contrast of Ali/Alix's invented worlds, and the 'real' one in which she receives her bookings. Winterson mimics fairy tales to show the boundaries of desire as encapsulated by Ali/Alix, who is at the end filled with madness and melancholy: 'The woman I love rode this way, carried off by a horseman. If I do not find her I will never find myself. If I do not find her, I will die in this forest, water within water.'[25] Ali/Alix's fascination with the story has turned her into the story itself. She is insistent and determined to be in the story and uses the e-story as a way to tell her client to challenge her current life; she is determined to be someone else even if just for one night. However, this fetishization has turned Ali/Alix towards delusion and madness.

The fairy tale element of Winterson's novels often juggles with the themes of history, reality, fantasy, love, loss and sex. For example, in *Sexing the Cherry*, Jordan tells the story of the Twelve Dancing Princesses which Winterson uses to challenge the expectations of a patriarchal, heteronormative society. The Twelve Dancing Princesses are imprisoned by their father: 'We all slept in the same room, my sisters, and I, and that room was narrower than a new river and longer than the beard of the prophet.'[26] However, they are clever and determined to seek freedom, so they find a way to get out of their father's prison: 'every night, we flew to a silver city where no one ate or drank. The occupation of the people was to dance. We wore out our dresses and slippers dancing.'[27] Unfortunately, they are caught by 'a clever prince [. . .]. He had eleven brothers and we were all given in marriage, one to each brother.'[28] Nonetheless, rebellious at heart and compelled by a strong spirit of freedom, they make their own choices and exert their preferences for their gender and sexuality. They are expected to marry and become dutiful wives, but while the princess who recounts their stories to Jordan says they all 'lived happily ever after', she adds: 'but not with our husbands.'[29] For instance, one of the princesses brings men to the lowest level, that of the powerless: 'There he is, just by your foot.'[30] The princesses have the liberty to make their own choice of love and happiness; two of the princesses choose to live outright as lesbians, while one of them ends up neglecting her husband, preferring to live with her lesbian partner.

Winterson uses other external elements, such as biblical references, entwining them through the multiple-strand technique with her fiction as a method of challenging the norms of narration. Her characters regularly interrupt the central narrative to tell another story, often extending the boundary norms into something more fluid and mobile than accepted views of gender, sexuality and identity. In *Oranges,* the orange demon acts as a mirror to Jeanette's internal urges, appearing only to her eyes and in humdrum circumstances: 'Leaning on the coffee table was the orange demon.'[31] This apparition acts as means for Jeanette to question her choice of gender, sexuality and identity, against the lessons imparted by her dogmatic mother and the evangelical church. Jeanette wants to push forward so that she does not stay in the ready-made world. Thus, the orange demon in the novel represents her double-consciousness, which reflects the presence of another desire, her love for Melanie: '"I want to help you decide what you want." And the creature hopped up on to the mantelpiece and sat on Pastor Spratt's brass crocodile.'[32] By deliberately sitting on the pastor's ornament, a tellingly vicious-looking crocodile, the orange demon intimates the struggles that Jeanette will have ahead if she continues to follow her desires.

Winterson's works, through their fetishistic narratives and the paradoxical use of imaginative memory, test postmodern aesthetics to their limits, going beyond boundary norms to represent post-postmodern notions of an individual's belief in their own agency; as Ali/Alix declares: 'I can change the story, I'm the story.'[33] Andermahr notes that 'Winterson's fiction is well known for its multiple border-crossings and fantastic journeys through space, time, genre and gender [that] blur the boundaries between masculine and feminine, past and present, material and magical worlds.'[34] Counter-memory correlates with the power of imagination, and its presence in *The PowerBook* is no exception. In this novel, the themes of boundaries, desire, love and loss are critical. These themes intersect at the borders of common sense in Ali/Alix's search for self-identity and sexuality; she believes you can be anyone as you can rewrite and reinterpret the story of your life: 'undress. Take off your clothes. Take off your body. Hang them up behind the door. Tonight we can go deeper than disguise.'[35] Thus, in Winterson's world, gender, sexuality and identity can be transformed as and when needed, depending on the situation, thus bodies are physically and psychically fluid and changeable. However, as discussed before, obsession, when practised overtly, can lead to dire consequences. This obsession can be seen as having a negative or positive effect on the body, but due to the power of imagination and the use of mental and emotion manipulation, Ali/Alix manages to return to her lost object through memory. Ali/Alix's love affair does not proceed as planned and, although she and her lover lie 'in bed together, watching the sun stream through the window', she knows in her mind that 'this was never going to work'.[36] Ali/Alix reminisces about what had happened back in Paris:

> I remember everything about Paris [. . .] With my fingers [. . .] I wanted it to be your lips. Kiss me. Yes. Always. Even when I never see you again. After speech, kisses. The silent movie of my feelings for you. Our lips say one thing and do another. We argue in English and we make love in French.[37]

The images of Ali/Alix's lover play in her psychic space as Ali/Alix imagines her body and its parts as a permanent symbol of her own pleasure and desire. Thus, Winterson dismantles normative and dominant stories and histories into smaller, fluid and mobile sections by processes of destabilization and stabilization. The lived and inscripted bodies are deconstructed through the concepts of memory and imagination, powered by language and knowledge.

Frankissstein was written and published during the time of great political uncertainty in the UK, namely Brexit. Winterson repurposes Mary Shelley's *Frankenstein* to create a multi-stranded response to the original, which interweaves an imagined account of Shelley's life with a parallel tale set in a high-tech, but eminently recognizable, twenty-first-century world. *Frankissstein* starts with the voice of Mary Shelley philosophizing about the relationship between material existence and intangible ideals: 'The world is at the start of something new. We are the shaping spirits of our destiny. And though I am not an inventor of machines I am an inventor of dreams.'[38] Her modern counterpart is Ry, a transgender doctor with a ready supply of cadavers and amputated limbs. In a similar vein to Shelley's original, Winterson's *Frankissstein* is based on the discovery and application of a science that threatens the established social order. Winterson makes the fluidity of gender the key issue, with individual freedom, hybrid bodies and androgynous minds as supporting topics. The effects that advanced technology and science will have on the world of sexual politics are uncertain; according to Winterson's Victor, robots are 'an intermediate species that will help humanity adjust to its coming role. The nature of that role is unclear.'[39] Winterson uses a characteristic non-linear structure to question and complicate the notion of progress, as these new forms may see the end of the human body. Victor believes this will be the future, saying that, 'Intelligence – perhaps even consciousness – will no longer be dependent on a body'.[40] He also plans to upload his brain before death to achieve a bodiless, digital immortality, which stands in stark contrast to his ongoing need for a fresh supply of body parts from Ry's hospital. This suggests that, though the body might become separate from the mind in future, in order to perform completely in society, the imaginary body would still be needed to navigate the post-human world.

The responsibility for surrogate sexual bodies in the novel falls to Ron Lord, the sex-bot mogul from the suggestively named town of Three Cocks in Wales. He deals in disassembled body parts for his business, which is consumer pleasure, and they arrive 'in separate bags like a chainsaw massacre'.[41] Although these body parts are robotic, they are simulacra of their flesh and blood counterparts, and despite a post-human world becoming rapidly immanent, Ron holds a traditional mentality when it comes to gender equality. He sees the female form as a sex object and his sex-bots are meant to replace women. He focuses on the body parts rather than the whole: 'Lovely slim arms. Then the legs. Look at the length! The shape!'[42] As Irigaray suggests, female bodies are a product of exchange in consumer societies, and Ron's sex-bots are sold and rented, in place of relationships with real women: 'bring her in for service once or twice a year, depending on wear and tear. Online you can order spare parts, if any of her got damaged, or too messy.'[43] The novel suggests that in the future, the robotic female body may be a fetish object (if, indeed, it is not already) and that fetish practitioners will still exist and provide a lucrative market to someone like Ron. His need for these prosthetics acts as a technological counterpart to Victor's requirement for real body parts from Ry. These are ostensibly for Victor's research into surgery to repair and replace limbs, but a similar fetishizing of the deconstructed body occurs, especially as Victor works towards a future in which he hopes 'we will be able to choose our bodies' as desired, and into which the brain can be uploaded.[44] This multi-bodied, yet disembodied, future causes Ry some hesitation, who embraces their bodily self, having been through the rigours of surgery to transition. Following sex between them and Victor, Ry thinks it is 'enough to sleep in the temporary forever of now', suggesting that not all future inhabitants will embrace the deconstructed body quite so much as Ron and Victor.[45] As Ry masturbates Victor, they cannot help finding the idea of a post-human existence a little disorientating: 'A man who wants to be without his body. And I am holding his body in my left hand.'[46] For Ry, to hold on to the body is to hold on to pleasure for a while longer.

Winterson's work suggests, then, that untold but possible stories, which exist outside of any official historical record, require a fictional treatment to reveal how they represent the supressed voices of those effaced from the dominant historical, or predictive, narratives. These untold and unpredicted stories stand as a representation of the other that is often portrayed, through the repeated act of telling, as an object of fetishism. Therefore, the act of reconceptualizing the dominant narrative is an act of alternative storytelling, dismantling the stories and histories through a rethinking of memory and imagination. The act of alternative storytelling becomes itself fetishistic, representing the diverse desires of telling and knowing through counter-memory and imagination for the body to convert negative and painful experiences into positive and acceptable ones. This versatile and fluid method of storytelling, via counter-memory, imagination and the multiple-strand technique, produces an alternative form of obsession as a fetish object. Consequently, the act of dismantling the texts is a gesture of alternative fetishism, as Winterson's stories break down into smaller units, giving a voice to particular minorities whose previously unheard histories are now transmitted through a constant cycle of telling and remembering.

In this section, we have seen how, through the correlation of the body and mind, and of the lived and inscribed body, Winterson's obsession with language is an act of fetishism. Her presentations of the body and desire reveal a bodily fetishism that is produced from the reconceptualization of first-wave and second-wave studies of fetishism. I have explored the way in which the psychical and physical correlate with both the interior and exterior of the body in society. The deconstructed body in Winterson's texts is an object of fetish, depicted through the psychological, physical and cultural drives of her characters, bound with complex exchanges of internal and external desires. Winterson transmutes normative acts of adoration into alternate operations of fetishism, showing that in society an individual's gender, sexuality and identity can exist outside of rigid categorizations, such as containing elements of both masculinity and femininity. Winterson believes that 'language is movement', and this mobility is a mechanism of fetishism that operates through her obsessive use of substitutes for something other.[47]

Bodies in her work are fluid and interchangeable, depending on the situation they encounter. They face a series of binaries while seeking to refuse and destabilize any and all established hierarchical pairings: surface/depth, inside/outside, passive/active, fantasy/reality, self/other. Through this struggle to resist established structures of power, Winterson brings about new combinations of meaning in language and strives for new forms of knowledge that are capable of articulating the essential fluidity of gender, sexuality and identity. In *Written on the Body*, Louise is like God for the Unnamed Narrator; similarly, in *The Passion*, Villanelle and Napoleon are more than human to Henri. In *Oranges*, Mrs Winterson submits her body, mind and soul to religion, while Jeanette transfers her obsession for the church to her lover, Melanie, as another body to worship. By these actions, normative ways of worshipping the other – in the latter case,

God – are remoulded by acts of obsession and replacement. Mrs Winterson's extreme ways of worshipping God represent pathological fetishism, while Jeanette's devotion to Melanie embodies contemporary notions of fetishism. By portraying both first-wave and second-wave notions of fetishism, *Oranges* demonstrates the alternative fetishism that arises from the combination of these depictions. In *The Passion*, Villanelle is described as androgynous, complicating the uses of the body that is desired by the self and the other. As the discussion showed, she desires, and is desired by, males and females, and her actions are mainly influenced by societal forces and the situations she faces. Likewise, in *The PowerBook*, Ali/Alix's body is deconstructed to complicate their gender and sexuality in order to challenge societal norms through imaginative fetishism, as Ali/Alix substitutes their inner desires to be the other through her e-narrative obsession. Cross-gender performances are prominent in Winterson's works as her characters show the importance of subjectivity and that materiality can be fluid when rethinking normative desires and pleasures. As Grosz argues, 'bodies speak, without necessarily talking, because they become coded with and as signs. They speak social codes. They become intextuated, narrativized; simultaneously, social codes, laws, norms, and ideals become incarnated.'[48] Thus bodies in Winterson's works are physically and psychically connected as the diverse and fluid gender, sexuality and identity of her character's form libidinal flows of excitement and adventure that seek extreme gratification of the self and the other.

Winterson's characters oscillate fluidly between masculine and feminine genders, and their desires are equally variable across the whole spectrum of sexuality. The characters' choices and preferences of extreme liking for something or someone, depicted either through physical, psychological and emotional means, are made clear to the reader through the multi-layered meanings and perceptions of the body as a fetish object that represents internal desires. The body's role as a fetish object through Winterson's fetishistic language has been shown in this chapter through her sophisticated presentation of obsession and worship, which intersect with madness, mourning and melancholy, depending on the individual's situation in society. The obsession and madness of the bodily self or the other is presented through the act of substitution, either permanently or temporarily, where most of the time it can be seen as a positive process. Bodies and minds in Winterson's work 'are not two distinct substance or two kinds of attributes of a single substance but somewhere in between these two alternatives.'[49] Winterson's texts transmute normative acts of bodily adoration into alternate operations of fetishism, showing that in her work an individual's gender and sexuality can exist outside of rigid binary categorizations and contain elements of both masculine and feminine physicality. This argument leads us further in examining other manifestations of the fetish object that also represent multiple dimensions of diverse pleasures and desires. The next section discusses how, through figurative language, food functions as a fetish object and how its preparation and consumption have many different meanings for Winterson's characters in relation to power, love, politics and psychology.

Part II

Food fetishism

The preparation and consumption of food have many different meanings in Winterson's writing, and the complex relationships between eating, politics and culture are revealed through her figurative language that interrogates how food can affect mechanisms of perception. This section argues that in the alternative fetishism of food in Winterson's texts, the erotic potential of food becomes the medium of communication for diverse desires, and food itself functions as a fetishistic substitute for a lost object. Food fetishism in her texts is not synonymous with eating disorders; rather, obsessive acts are described through the use of food terminology, revealing an alternative mode of fetishism that also crosses gender lines. Winterson's fetishistic use of language turns food into a major fetish object in her texts, informing the fluid gender, sexuality and identity of her characters. Winterson's works explore the connections and conflicts in people's diverse ways of behaving in relation to choice and preference, and I focus here on food as a significant tool for communicating to the other; as Winterson says: 'Food is all the love you can eat. Real food, like love, takes time, imagination, passion, good humour, a willingness to learn, and not too much distress over upsets. Things go wrong. Things go right.'[1]

Much significance is given to the feeding body in Winterson's novels, regardless of its gender and sexuality, and the language in Winterson's works often utilizes metaphors associated with feeding and eating because such acts have distinct and emotive power in describing culture, behaviour, the psyche and the physical body. Consequently, there is a close relationship between food and the productions of gender, sexuality and identity. Ina Schabert argues that eating is more than just an 'obvious way for a person to carry on an exchange with the outer world through the body, to incorporate things from the outside'; it is also 'a powerful and macabre method of communication between human beings'.[2] In this vein, food in Winterson's writing can function as a metaphoric device to illustrate the fluidity of the subject. It also accords with Carole Counihan's belief that one can 'influence others through manipulations of the symbolic language of food'.[3] In Winterson's texts, characters regularly attempt to influence others through food, as they are themselves subject to its symbolism and signification. In her fiction, food assumes the symbolic function of communicating the diverse desires of the body, through seduction and the arch-component of fetishism: substitution. That is, food in Winterson's writing, whether as object, theme or metaphoric vehicle, often provides a temporary or permanent replacement for a lost object, and this act of disavowal for diverse desires in daily practice enables an alternative form of fetishism. This section is divided into four chapters, each focusing on a particular text in detail: *Sexing the Cherry*, *The Passion*, *Written on the Body*, and *Boating for Beginners*.

When conducting a nuanced reading of Winterson's works through the lens of fetishism, studying her use of food terminology is important because it is so often used to denote the fluidity of gender, sexuality and identity and the ever-shifting boundaries between the body, desire and pleasure. Food acts as a signifier of a diverse pleasure and desire, as either a temporary or permanent substitute for an absent object. Therefore, food becomes a required item and acts as a fetishistic object for the self in relation to the other. Gamman and Makinen rightly apply the Marxist theory of commodity fetishism to the relations between people; when products or goods produce a use-value, it is seen as necessary and/or desirable by others, as use-value transmits some sort of 'mystical' power. This is because:

> [i]n commodity production, the value of the products is displaced from the labour that produces it and is thought to emanate from the product itself. Thus, in the commodity, the social relation between 'men' (i.e., the social relations of production and exchange) assumes the 'fantastic form of a relation between things'.[4]

This mystical power compels the subject to exhibit fetishistic behaviour with regard to those valuable objects, and the concept of commodity fetishism can be used to measure how 'capitalism converts people and things into abstractions'.[5] In turn, this fetishism allows – encourages even – the articulation of metaphor. This conversion is apparent in Winterson's use of food terminology, which demonstrates alternative fetishistic behaviour by the dismantling and destabilizing of the metaphorical meaning of food and its consumption. Further, commodity fetishism can also be used to analyse the connection between products and their values, in this case food, as experienced by people:

'processes of mystification and reification as part and parcel of the fetishism of commodities'.[6] Accordingly, the processes of mystification and reification are acts of imagining and desiring something as a substitute, either temporarily or permanently, for an actual object.

As Anna Freud demonstrates, food is an object that fills the hunger of our emotions as well as our bodies, and it also has powerful sexual associations. Its significance is rooted back in the child–mother relationship, where awareness of hunger and being fed are the first sensations of lack and pleasure experienced by the child. She explains:

> The appeasement of hunger through the intake of nourishment is felt as satisfactory and is accompanied by pleasure. Since the infant's behaviour is dominated by the urge to avoid pain and discomfort and to gain pleasure the urge for self-preservation through feeding is reinforced by the urge to gain pleasure through feeding.[7]

Hence, food is a foundational way in which the self shows physical, emotional and psychological connections with the other to satisfy its inner desires. In this connection, food in Winterson's writing acts as a vehicle to convey ideas of fluid gender, sexuality and identity. Further, Winterson's use of the terminology of food and its consumption links both to the body, pleasure and desire, conforming with Counihan's observation that 'people articulate and recognize their distinctiveness through the medium of food'.[8] Probyn states, 'the boundaries between food and sex are currently being blurred', and this is enacted textually in Winterson's use of food to represent fluid and mobile gender, sexuality and identity.[9] In relation to the ideas of signifiers, MacClancy says:

> Food as identity, as our physical selves, as a way of thought, as sex, as power, as friendship, as a medium for magic and witchcraft, as our time-controller – in all these different ways and more, food pervades our culture and gives meaning to our lives.[10]

Food absorbs and reflects a person's presentation of gender, sexuality and identity through the cultural practices and beliefs performed in their daily life. Food and fetishism in Winterson's works reveal the power relations and conceptions of a person's own unique choices and preferences of their gender, sexuality and identity. In her novels, food acts as a mirror of the self and the other, one that multiplies and magnifies meaning and interpretation, and provokes a fetishistic discourse between the body, love, loss, power and sex. For Winterson, food is no mere background detail in her fiction – it plays a vital role in representing interchangeable modes of gender, sexuality and identity. As Counihan says, 'one of the significant domains of meaning embodied in food centers on the relation between sexes, their gender definitions, and their sexuality'.[11]

Foodstuffs in her work are objects and subjects, used as temporary and/or permanent substitutes, that release the unspoken desires and pleasures of the bodily self. At times food can also act as a performance of denial to the bodily self and the other. Consequently, this chapter deconstructs normative ideas of food into alternative ideas of gender, sexuality and identity by revealing that food is an object of substitution of desire of the self and the other in Winterson's works. This relates to MacClancy's ideas of food and sex metaphors:

> Men speak of hunting the (edible) object of their desire and of cornering their prey. [. . .] a woman is said to have a 'bun', a 'breadbasket', a 'snapping turtle', or, to use the Ancient Greek phrase, a 'bowl of sauce'. On her chest she has a pair of 'fried eggs', 'apples', 'oranges', 'grapefruits', or 'melons'.[12]

Although food terminology is not a new medium for writers to voice, challenge and compare the body, sex and desire of the self and the other in their works, Winterson's texts destabilize the normative into an alternative way of looking at the subject from a new perspective. Food and its language contain unique metaphorical traits correlating the bodily self and the other with respect to fluid pleasure and desire. Following on from the previous section that discussed the body as a fetish object, I argue here that food is another central fetish object in Winterson's works. Feeding and eating relate to culture, the psyche and the physical body in distinct and emotive ways. Resultingly, food is closely linked with the formation of gender, sexuality and identity. Winterson reconceptualizes fetishism through her depictions of extreme obsession, which often rely on substitutes for the individual's internal and external desires. These substitutions enable a fluid reordering of situations, a repetition-with-change that limns and supports the subject's physical, psychological and cultural being. Food in Winterson's invented reality signifies the disavowal and substitution of normative desires for something more peculiar when looking into the desires of the body. That is, the use of food terminology functions as a metaphor for the temporary or permanent replacement of an actual object and as an act of avowal for diverse desire in daily practice.

4

Fluid fruits

Sexing the Cherry is Winterson's fourth novel, largely set against the historical background of seventeenth-century London, and it depicts the fluidity of identity, gender and sexuality. The very title, *Sexing the Cherry*, invokes the relationships between sexuality, gender and food, before the reader even needs to open the cover. 'Cherry' has long had sexual connotations of the hymen, 'popped' in the idiomatic expression for when a female loses her virginity. Suitably for a discussion of Winterson's fluidly gendered texts, there are also instances of 'cherry' being used to describe part of the male sexual organ; in *Imagining Sex: Pornography and Bodies in Seventeenth-Century England*, Sarah Toulalan quotes from *The School of Venus* (1655): 'There's a fold of skin towards the tip of it which draws back and uncovers a head like a huge red cherry – as pleasant to the touch as anything could be.'[1] The double signification of 'cherry' is matched by the possible interpretations of 'sexing'; it nominally means the process of ascertaining the gender of something (literally performed in the novel on cherries that have been produced by grafting, thanks to advances in botanical science), but it also idiomatically suggests an attempt to arouse the sexual urges of another.

The narrative is interspersed with fairy tales as part of the spectacle of the story and injected with grotesque themes to further challenge the normativity of life. *Sexing the Cherry* has multiple narrators, including Dog-Woman, a giant-sized woman who possesses superhuman strength, and her adoptive son, Jordan, who spends his life wandering the seas, searching for love and self-knowledge. The novel describes an early public appearance of a banana in Britain; the excitement of this unusual sight inspires Jordan's wanderlust, which later results in him bringing the first pineapples into the country. I focus here predominantly on the use of fruit pictorial icons at the beginning of each chapter, which represent the fluidity and versatility of each character's gender, sexuality and identity, as they contest normative expectations.

The icons for each narrator are: a banana for Dog-Woman, a pineapple for Jordan, a split banana for the Nameless Ecologist and a split pineapple for Nicholas Jordan. The fruit iconography acts as a vehicle of substitution and disavowal of given gender and sexuality through the process of substitution. Laura Doan argues that Winterson successfully disrupts her own narrative 'by aligning each character with a fruit against conventional expectations'; however, more can be said about Winterson's use of fruit icons to contest historical and normative views of masculinity and femininity.[2] Winterson not only writes against the conventional expectations of gender through her characters, as claimed by Doan, but she also offers a further challenge to identity and sexuality norms by reconceptualizing ideas of the subject through alternative fetishization. The combinations of narrator and their fruit challenge normative expectations of given gender and sexuality as the physical characteristics of the fruit are contrasted with the subversive signifiers of gender and sexuality attached to the novel's characters.

Elizabeth Langland observes that in this novel Winterson has managed to portray the 'imaginary woman' whom 'Butler cannot quite manage to convey with drag performance – that is, the way performativity, or the ritualised repetition of gender norms, can have a destabilising effect'.[3] Langland further notes the performative destabilization of convention and tradition accomplished through 'Winterson's parodic text', where, she claims, 'women's bodies are at once a site for the inscription of conventional meanings and a locus for their disruption'.[4] However, Winterson's remapping of gender and sexuality exceeds Langland's observations. For instance, even though Dog-Woman is female, she possesses a masculine power, and her characteristics are those of a giant. Winterson uses the banana to signify Dog-Woman, although it is usually associated with the male phallus, symbolic of masculine power. Dog-Woman makes this link herself, albeit a little dismissively, upon seeing a banana for the first time: 'I swear that what he had resembled nothing more than the private parts of an Oriental. It was yellow and livid and long.'[5] In this way, using a banana to introduce a character strongly suggests they would be male. However, typical of Winterson's works, which always challenge the boundary norms of gender, sexuality and identity, she uses the banana to shatter gender stereotypes, as it represents here a female character. This swapping of characteristics serves to complicate regular expectations of gender and sexuality. For example, Dog-Woman's narration indicates she consider herself capable of giving birth but that the men she is aware of are physically incapable of inseminating her: 'I would have liked to pour out a child from my body but you have to have a man for that and there's no man who's a match for me'.[6] She is not feminine by any typical expectation of gender performances, and her physical body deconstructs ideas of feminine form; she exceeds Butler's concept of drag to present an alternative portrayal of female body, gender and identity. Therefore, through Dog-Woman, Winterson offers an atypical description of femininity, whether in physical, emotional or psychological terms.

Dog-Woman is first introduced in the novel by her adopted son, Jordan, who describes her as gigantic and dishevelled, but loving. Her grotesque size and insanitary nature are confirmed by her own description of Jordan sitting on her 'much as a fly rests on a hill of dung'.[7] Her body challenges all expectations of gender and sexuality norms and, consequently, the boundaries of desire. The use of the banana, thus, is a representation of her masculine side and a representation of her as a powerful woman. This reversed representation symbolizes those who fight for their right to exist. Dog-Woman persists in what she believes, and she practises what she thinks is sufficient for her and for others with the masculine traits present in her body, mind and soul (this behaviour is also reflected in the Nameless Ecologist, whom I will discuss further below).

Jordan, who is male by biological sex, is more feminine in nature, and his icon is the pineapple, whose curves may be better suited to stereotypically representing a female character. He was found by Dog-Woman on the bank of the Thames and she had to wash him so that she could 'find out what his sex was' because his body was 'caked in mud'.[8] He has to be cleaned up to reveal whether he is male or female, introducing a note of sexual ambiguity in his character from the start. The pineapple represents Jordan's experiences in the feminine world, where he has the opportunity to become the other, by learning the language and culture of women. His gender-blurring acts of performing female experiences contest normative behaviour and offer an alternative mode of living. Therefore, the pineapple is not simply a fruit but a substitute that represents Jordan's inner desires and alternative gender performances. Jordan's high-pitched voice gives him the opportunity to explore his feminine side by passing as a woman; in combination with his cross-dressing, he is able to leave his male existence behind, live as a woman, and 'escape from the weight of the world'.[9] This 'weight' suggests how the patriarchy also has a deleterious effect on the men who live under its oppression. He has the opportunity to be the other through his adventures in the world of women by learning their culture and language. Jordan observes how women view men: 'I never guessed how much they hate us or how deeply they pity us. They think we're children with too much pocket money'.[10] He also experiences how women band together to survive:

'The women who owned the fish stall warned me never to try and cheat another woman but always to try and charge the men double or send them away with a bad catch.'[11] By masking his maleness and adopting a feminine appearance, Jordan substitutes the alternative for the normative. His character suggests that each human being has masculine and feminine traits and so can embrace an alternative interpretation of gender, sexuality and identity, one that refuses fixity. Thus, the pineapple is not just a fruit, but it is a substitute object that represents Jordan's inner desires and alternative lifestyle.

As discussed, each fruit hints at a character's inner qualities, challenging gender and sexuality expectations. Through the diverse pictorial icons of the fruits accorded to each of these characters, gender expectations are loosened and subjective boundaries challenged. In this way, Winterson opposes established norms by allowing her characters to perform a range of gender roles with conflicting sexuality and gender identities. This enables her characters to experience the other's body, language and behaviour, while still inhabiting their own bodily self. Consequently, the fruit icons hint at fluid articulations of gender and sexuality for each character. They act as a semiotic force for altering the normative, which confuses and complicates the subject and acts as a symbolic carrier of alternative fetishization. In this way, Winterson deconstructs the notions of first-wave and second-wave fetishism: first, by admitting women into fetishistic substitutions and, second, by displacing assigned masculine and feminine roles. The substitution of an icon for a character's inner sexuality and gender performances reveals a third, alternative, mode of fetishism that offers freedom rather than repression. Winterson's characters show that each human being can have masculine and feminine traits from any point along the gender spectrum, and their lived experiences undermine and destabilize any notion of gender, sexuality and identity being static positions. Winterson regularly uses food in her texts to convey that gender, sexuality and identity can be fluid, mobile and interchangeable, depending on the situation encountered. Fruits, in Winterson's texts, are a semiotic force of alterity; in *Sexing the Cherry*, the normative symbolism between fruit, femininity and masculinity is rethought, and fruit functions as a disavowal of normative desire and concurrently as an avowal of alternative desires and gender identities. Thus, this act of disavowal and avowal represents the complication of the normative and alternative fetishization of the subject. Food's ubiquity in society imbues it with wide and deep powers of signification; MacClancy says, 'It plays a central role in our societies, and provides us as much with intricate symbols and metaphors as with nutritional substance.'[12]

The behaviour of the characters in Winterson's novels is largely directed by their diet. If there is not enough food, they respond negatively and seek retaliation on the self and the other. Women who are treated poorly, like the Twelve Dancing Princesses, Dog-Woman in *Sexing the Cherry* and Sarah Device in *The Daylight Gate*, are all pushed to the limits of their gender and sexuality because they do not control their food supply. Those who regulate food and 'its production, distribution, and consumption can control others'.[13] For example, those in power, the male elite, dictate who eats what and when, as 'maleness and femaleness in all cultures are associated with specific foods and rules often exist to control the consumption of those foods'.[14] This manipulation of power through food, meat in particular, will be discussed further with regard to *The Passion*.

In *Sexing the Cherry*, fruit is a significant element relating to voices of the past and present. We have already seen that particular fruits are associated with certain genders and sexualities and that Winterson challenges the normative boundaries of the subject by complicating it through unorthodox choices of fruit iconography. Winterson's female characters often have to act monstrously and be physically, emotionally and/or psychologically rebellious to gain their independence or freedom from those in power. This is evident from Dog-Woman and the Twelve Dancing Princesses, and it can also be seen with Alice Nutter in *The Daylight Gate*. *Frankissstein* shows Winterson crossing the gender binary even further with Ry, 'who lives with doubleness', as a female-born, male-presenting, transitional character. These examples show that society fears and shuns strong and independent women, because they possess a power deemed suitable only for men. Thus, a powerful woman needs to reject and counter phallocentric oppression. The actions of Dog-Woman, Jordan, Ry, Victor, or almost any of Winterson's characters for that matter, are not conventional or normative for women or men. Instead, they offer the possibility that people may be able to move beyond the gender binary to transgender, transhuman identities, which may ultimately become post-gender in a post-human world. Winterson's texts argue that, male or female, a person has the free will to choose what gender, sexuality or identity they wish to be in society.

In relation to Jacques Lacan's concept of the 'mirror stage', the split banana and pineapple – associated with the Nameless Ecologist and Nicholas Jordan, respectively – reflect the stage where one realizes the issues with the self and the body as a coherent, self-governing being.¹⁵ Even though it is still an imperfect self, this creates a desire on the part of the subject to have something beyond what they already have. Consequently, it creates a desire for the other. To extend this concept to Winterson's reversal technique, the split fruit represents the other, the desire to own the other, whether in terms of gender, sexuality or identity, through the deconstruction of the bodily self. The splitting of a fruit in half is used as a way of challenging the conventional notion of the self and the other, which deconstructs normative notions of gender, sexuality and identity. By doing this, Winterson twists expectations of masculinity and femininity, suggesting that identity can be multiple, deconstructed and performative.

The Nameless Ecologist is trying to save the earth from modern technology and the cruelty of the factory system, while Nicholas Jordan loves building boats in his spare time. Their voices are significant factors in illustrating the issues of gender and sexuality in their contemporary settings; for example, the pineapple is again represented as a male voice, even though this is a different century. Nicholas Jordan has kindred interests with the Jordan from the past: boats and sailing. He is '[f]ive foot ten. Dark. Makes model boats and sails them at the weekend.'¹⁶ Like Jordan, he also has a feminine side, but instead of this being displayed by his physical stature or by cross-dressing, his femininity is manifested through his empathy for, and vocal defence of, women. He appreciates their subaltern status and treats them more fairly than other men do: 'My mother has often been labelled as strange but that's because she says things people can't possibly believe. Mostly she's right.'¹⁷ In another incident, he praises the Nameless Ecologist, viewing her as a hero while others disparage her, as she fights for what she believes in and seeks to effect change: 'surely this woman was a hero? Heroes give up what's comfortable in order to protect what they believe in or to live dangerously for the common good.'¹⁸ Similarly, there is a split banana to represent the Nameless Ecologist, the alter-ego of Dog-Woman in the future. She protests against hypocritical people in power, like owners of multinational business conglomerates, to stop them destroying the earth. She is against banks, which she believes fund the big businesses that are destroying forests to set up factories, and she is also opposed to the security department because she believes that the government budget for the defence ministry supports wars around the world. These funds, she thinks, would be better spent fighting poverty. In her imagination, she is a monstrous woman (reflecting Dog-Woman) and stands against modernity. For her, modernity is tantamount to murdering the planet, so through her actions she stays strong to her beliefs and continues her fight to save the earth. Like Dog-Woman, she tries her best to save powerless people from becoming victims of the powerful.

Consequently, the use of split fruit in Winterson's works is intended to question the existence of the gender binary and to challenge conventional notions of gender and sexuality. The split fruit illustrates contrary views of gender and sexuality and, consequently, demonstrates that both males and females have their own issues to deal with in the struggle against internal and external influences, such as emotions and environment. Many of Winterson's female characters are born fighters, brave enough to challenge the injustices done to them. Conversely, not all her male characters are strong and imbued with manly attitudes that conform to social expectations. There are men who are feminine in appearance, who are seen as weak and passive. This opposes the conventional idea that there is 'an essential difference between man and woman'.[19] To Winterson, people have their own choices and preferences in life, be it gender, sexuality or identity. However, due to societal pressures, most people are compelled to follow orthodox understandings of gender, sexuality and identity. If people do go against the norms, they are seen as different and condemned as sinners or deviants (this will be examined further in the 'Sexual Fetishism' section). The fruits in *Sexing the Cherry* are icons that challenge this orthodox view and represent the fact that there is often a choice in life.

Through her use of food terminology, Winterson demonstrates that desire, pleasure, love and power are not inherently gendered – men, women and all positions along the gender spectrum can experience them. Thus, masculinity and femininity are fluid in every individual. The unconventional lives led by Dog-Woman, Jordan, the Nameless Ecologist and Nicholas Jordan challenge the boundary norms, and society in general might find them abhorrent or perverse. The unfair treatment of women or the unfortunate other by those in power is particularly challenged by Jordan's voice. Through Jordan, Winterson facilitates a break from the imposed restrictions of gender, sexuality and identity. By the use of the banana and pineapple icons, both whole and split, Winterson expands the metaphorical significance of these fruits and reveals alternative ways of representing fluid gender and sexual identities. Winterson's customary style is to unravel the inner desires and pleasures of each of her characters by opposing orthodox viewpoints, and each of her characters has a certain level of agency to perform their desired gender roles from a re-invigorated ethical stance.

5

Meat as power

The Passion, Winterson's second serious work of fiction, intertwines the boundaries of love, memory and fantasy with the spectacle of history during the Napoleonic era. The story reveals the role internal and external desire plays in surviving in society, and I discuss here the significant relationships between meat, morality and power. Winterson's frequent and distinctive use of food to metaphorically represent the fluidity of gender, sexuality and identity by dismantling or reconceptualizing the normative view provides a means of rethinking the processes and outcomes of fetishization. Whereas *Sexing the Cherry* uses fruit iconography to present the body's diverse desires and the fluid nature of gender and sexuality, I argue that *The Passion* turns animal flesh into an eroticized symbol of material pleasures. The novel's obsession with meat marks the body as an object and subject of power relations in society, and the production, distribution and consumption of meat in the text symbolizes the unequal forces at large in Napoleonic France. The power of a person can be measured through the food they produce and consume. In *The Passion*, the dominance of aggressive men, such as Napoleon and the Meat Man, over the less powerful is strongly linked to the supply and consumption of meat. In terms of what meat signifies for the gender difference in power structures, Adams argues that

> [e]ating animals acts as mirror and representation of patriarchal values. Meat eating is the re-inscription of male power at every meal. The patriarchal gaze sees not the fragmented flesh of dead animals but appetizing food. If our appetites re-inscribe patriarchy, our actions regarding eating animals will either reify or challenge the received culture. If meat is a symbol of male dominance then the presence of meat proclaims the dis-empowering of women.[1]

Winterson uses food terminology in *The Passion* to present the unequal relationships between the sexes. In this novel, meat is a metaphor for women, who are objects for men to gaze at and consume. Women such as the *Vivandiéres* are perceived as passive things who become subjects of male domination. The flesh of these oppressed women, through their sexual exploitation, becomes a meat to be consumed by the powerful others. Food plays an important role in *The Passion*, as it does in *Sexing the Cherry*, in the production, categorization and regulation of gender, sexuality and identity. Hence, alternative depictions of food and power, and their concomitant effects on gender and sexuality, reveal an alternative fetishism of food that underpins Winterson's obsessive gastronomic focus. The power of a person can be measured through the food he or she produces and consumes. Men in *The Passion* are often the providers and distributors of raw food to women, who cook it. Men master the supply of meat because

> [t]he male prerogative to eat meat is an external, observable activity implicitly reflecting a recurring fact: meat is a symbol of male dominance. Meat is king; this noun describing meat is a noun denoting male power. Vegetable, a generic term meat eaters use for all foods that are not meat, have become as associated with women as meat as with men.[2]

Food, and meat in particular, is a weapon for those in power to maintain their strength over others. As we saw in *Sexing the Cherry* with fruit, in *The Passion* meat plays a similar role in articulating gender, sexuality and identity. However, in *The Passion*, meat is the main element used to represent the power, sex and gender one holds in society. Meat in the novel signifies normative gender, sexuality and identity. Yet by challenging and destabilizing this normative status, through highlighting how meat is so often a substitute for some other object, Winterson presents an act of alternative fetishization. Hence, by altering the significations of meat in *The Passion*, it comes to stand for a disavowal of power, sex and desire.

Food is, of course, necessary for the individual body to stay strong and alive; however, Adams also argues that 'class, caste, race, and gender hierarchies are maintained, in part, through differential control over and access of food'.[3] Although Winterson uses food to represent the desire for power, and she shows that the control of food and power are closely linked in patriarchal governing societies, food in her novels can still play a part in resisting oppressive moral and legal codes. Her use of food to represent metaphorically the fluidity of gender, sexuality and identity, by destabilizing or dismantling normative views, enables a rethinking of fetishism. More precisely, through her fictional characters, Winterson employs food and its consumption as prominent elements to represent diverse desire, love, loss and power in order to challenge and subvert patriarchal and heteronormative assumptions in society.

The characters in *The Passion* include Villanelle, a bisexual woman; Henri, a village boy who becomes a soldier; and the Meat Man, who works in Napoleon's kitchen and is later also a supplier of meat. The story is all about taking risks in order to emancipate the self and the unfortunate other from a patriarchal society and from those in power. Men in society use meat to display patriarchal power, conforming to Adams's claim that 'people with power have always eaten meat'.[4] Adams describes a painting of Henry VIII eating a steak-and-kidney pie, appearing proud and in control, and contrasts it with the portraits of each of his wives in which they are depicted holding a fruit or a vegetable, rather than meat or any other food that is believed to be illustrative of masculine power.[5] This suggests that meat represents strength and power, and thus those who consume meat are considered superior to those who do not have the opportunity to eat it. Napoleon Bonaparte, who is preoccupied with chicken, women and winning the war, is shown to be an ambitious and powerful man. He is obsessed with power and possessed by it. For him, others are only objects of his obsession with success. He treats the other without any sympathy; the only things he loves are his wife and poultry, the two things often seeming to merge in his desire: 'He liked no one except Josephine and he liked her the way he liked chicken.'[6] He is selfish and wants only to be on top, either in battle or bed. Winterson illustrates that only meat can assuage Napoleon's extraordinary appetite as, to quote MacClancy, '[m]eat is strength. Meat is power. Meat is life. It is the very king of foods.'[7] Napoleon's obsession with chicken metaphorically represents his characteristic greed for power and his treatment of others, especially women. He has such 'a passion for chicken that he kept his chef working around the clock'.[8] He makes his men work as hard as he pleases, regardless of whether it is day or night; at any time, whenever his appetite so desires, he will ring the bell 'like the Devil himself is at the other end'.[9] Napoleon's greed when eating his meal represents his desire for global domination: he wants to own the world, and he fantasizes about having it in his grasp, 'holding it tenderly with both hands as if it were a breast'.[10] In his mind, the world and the countries he has conquered are so small they can be held in both his hands, and the breast could be a chicken's as much as Josephine's.

The meat he consumes represents his power over the countries he has conquered, and it is also a metaphor that indicates his domination and cruel control of those under him, particularly the women he keeps for the sexual satisfaction of his armies. The women he conquers are passive objects, ready for direct or indirect submission to his might. The breast is a fetishized body part that acts as an object to stimulate his erotic activity and, thus, countries and women are, to Napoleon, subdued and submissive before him. His extreme obsession to control and conquer is itself a fetishistic behaviour, imagining the world as a stimulant to his desire for power. Winterson's text illustrates that Napoleon's mania for chicken is an extreme obsession: the cooked bird acts as a fetish object to sate his hunger for world domination and to divert, albeit temporarily, the stresses produced by this quest. This reformulation of greed and selfishness reveals an alternative fetishism in operation, as the symbolic substitution of chicken for the lands and people Napoleon wishes to devour acts as a defensive strategy. His internal desires for conquest, and his fears of failure, are transmuted by the consumption of chicken into acceptance and a psychical integration that benefits his mental and emotional processes. In other words, his appetites for food, meat in particular, closely resemble his greed for power. Napoleon's obsessive desire to subjugate enemy nations, in order to wield the power to control the other, is itself a fetishistic act. It is his pleasure and desire to own all the different countries in the world as he owns all his soldiers and women.

Napoleon's greed is further portrayed when he is shown to prefer dining alone, just as he plans his military campaigns alone. His plans are made quietly as he eats his meals greedily and with impatience, as if he had not eaten for a week: 'As soon as I'm gone he'll lift the lid and pick it up and push it into his mouth. He wishes his whole face were mouth to cram a whole bird', says Henri.[11] How a person eats his food offers an insight to their personality and so Napoleon's table manners strongly suggest he is impatient with everything, including winning the war and women. This relates to the patriarchal domination of certain foods as explicated by Adams: 'meat is always the food for the king and those in power.'[12] Napoleon's meals consist of only meat. Not once in the novel is there a mention of any other food. His kitchen is scattered 'with [chicken] in every state of undress; odd to be so governed by an appetite'.[13] In addition, the word 'chicken' stands for something more than just meat, especially in their state of 'undress', as they feed a certain appetite. Napoleon behaves fiercely towards others, and they cannot voice their unhappiness or rebel against him; instead, the others become fodder for the hunger of his passion and obsession, and, in the face of his naked ambition, it is they who are 'undress[ed]' by his actions. Despite 'being governed by an appetite', Napoleon is the one who actually dictates the movements of this appetite.

Napoleon's hunger for chicken reflects his attitude towards power, women and sex. He controls every movement of the others below him using his power as a leader, and the women in his world are perceived as sexual objects. He even divides these women into categories of sexual slaves. He treated the *Vivandiéres* as the lowest category of prostitutes: 'Unlike the town tarts, who protected themselves and charged what they liked and certainly charged individually, the *vivants* were expected to service as many men as asked them day or night.'[14] Not only does he categorize these women, but the food that he instructs be given to them is 'often worse' than the food consumed by his soldiers, even though these women give his army sexual pleasure.[15] Some of them are too weak to serve in this capacity because not only is their food always poor, but they are paid hardly any money for their services. Napoleon creates laws to police the women's bodies, such as issuing shawls, but proclaiming that any of them 'found covering herself on duty could be reported and fined'.[16] This is to show how disadvantaged and devalued people, usually women, are kept in subordination due to gender hierarchies in society. While this exemplifies a patriarchal system of oppression and abuse, Winterson deconstructs the normative gender hierarchy to a certain degree by showing how the women themselves resist internalizing and accepting the hierarchical system of grading the prostitutes. The acts of kindness by the 'town tarts' to their unfortunate counterparts in the army camps, such as bringing them loaves of bread, reveal a female solidarity and community that cannot be wholly extinguished by the despotism of Napoleon and his imperial rule. This illustrates that men in power assert and maintain their position partially through easy access to good food but that they display little communal charity. By contrast, those women in a comparatively higher position to others of their sex adopt a more humane and distributive approach to the resources they have access to, including food. The particular status of the men in power is determined in part by the quantity and quality of food under their control, while conversely, the greater the struggles faced by women and the unfortunate others, the lower their position is on the social scale.

In times of war, meat always becomes less available, but Napoleon can eat it any time he desires, day or night. His army gets meat, and though their portions are meagre, it still surpasses what is given to the women:

> We got most of our meat from nameless regions and I suspect from animals that Adam would not recognise. Two pounds of bread, 4 oz of meat and 4 oz of vegetables were rationed to us daily. We stole what we could, spent our wages, when we had them, on tavern food and wreaked havoc on the communities who lived quietly round about ... [The *vivandiéres*'] food was often worse than ours.[17]

Napoleon's control of food and its consumption is an established strategy to maintain 'power by keeping the poor debilitated and dazed'.[18] As Adams notes:

'during wartime, government rationing policies reserve the right to meat for the epitome of the masculine man: the soldier.'[19] Napoleon's policy of near-perpetual war ensures that the military prioritizing of the meat rations becomes a normal situation in his empire. Napoleon wields the highest authority in the land, and, thus, he reserves the right to have more meat than anyone else as a symbol of this masculine power. Winterson acknowledges such male domination over the passive other but later deconstructs and destabilizes such apparent mastery through her female character, Villanelle, in order to challenge patriarchal and heterosexual hegemony. Therefore, food holds the power to manipulate others and also acts as a mirror of the power of the sexes more generally.

Food as an indicator of gender politics can also be traced in *The Daylight Gate*, where the unfortunate others, like Sarah and Jennet Device, are victims of hunger. For example, Sarah turns monstrous because of it: 'She felt [Robert's] tongue in her mouth. She was dizzy. She hadn't eaten for two days.'[20] So she bites his tongue in a desperate, cannibalistic deed. Jennet is used by her brother and mother in sexual transactions for the convenience of their bellies and other economic purposes, such as procuring clothing. Food is important in life as mentioned above, thus 'hunger – like poverty – is far more likely to strike people in disadvantaged and devalued social categories', and so women and the unfortunate others can be transformed into the monstrous.[21] Therefore, such people 'often suffer hunger and famine more severely than men because of their socioeconomic and political subordination'.[22] In other words, power indicates what, and how much, food a person can consume. The immense quantity of chickens that litter Napoleon's kitchen is analogous to the number of women he abuses and seduces, resulting in women becoming objects for him to collect and conquer, just like winning the war and conquering other countries. His consumption pattern differs from that of other people below him. This makes it easy for him to impose rules on others, like poor food for his soldiers, and even worse fare for the prostitutes. Napoleon's control of meat in the novel represents Kate Millet's definition of 'politics': 'power-structured relationships, arrangements whereby one group of persons is controlled by another'; in this case, the politics of food means everyone has to negotiate their place in society largely based on their ability to produce, procure and consume meat.[23]

As mentioned, certain characters in *The Passion* have an ambiguous nature that is reflected by the food they eat. Villanelle is born with webbed feet and androgynous characteristics, so she creates self-confidence by switching gender roles depending on the situation she is in. She is comfortable with her chameleonic nature, though she uses most often the feminine side of her inner desire. It is a compliment to Villanelle's fluidity that is sufficiently able to navigate and survive the patriarchal society in which she finds herself. However, Winterson still shows that meat is power and only controlled fully by men in authority. Giving Villanelle the power to consume meat places her on the side of male power in a masculine world and her carnivorous actions undermine and threaten to subvert the patriarchal order, but this is only temporary, for as long as the meal lasts. In this time, the obsessive focus on meat's ability to stand in for male-associated freedoms to Villanelle transforms the everyday activity of eating into an act of alternative fetishization. An example is of this is when Henri recalls his first meeting with Villanelle, in a scene that revolves around meat:

> Patrick was waiting for me with a woman I had never met. She was a *vivandière*. Only a handful were left and they were strictly for the officers. The pair of them were wolfing chicken legs and offered one to me. [. . .] 'Where did you get them?'[24]

Villanelle answers with confidence and without hesitation: 'I fucked for them, the Russians have got plenty and there's still plenty of Russians in Moscow.'[25] It is clear that meat is the king of all foods and represents power, and thus Villanelle is prepared to sacrifice her body to have meat in her diet and to survive. Her cross-dressing and her determination to consume meat play an important role in her participation in a patriarchal society. Villanelle eats in a similar manner to Napoleon, 'wolfing' her meal down, and this is because meat has power: '[it] increases our potency, adds edge to our aggression, heats our passion.'[26] According to this belief, those who consume meat think and act more aggressively, which are useful characteristics for a woman in a patriarchal, militarized society that is at war. According to Adams, there is an obligation for a masculine man, such as a soldier, to eat meat.[27] Villanelle's vacillation between dressing as a man and as a woman confuses her sexual objectives and aims, but, rather than depressing her, this ambiguity allows her to take pleasure in both her identities. As mentioned earlier, Villanelle's insistence on periodically consuming meat is itself a fetishistic act of male power. Villanelle performs contradistinct gender and sexuality roles; her fetishization of male power is displayed by her desire to gain it and use it against those in positions of high authority in the patriarchy. As such, her desire for meat and her desire for agency in a male-dominated society become superimposed.

Food, Probyn says, is 'imbricated in nation-building, the reproduction of the family, constitutes a major site of the division of labour, and is central to the production of geopolitical inequalities'.[28] These are plentiful reasons for why food is one of Winterson's foremost literary concerns. Henri, raised mainly by women and friendly with a priest, is not a habitual meat eater. This influences his behaviour and his treatment of others, especially women, to whom he shows respect and kindness. For example, in the brothel, Henri avoids engagement with the prostitutes: 'I told her I had a headache and went to sit outside.'[29] On the other hand, the carnivorous Meat Man behaves in a cruel and desperate manner, deeply affected by his experiences of the brutalities of war. This unleashes in him an animalistic desire to be aggressive and domineering. Similarly, Napoleon's abusive behaviour can be regarded as a direct consequence of his military power, as the establishment of the military and the forces of war become tools in the metamorphosis of people; he, too, relishes his meat to the point of obsession. Foucault writes of the nature of power and warfare before the atomic bomb:

> Power was exercised mainly as a means of deduction (*prélèvement*), a subtraction mechanism, a right to appropriate a portion of the wealth, a tax of products, goods and services, labour and blood, levied on the subjects. Power in this instance was essentially a right of seizure: of things, time, bodies, and ultimately life itself.[30]

Food in *The Passion* is a fetish object because it can substitute for the sword in wielding the power of life and death. Known as the heart of most meals, 'meat is so central to our ideas about nourishment that the very word can stand for all food in general' and, therefore, it represents strength and control, whether physical, emotional or psychological.[31] Nonetheless, Winterson's obsession with food does not end with *Sexing the Cherry* and *The Passion*. Even though each of her novels uses food imagery and terminology differently, a consistent thread running through them is how food is linked with the deconstruction of bodies and the reconceptualizing of gender and sexuality. The alternative fetishization of food offers a substitute replacement for the lost object – be it power, agency, a loved one, or whatever – that enables unorthodox individuals and non-normative desires to exist, and even flourish, in the world.

In *Frankissstein*, Winterson engages with matters of the flesh in a transgender and transhuman reimagining of Mary Shelley's *Frankenstein*. Once again, meat is strongly linked to masculinity and generally eaten only by male characters in the novel, such as Ron Lord and Victor Stein. However, the complexities of gender and sexual politics are increased by Ry's transgender status. Ron Lord, a stereotype of boorish and bigoted masculinity, cannot adequately process Ry's existence and so tries to force them into one or the other categories in the strict male/female binary he has in his mind. Although Ron believed Ry to be male in their first meeting, having a penis appears to be his pre-eminent qualification for manhood as Ry's subsequent declaration regarding the contents of their trousers alters Ron's view: 'OK, no dick. So you're not a bloke really.'[32] However, Ron is still confused by Ry's blurring of gender boundaries, as other physical characteristics do not entirely accord with Ron's ideals of femininity: 'What big hands you've got [. . .] You've got a bloke's hands, says Ron.'[33] It is telling that Ron's final test regarding Ry's gender concerns the eating of red meat:

> Tell you what – I'll take us all out for something to eat. Prof! Ryan? I could murder a steak.
> Good job it's already dead, I say.
> Ron looks at me more in sorrow than anger.
> Ryan, I am extending the hand, he says.
> Thanks, Ron, but I'm vegetarian.
> I knew you wasn't a bloke, says Ron.[34]

Vegetarianism is the final piece of evidence that confirms Ry's lack of masculinity to Ron. As Adams states, 'Men who decide to eschew meat eating are deemed effeminate; failure of men to eat meat announces that they are not masculine.'[35] Ron's response suggests that had Ry embraced the idea of going for a steak, Ron might have been able to overlook the absence of a penis. As it is, Ry's vegetarianism now combines with their genitalia to bar them from Ron's mental categorization of 'man'. The steak could have been a fetishistic phallic substitute for Ry's non-existent penis, allowing Ron to deal with Ry's transgressive being, but by refusing to have a steak, Ry also refuses the masculine values encoded within the patriarchal semiotics of meat.

Victor's relationship with meat and masculinity is a little more complicated than Ron's, and perhaps even more revealing. During his first encounter with Ry, Victor leaves a toasted cheese sandwich untouched, on the premise of not mixing carbohydrates and protein. This particular concern with diet and health adds to the air of vanity, if not indeed narcissism, attached to Victor following Ry's initial assessment that he has had Botox or some other form of cosmetic surgery on his face (it is unlikely Ron Lord, that cypher of unreconstructed masculinity with his ill-fitting shirts and urine-stained trousers, similarly worries about mixing food groups or reducing wrinkles around his eyes). However, Victor also enjoys steak, mentioning it twice during this first encounter with Ry in Arizona, which would confirm his masculinity by Ron's criteria. Further masculine behaviour by Victor makes the subsequent sex scene with Ry problematic due to its reliance on gender stereotypes from both parties – Victor as cis-male and Ry as 'anatomically' female.[36] When Victor discovers that Ry is trans, he stares as though he was 'scanning' them.³⁷ Despite his obvious attraction to Ry, when Victor is asked 'Do you want to touch me?', his immediate response is 'I'm not gay'. Like Ron, Victor is also curious about Ry's genitals and questions them:

> His finger was inside me.
> This is . . .
> As it always was, I said.
> And this?
> The clitoris gets much bigger with testosterone.
> Is it sensitive?
> I have 8,000 nerves in my clitoris. Your penis gets by on 4,000. Yes, it is sensitive.³⁸

It seems Victor needs to be reassured that Ry's vagina is original, and thus she remains essentially female, to ensure their lovemaking transgresses the boundaries of heterosexuality as little as possible. This has followed on from Ry behaving in a passively feminine way towards Victor: 'It is easy to be controlled by someone who is controlling and charming. And, outside my job, I dislike decisions. I'll go with the flow on this.'³⁹ It seems the stereotypical associations of meat-eating and vegetarianism with masculinity and femininity coincide with the thoughts and actions of Victor and Ry; what could have been a truly novel and transgressive situation becomes, instead, a heterosexual love scene, to all intents and purposes. All of which show Victor to have an ongoing concern for regulatory matters of the flesh that sit uneasily with his plan to upload consciousness and achieve immortality through bodyless, digital means. Perhaps the future Victor is actively trying to create, in which human minds 'will no longer be tied to a body that is a substrate made of meat', still holds some fears or drawbacks for a steak-lover like himself.⁴⁰

In addition to the discussion in Part I about gazing at the body, Adams believes that 'food in general and meat in specific, like the female body, is a "site of visual pleasure or lure of the gaze"'.⁴¹ The following chapter will show how food is compared with the body: the body is an object and subject of obsession with the self and the other; it is hunted, produced and appreciated through the acts of looking, touching and consuming. Recalling Freudian and Foucauldian notions of the body as discussed previously, the eyes act as a scanner for the pleasure of the nose before the hand picks up the object for the pleasure of touch, conveys it to the mouth for the pleasure of taste, and, finally, the mouth consumes it for the pleasure of the stomach. This process that seemingly relies on separate areas of the body operating interdependently to achieve a unifying goal leads to an extension and broadening of definitions of food and sex in Winterson's work.

6

The boundaries of food

In this chapter I discuss how an obsession with food is transferred onto the body, and vice versa, with a main focus on *Written on the Body*. I argue that acts of looking, touching and consuming in Winterson's works make food and the body comparable objects and subjects of obsessions in the self and the other. Erotic pleasures are imagined, produced and appreciated through food and its consumption, uncovering the poetics of desire within Winterson's writing that obsessively propel the emotional power of her stories. The consumption of food becomes a fetishistic act, a necessary displacement for the self to release its desire for someone or something else. As my analysis of *Written on the Body* demonstrates, food and sex are intimately connected by the body: eating is often portrayed in sexual ways, and sex is often described by a metaphoric language of eating. The role of food in Winterson's texts contests the idea that 'in many cultures, eating is a sexual and gendered experience throughout life'.[1] While it may agree with the first half of that statement, her writing indicates that the particular circumstances of every situation direct the choices a person makes, rather than their gender, and that their pursuit of pleasure is fluid and contingent. *Written on the Body*'s narrator has no name or specified gender, despite all that the reader learns of their sexual and culinary tastes. This aligns Winterson's work with the thinking of Deleuze and Guattari, who state, 'what regulates the obligatory, necessary, or permitted intermingling of bodies is above all an alimentary regime and a sexual regime'.[2]

Written on the Body remains one of Winterson's most controversial work. Many of Winterson's fans and critics, especially feminists, were shocked by Winterson's apparent promotion of individualism, rather than feminism, with some feeling 'cheated' by its unnamed and ambiguously gendered narrator.[3] However, *Written on the Body* underlines a main concept present in all of Winterson's novels: pleasure and desire know no boundaries and are not contingent on sex. Winterson uses food terminology to express her belief that food, sexuality and identity are not gendered. Rather, experiencing pleasure or desire, temporarily or permanently, depends on the choices made, and the metaphorical overlapping of meaning around gender, sexuality and identity are fluid and depend on the situation. Consequently, Winterson displaces the language of love, loss, pleasure and desire into food to illustrate that pleasure and desire are not gendered but free-floating. What does remain constant is the central role of the body as *the* object to represent the discourse of fluid pleasure, desire, love and loss. Through food, Winterson uses the body as a medium to communicate diverse pleasures and desires and to destabilize heteronormative conventions.

Food and sex are connected by the body, and the Unnamed Narrator shows that certain foods are a wild delectation to the mouth as they are eaten; for instance, remarking of Louise: 'After sex you tiger-tear your food, let your mouth run over with grease.'[4] This reflects Foucault's linking of food and sex, in which pleasure is stimulated by 'contact with the mouth, the tongue, and the throat (for the pleasures of food and drink), or contact with other parts of the body (for the pleasures of sex)'.[5] Thus, through food, the body is a medium of communication to express pleasure and desire of the self and the other, in order to, in the words of Probyn, 'lose oneself, to have oneself rearranged through sex'.[6] Thinking and fantasizing about food is one mode of substitution of the actual object, and it is an alternative way of fetishization performed by the bodily self in Winterson's work; as Massimo Fusillo states, 'fetishism always works on the detail, granting it value, rendering it infinite, penetrating its microcosm with an entire macrocosm of passions and narrations, employing procedures that have a great deal in common with literary composition and artistic creation'.[7] Food is also used as an object to seduce as it provokes ideas of eroticizing, imagining and pleasuring the self and the other. Gamman and Makinen claim that, 'food is frequently used to explain sexual practice' and 'is metonymically connected to courting'.[8] MacClancy goes further in highlighting the food/sex link, saying that '[f]ood can also be a sexual aid, stimulating one's desire for another [. . .]. Among some groups, a meal together is seen as a form of sex, and it is intended that eating should lead to intercourse'.[9] The Unnamed Narrator observes: 'It's well-known that molluscs are aphrodisiac, Casanova ate his mussels raw before pleasuring a lady'.[10] A further example of the link between the body and sex is when the Unnamed Narrator reminisces about their time with Louise: 'We will fall like ripe fruit and roll down the grass together.'[11] Food acts as a substitute to replace sexual desire and pleasure of the self and the other. Consequently, the consumption of food becomes a fetishistic act, a necessary displacement for the self to release its desire for someone or something else. Also, the use of food words makes the reader see things imaginatively and transformatively. The Unnamed Narrator wishes at one point to be a vegetable just so that they can be held, chewed and eaten by Louise, to be close to her, to feel her, to taste her, if only through her cooking. The Unnamed Narrator also wants to be tasted by Louise so she will know how they feel about her: 'You affect me in ways I can't quantify or contain. All I can measure is the effect.'[12] With regard to infantile development, Freud writes about a baby's satisfaction with food:

> [it] persists as the prototype of the expression of sexual satisfaction in later life. The need for repeating the sexual satisfaction now becomes detached from the need for taking nourishment – a separation which becomes inevitable when the teeth appear and food is no longer taken in only by sucking, but is also chewed up.[13]

This action of consuming food, or at least certain foods, is a pleasure and a desire for the self and the other, which is prominent throughout *Written on the Body*. This is because when talking about eating food, we are frequently doing so as an act of substitution, to metaphorically express desire, pleasure and sexual activity. For example, MacClancy illustrates the connection between food terminology and the male body:

> Food metaphors for the male torso imply masculine muscle and strength, while those for the female form suggest pleasure – men's possessive pleasure of female bodies. A man can be 'beefy' and has a 'hot dog', 'sausage', or 'piece of meat' between his legs, together with a 'couple of nuts'.[14]

As argued throughout this book, Winterson's fetish objects rely on her precise, yet suggestive, writing style. She deploys in her novels a distinctive language of sensuality and sensuousness, while simultaneously fearing its decay and atrophy: 'Delicate words exhausted through overuse.'[15] Thus, she creates a new meaning for words, in this case gastronomic words, replete with connotations of desire, pleasure and sex, suggestive of a fluidity of gender and sexuality. For example, in *Written on the Body*, she compares the body, religion, food and consumption with the boundaries of pleasure and desire: 'The pomegranate was the real apple of Eve, fruit of the womb, I would eat my way into perdition to taste you.'[16] Consequently, the body becomes the site of discourse for desire, sex and love, and food becomes the subject that is responsible for developing that body: 'Written on the body is a secret code only visible in certain lights; the accumulations of a lifetime gather there.'[17] Thus, 'every object carries a different significance', especially food, in the form of the desire to eat something, and the pleasure when it goes through the mouth, down the throat, and into the stomach.[18]

MacClancy says, 'Freudians claim that food and sex are so often linked because our first pleasurable sensation comes from feeding at the breast.'[19] Therefore, not only does the body feature prominently when discussing food but also body parts and organs. For example, the Unnamed Narrator draws parallels between their sexual pleasure and terms of consumption: 'Scoop me in your hands. [. . .] Eat of me and let me be sweet.'[20] The Unnamed Narrator also uses food to represent or replace body parts as a substitute in order to generate sensual and sensuous language: 'My lover is an olive tree whose roots grow by the sea. Her fruit is pungent and green. [. . .] The little stone of her hard by the tongue.'[21] Louise's body is compared to an olive tree, the little stone representing her clitoris. Food is also used for sexual arousal, for example 'the stimulating powers of hot chocolate'.[22] Correspondingly, Winterson uses the language of consumption to develop a more nuanced appreciation of sexual desire and foreplay: 'There could not be a more unromantic moment than this and yet the yeasty smell of raisins and rye is exciting me more than any *Playboy* banana.'[23] Food seems to activate sexual drives and desires in *Written on the Body*: 'One night, after a seafood lasagne and a bottle of champagne we made love so vigorously that the [bed] was driven across the floor by the turbine of our lust.'[24] Louise is both the sexual object and sexual aim for the Unnamed Narrator; this type of fluid and mobile act of sexual obsession will be discussed further in the next section.

Louise's physical gestures while cooking and eating in the kitchen are arousing to the Unnamed Narrator, drawing them into an ecstatic appreciation of her body. They later fantasize about Louise through the imagery of food in an act of alternative fetishism. When the Unnamed Narrator eats, the action is filled with meaning and drama: 'each bite burst war and passion'.[25] The Unnamed Narrator strips off any given gender and sexuality and allows the self and the other free will to live as they please; they challenge orthodox thinking about pleasure and desire, though this desire occasionally acts as a fulfilment of pleasure by the temporary substitution of the terminology of food and its consumption to perform a cycle of disavowal and avowal by the bodily self. As Gamman and Makinen argue, 'some women may develop food fetishism as a coping mechanism to disavow certain anxieties about identity'.[26] The Unnamed Narrator, whether male or female, does not feel secure in their position as Louise's lover, so they keep fantasizing about Louise through anything and everything around them. In this way, food is a temporary means to cope with the extreme feelings they have towards Louise. Not only has Louise 'charmed everyone' with her food, but she is also clever and beautiful.[27] The Unnamed Narrator would like to have, keep and even consume her. Thus, the Unnamed Narrator cannot stop thinking about Louise, and their pleasure and desire for her is a kind of torture.

The Unnamed Narrator's behaviour becomes an act of fetishization that seeks to disavow Louise's distance and difference from them. The Unnamed Narrator performs an act of disavowal by substituting Louise with another object in their mind. As mentioned earlier, an object or subject such as food can be used as a method to cope with the intensity of a desire: 'I could make a smoky tea and sit in my usual place and hope that the wisdom of objects would make some difference to me.'[28] They also seek to replace the pleasure of sex with another temporary desire, such as food: 'Well here I am at half past four with fruit bread and a cup of tea and instead of taking hold of myself I can only think of taking hold of Louise.'[29] Even though the substitution is 'peculiar', it is 'appropriate' as it still satisfies the hunger of the body.[30] The Unnamed Narrator conjures up a food fantasy to replace their desire for Louise: 'I cut a slice of fruit bread. If in doubt, eat. I can understand why for some people the best social worker is the fridge.'[31] Not only food but anything related to food or its consumption is a substitute object of disavowal. Everything around the Unnamed Narrator is a pleasure that is replaceable with anything else.

In relation to language and food, Winterson uses the lexis of consumption to develop a more profound appreciation of food as an alternative fetish object. However, this can only be achieved by fantasizing about Louise as the food which the Unnamed Narrator consumes, even 'the yeasty smell' that arouses them.[32] All these imaginations are playing out in the space of their mind as an act of temporary satisfaction of desire. For example, instead of focusing on their relationship with Jacqueline, the Unnamed Narrator keeps thinking about Louise. The Unnamed Narrator blames the food Louise cooked and everything around them: 'It's the food that's doing it.'[33] To return to Anna Freud's comments on hunger, feeding and ego-development, the Unnamed Narrator displays child-like behaviour in their relationship with food. The Unnamed Narrator realizes their body needs the satisfaction of the other body that they yearn for as they are 'drowning in inevitability' when they attempt to direct their passion away from Louise.[34] The Unnamed Narrator desires Louise and cannot control their need to be with her. They become obsessed, picturing her everywhere: 'on every hoarding, on the coins in my pocket'.[35] The food prepared by Louise becomes a schema in their imagination to search for Louise, a way to fulfil their desire through a fantasy of Louise, even 'if only through [her] cooking':

> She had been here, there must be something of her left. I would find her in the oil and onion, detect her through the garlic. I knew that she spat in the frying pan to determine the readiness of the oil. It's an old trick, every chef does it, or did.[36]

Louise, on the other hand, utilizes her female power to feed and satisfy hunger through her cooking for the Unnamed Narrator; as Counihan says: 'giving food to a great extent defines the nature and extent of female power.'[37] In this context, Louise uses her knowledge to manipulate the other through food and sex, intertwined with the beauty of her body, to satisfy her own desire and pleasure. The Unnamed Narrator uses this as a clue to navigate Louise's preparation of food. They enjoy the pleasure of unravelling the clues Louise offers, each of which has multiple emotional and sexual interpretations. This search for pleasure is like a game in which victory comes from the knowledge of how to achieve desire. This is because Louise, as acknowledged by the Unnamed Narrator, is a smart and beautiful woman who knows the connection between food and sex, and she is able to seduce the Unnamed Narrator by using this cognizance.[38] In Counihan's notion of feeding and consumption in food symbolism, she claims an adult satisfies and communicates with children through feeding their hunger. Thus, Louise, who is aware of the connection between food and sex, utilizes it to control the Unnamed Narrator by feeding their hunger emotionally, physically, psychologically and sexually with food. Therefore, it is appropriate to categorize food as a subject of commodity fetishism, one that is necessary in daily life and seems to be an instigator of sexual pleasure and desire. As Foucault states, 'food and drink serve to compensate' for desire, including diverse sexual desire; this will be elaborated in the next section.[39]

Having established the link between food and the act of sex, Winterson also uses food and consumption terminology to represent the thought of sex; Probyn states that 'food is the opportunity to explore the tangible links between what we eat, [and] who we think we are.'[40] In Winterson's texts, certain foods produce a kind of unspeakable pleasure and desire. Her imagery echoes Probyn's view that the lines between thinking about sex and food are inevitably blurred because through food, one can understand the self and the other, as food is something to be felt, touched and explored, which is similar to sexual activity. Probyn argues that food is always bound to values of power because 'the vector of food soon leads into other areas', such as sex.[41] Also, as Foucault believes, 'thinking about sex through food is compelling for the ways that it focuses our attention on the interrelation of various corporeal dimensions'.[42] Certain foods contain a range of warm effects for the body – 'raw mussels' and 'chocolate' can make one feel energetic. Thus, raw foods can give a person energy and make the body hot. Raw food, especially meat, is also connected to animal instincts because raw meat is usually eaten by animals. This suggests that a human being who eats raw food, especially meat, could have animalistic sexual urges. Consuming raw foods can also be a metaphor for love-making; the Ilahita Arapesh people of Papua New Guinea make the link between food and sex: 'cooked meat in the mouth and down the body: raw meat goes in the vulva and up the body'.[43] Keeping this statement in mind, a discussion about food nearly always compares with or leads to a discussion about sexual intercourse. Probyn further claims that 'within certain cultures of eating it seems that sex can explain everything'.[44] This mutual relationship is apparent in Winterson's writing from the way food and sex are used to depict the emotional and psychological status of her characters.

Winterson utilizes culinary terms and those of consumption to reconstruct the language of pleasure, desire, love, loss and sex:

> When she lifted the soup spoon to her lips how I longed to be that innocent piece of stainless steel. I would gladly have traded the blood in my body for half a pint of vegetable stock. Let me be diced carrot, vermicelli, just so that you will take me in your mouth. I envied the French stick. I watched her break and butter each piece, soak it slowly in her bowl, let it float, grow heavy and fat, sink under the deep red weight and then be resurrected to the glorious pleasure of the teeth.[45]

The Unnamed Narrator is desperate to fill Louise, fantasizing about everything that could be inside her. They would happily be a food so that they could be seen, eaten and chewed by Louise. They desire to be as intimate with Louise as the food she eats. Everything around them becomes a seductive object that triggers their desire for Louise. For example, the smell of certain foods reminds them of Louise: 'The yeast smell of her sex. The rich fermenting undertow of rising bread. My lover is a kitchen cooking partridge.'[46] The Unnamed Narrator uses the language of food to describe their lover and sex; thus, food, desire, sex and love are not only interconnected, but they are also important elements of substitution as fetishistic acts – elements required for the stimulation of desire and achievement of pleasure.

Addiction to certain foods can be a temporary act of disavowal in the imagination, a stage before one might approach the actual object that one desires. Winterson further layers pleasure and desire by deconstructing conventional expectations of the body through the use of split fruit, as discussed above in relation to *Sexing the Cherry*. The splitting of fruit is a metaphor for plurality or multiplicity in *Written on the Body*; when Louise 'split a pear, one of her own pears from the garden', it reflects the Unnamed Narrator's divided sexuality.[47] The Unnamed Narrator has had both male and female lovers, and they enjoy relationships with both sexes in their quest for pleasure. This is also Louise's experience, for though Louise is still very much married to her husband Elgin, she has an affair with the Unnamed Narrator. Split fruit demonstrates that one can exercise sexual choice to shape one's desire.

The close relationship between food and sex runs throughout *Written on the Body*, beyond just the Unnamed Narrator and Louise. The other women who have had sexual relationships with the Unnamed Narrator also show that desire and pleasure connect sex strongly with food: 'off with the business suit, legs apart, pulling me down on them, a pause for champagne and English cheese'.[48] That is to say, the pleasure of having both food and sex is an expansion of ambivalent desire, rather than a repression. At one stage in the novel, the pleasure of intercourse is portrayed through an image of lobsters; the bodies of the Unnamed Narrator and their lover are crammed in close to each other, and they 'can't move, caught like lobster in a restaurant aquarium'.[49] The restaurant lobsters, with shackled claws, and only one gesture away from a boiling pot, are a metaphor for the bodies that are trapped in a dangerous ecstasy of intense desire and pleasure of the bodily self and the other. Again, food acts as a signifier of, and as a vehicle to convey, diverse desire; so, the rethinking of food's normative associations creates a mode of alternative food fetishism.

Winterson creates depth in her narrative by paying attention to the ways in which language itself is capable of bringing forth more textured, nuanced interpretations of her characters' internal and external lives. She also uses symbols as substitutions for objects that are not described straightforwardly but suggested by indirect, albeit related, language. For instance, the repeated use of the word 'flesh' in *Written on the Body* emphasizes its importance in the repertoire of pleasure and desire. Flesh becomes a subject which can produce and consume, as well as an object of production and consumption: 'I didn't only want Louise's flesh', 'Your flesh is my flesh', 'I want your moving breathing flesh', 'Flesh of my flesh', 'Her thick-fleshed salt-veined swaddle stone'.[50] Flesh in Winterson's work is often used to feed a hunger one has for the other. For example, in *Gut Symmetries*, it connotes a larger meaning and recalls Adams's representation of patriarchal values in which, 'language distances us from the reality of eating, thus reinforcing the symbolic meaning of meat eating, a symbolic meaning that is intrinsically patriarchal and male-oriented'.[51] The central male character, Jove, is a respectable scientist who has an affair with a young physicist, Alice, who then falls in love with Jove's wife, Stella. Jove occupies a powerful position in a male-dominated society, and he symbolizes the power of the patriarchy over female passivity. However, when his wife has an affair with his mistress, he feels that his power as a man has been reduced, reflecting Adams's view of the threat posed by the withdrawal of flesh: 'To remove meat is to threaten the structure of the larger patriarchal culture.'[52] This is shown when Jove resorts to cannibalism to survive when he and Stella are stranded in the middle of the sea; eating his wife's flesh is symbolic of reclaiming his male power over her:

> I made the cut so carefully. I made it like a surgeon not a butcher. My knife was sharp as a laser. I did it with dignity, hungry though I was. I did it so that it would not have disgusted either of us. She was my wife. I was her husband. We were one flesh. With my body I thee worship. In sickness and in health. For better or for worse. Till death us do part. Till death us do part. I parted the flesh from the bone and I ate it.[53]

This mentality can be traced throughout the novel by Jove's cruelty towards Stella. His greed for power is obvious; he eats his wife's flesh because he wants to stay alive, and his fetishistic act of consuming her flesh emphasizes his mastery over the other. On the one hand, Stella's weak body renders her unable to fight for her rights or to defend herself at the time, in a stereotype of female passivity. She represents all the women who have been excluded from positions of authority, acting as an object of female passivity subjected to Jove's selfishness, which in turn derives from the patriarchal practices in their society. Stella's survival from her ordeal is a powerfully symbolic act that contradicts the stereotype of female passivity and surrender. The normative associations of meat-eating in a patriarchal society, such as male dominance and a position at the top of the food chain, are challenged and undermined by her continued existence, and even the physical traces of the attack are erased following plastic surgery. Stella represents an oppressed and abused section of society that fights to reclaim its freedom and equality in a masculine world, and her survival also suggests queer resistance, as, following their rescue, she rejects her husband to live with Alice instead. Despite Jove's desperate attempt to claim Stella as his property in the most extreme and taboo way, it is to Alice that Stella willingly gives her body, resisting the power of the male other and its fetishizing of meat in a defiant act of same-sex love.

This discussion has illustrated that food and consumption are important elements in the representation of the boundaries of sex, power, desire and pleasure. Therefore, thinking about food and sex is to explore the boundary norms of pleasure and desire of the bodily self and the other. Through the adventures undertaken by her characters, Winterson complicates conventional ideas of foods with fluid notions of gender and sexuality to show how the body, pleasure, power and desire are interconnected. Through food, she remaps gender and sexuality norms and deconstructs the body to represent multiple views on gender identity and the sexual choices and preferences of the self and the other, allowing their performance beyond boundary norms. Hence, desire and pleasure become fluid and resist any given demarcation of gender and sexuality. Instead, they freely float between the desire of the body and the pleasures of both the self and the other. The following chapter will discuss in detail how food is used as a metaphor to represent the choices and preferences of normative and alternative views of gender and sexuality.

7

The sexual politics of food

The politics of food is learned by people in every culture through experience of its acquisition, preparation and consumption; Winterson has stressed in interviews that consuming food is the most political thing we do in our daily life.[1] As Counihan rightly points out, 'food is so essential and so frequently used to affirm connection, it takes on rich symbolic meaning'.[2] Consequently, Winterson uses food terminology in her texts as one way to complicate normative definitions of gender, sexuality and identity through the metaphorical meaning of the subject; thus, she shows how food is interrelated with power, desire, sex and loss. Overloaded with metaphorical associations of gender and sexuality, food in *Boating for Beginners* (1985), as in all of Winterson's novels, is able to transform one meaning to another. For example, food and its consumption in this novel is another way of representing sensitive or taboo issues around gender, sexuality and identity. In her autobiographical writing, Winterson reveals herself as obsessed, almost to the point of worship, with food and its quality; from an early age, she had questioned where all this food came from:

> I learnt about the politics of food through eating it. I got curious about where everything had come from and how it was grown and harvested. I was one of those mad people who did early recycling by unpacking it all at the supermarket till – so annoying for everyone behind you. I wasn't a saint or a do-gooder, or even much of an activist, but it seemed to me that food was more important than anything.[3]

Winterson has always challenged orthodox views of boundaries, pleasure and desire of the self and the other. *Boating for Beginners* is an early example of Winterson's fluid approach to genre; it is a comic satire based on the biblical myth of Noah's Ark. Makinen believes that

> Winterson in *Boating for Beginners* is playing a number of different games with the story of Noah's Ark, but she also mocks a number of other more

contemporary aspects alongside fundamentalism – fashion, publishing and the food business, the romance genre, literature and literary criticism.[4]

In the novel, there is a reconceptualization of gender, sexuality and identity as the characters are divided into oppositional factions by the opposing ideologies of two companies. These communities enact political arguments of gender, sexuality and identity between historical, normative and alternative views in the current era. The companies are called 'NAFF' ('No Artificial or Frozen Food') and 'SCOFF' ('Society for the Celebration of Frozen Food'), representing their political beliefs and practices concerning food and its consumption. The tension and contrast between traditional, fresh, home-cooked food (henceforth, 'traditional food') and processed, factory-farmed, convenience food (henceforth, 'industrial food') in *Boating for Beginners* illustrates how choices and preferences of gender and sexuality became a prominent theme early in Winterson's career.

Although in a markedly different manner to *Oranges*, *Boating for Beginners* continues Winterson's interweaving of biblical stories with her personal experiences to engage with ideas of fluid gender, sexuality and identity through fiction. And like her first novel, although to a far greater degree, Winterson demonstrates both normative and alternative views of the subject by the medium of food. Preparing and consuming traditional food in *Boating for Beginners* represents the normative view and conventional ways of living espoused by NAFF and its followers, such as Noah, Mrs Munde and Bunny Mix. On the other side, industrial foods typify the modern and alternative lifestyles championed by SCOFF and their members, which include Desi, Marlene and Gloria. As Probyn suggests, a 'representation of contemporary existence is implied in the consciousness we have of the function of food'.[5] However, this is one example of progress that Winterson herself is against; she does not 'see the point of being alive if we cannot eat real food. If food is processed, manufactured, convenience, instant, frozen or factory farmed, forget it.'[6] In an article in *The Guardian* in 2014, Winterson says that the problem of obesity results from factory-made foods. She writes that 'the UK government spends a mere £14m a year promoting healthier lifestyles', while 'food companies in the UK spend a mighty £1bn a year bombarding us with ads for processed foods and snacks'.[7] In this connection, since food is vital for the sake of a healthy body, Winterson is outraged with the way modernity has replaced the era of fresh and home-cooked food:

> Getting closer to our food would be a saner way to live, and although most of us cannot do it by living in the country, we can visit small specialist shops, whether butcher or grocers, and become keenly interested in just what it is we are eating.[8]

In this relation, Winterson's fiction often opposes her personal views of certain subjects, such as how the playful and complicated world in *Boating for Beginners* stands in contrast to her own beliefs on food and its consumption. As she says, her fiction and her personal life are not the same: 'judge me on my work, not my shopping habits, not my sex life.'[9]

Counihan claims that due to the demands and developments of modernity, 'women are losing an important source of their traditional prestige and losing the manipulative power of food'.[10] It is possible for women to achieve a certain type of power, symbolic or actual, through the preparation and cooking of food. If this power is taken away by industrial food, like it is in *Boating for Beginners*, the question then arises of what is left for women who may become little more than passive objects of oppression. Counihan states that 'women clearly felt ambivalence and conflict about their declining role in food provisioning' as the industrialized food industry took over their role as the main provider of food to others.[11] The destabilizing conflict in *Boating for Beginners* offers a counterpoint to this erosion of heteronormative gender roles by placing it in opposition to the liberating opportunities to express diverse gender, sexuality and identity made possible by industrial food.

Ideological stances on the politics of food are embodied by the central characters in the novel: Noah, who runs his own business called 'Boating for Beginners'; Gloria, who dreams of working in the city, but is controlled by her mother, Mrs Munde; and Bunny Mix, the novelist who has written almost 'one thousand novels' and 'a cookery book'.[12] Through Noah, Mrs Munde and Bunny Mix, Winterson interrogates the choices brought to society by modernity which includes Noah's worry that, with 'convenience foods and ready-mixed cocktails there was too much time for agitation and revolution'.[13] This concern about the wider political and social implications of changes to food production can be analysed through the work of Appadurai, who discusses 'the particular social contexts' of food.[14] Appadurai argues that 'the cultural notion that food has an inherently homogenizing capacity [is] converted from a metonymic hazard into a metaphoric convenience in the contexts where sharing, equality, solidarity, and communality are, within limits, perceived as desirable results'.[15] The metonymy that powers the 'metonymic hazard' includes beliefs such as 'you are what you eat', while the hazard is the effacement of difference such a mantra implies for those who eat the same things. This warring combination offers the possibility of a potentially volatile group formation from individual relationships with food. This hazard can be transformed into a 'metaphoric convenience' by the social and cultural sanctioning of shared food matters in the 'contexts' where positive concepts of group harmony are 'perceived as desirable'. For Noah and NAFF, their established cultural codes around traditional food have long converted its universalizing properties into a metaphoric convenience which binds society together, and for the better, in their eyes. SCOFF comes into being, thanks to technological progress, and it functions as a counter-cultural response to traditional food. In contrast to the hegemonic NAFF, SCOFF lacks the cultural legitimacy to convert the communal aspects of food into a metaphoric convenience. Instead, the process described by Appadurai is reversed and those grouped together under SCOFF's umbrella constitute a metonymic hazard. As such, NAFF fears SCOFF because their alternative food choices – and lifestyles, by metonymic extension – create an antagonistic group who want modernity, industrialization, convenience and, possibly, as Noah fears, revolution.

Mrs Munde acts as a catalyst for promoting the traditionalist viewpoint after she loses her arm to Noah's hamburger machine. She works as an editor at a NAFF-sponsored newspaper, promoting the originality of food provisions in a traditional way for the self and the others. She lost her arm in a machine that produces industrial food, so she campaigns against SCOFF, believing that the food it endorses has 'led to disruptions of the marital home'.[16] However, she also believes, in an act of apparent cognitive dissonance, that the loss of her arm is only a 'little incident and put[s] it down to an act of God'.[17] To Mrs Munde, industrial food is evil, though alluring, and her dreams about it cause her to feel a religious guilt: 'she had dreams [of] working in a huge automated kitchen with electronic egg-slicer and pre-programmed French dressing. [...] She always repented after such dreams, worked extra hard cleaning [...] and make unnecessary trips to the cesspit'.[18] In her repressed, waking life, she links industrial food to progressive – and so, to her, transgressive and immoral – movements, such as feminism. In an exchange between Mrs Munde and a SCOFF proselytizer, a member of the crowd asks: 'Where would feminism be today without the deepfreeze?' Mrs Munde replies: 'Liars and hypocrites, the lot!'[19] The connection between industrial food and issues of non-normative gender and sexuality is delivered in more metaphorical terms by her opposite number in this exchange, but the language he uses is telling: 'What's so corrupting about mixed veg?'[20] The innocence of a bag of mixed vegetables – an intermingling and cohabitation of different types – is rhetorically proposed through the term 'corrupting', a word so replete with suggestions of sexual transgression.

The negative associations between industrial food and unorthodox behaviour are made explicit by the homophobic pamphlets Mrs Munde gives out, in which a supposed confession from a schoolboy attempts to establish a causal link between gay activity and the comfort eating of frozen food: 'You get depressed at school, or something goes wrong with your girlfriend, or you find out your maths teacher is a homosexual, and you think: I'll just have one little slice to keep me going. Next thing, you've eaten nearly a whole gâteau.'[21] Being different is often considered to be taboo in society, especially if it is against heteronormative beliefs and practices. SCOFF opposes everything NAFF campaigns for, and it believes that industrial food is the way forward for a modern lifestyle and should replace traditional methods of food processing. SCOFF continues to promote an easier, more convenient, lifestyle for the sake of modernity. Recalling Winterson's use of figurative language, what SCOFF is fighting for and promoting are the choices and preferences a person in any culture should have, especially in terms of their gender and sexuality. The allegorical nature of this novel suggests, through food, that no one should be discriminated against for their sexual orientation: 'This woman had no right to tell any of you how to spend your money or your time. What is wrong with diced carrots?'[22] Even though ideas of different choices and preferences of gender and sexuality have long been debated, these subjects are still taboo for many. In this way, Noah, Mrs Munde and Bunny Mix strongly consider that food provisioned in a traditional way by women is pure food, and they believe that women who do not perform this function are lost in the eyes of normative communities. They also argue that storing food, whether processed or not, affects the community because people will then rely on its instant availability for consumption, instead of coming together to prepare it. The established social order will, they fear, disintegrate and be replaced with isolation and alienation:

> Mrs Munde felt that being able to store food for longer periods had broken down the community spirit. There was no need to share now, no need to meet every day, gathering your veg or killing a few rabbits. The day-to-dayness has gone out of life. Everyone lived apart in their own little house with their own little fridges.[23]

On the other hand, through Gloria, industrial food is made to represent alternative ideas about choice in gender, sexuality and identity. As mentioned earlier, in the novel, NAFF and SCOFF represent rigid, traditional and fluid, contemporary schools of thought in the subject of gender and sexuality, respectively. Gloria finds it difficult to connect or even communicate with her mother because she has different views from those expected in normative society, which includes the reactionary beliefs of Mrs Munde. Gloria's experiences are similar to those of other young characters in Winterson's novels, for example, Jeanette in *Oranges* and Silver in *Lighthousekeeping*, who both battle with their old-fashioned and close-minded mothers.

For Noah, modernity is a virus and a burden on society. He represents an orthodox school of thought, such as stating that 'a simple diet [is] more important than gold'.[24] The text makes clear that Noah understands this to be a metaphor only, indicating the grasping hypocrisy behind his slogans. His conservative approach to food is mirrored by his attitudes to gender and sexuality, and he links food, religious beliefs and heteronormative patriarchal practices in the domestic sphere when he says: 'A simple diet prepared by a simple wife, these are the corner-stones of a godly life.'[25] Noah wants women to be as plain as his taste in food, and so during the shooting of his film about the world's creation, he ensures his female cast is 'as ugly as possible': '"You're too pretty," he shouted. "Can't we get a wig or some false teeth?"'[26] Recalling Adams's notion of meat and patriarchy, Noah's domination of power over women can be traced through his diet. As discussed above, meat is the central food for the enhancement of masculinity; it is the food of the upper class in society and for those in power, like Noah. Mrs Munde clearly sees the link between Noah, God and meat when she explains the source of Noah's wealth to Gloria: 'He's being guided by the Unpronounceable. [. . .] Besides, meat's popular. He's always been involved in meat.'[27] In other words, 'meat becomes a symbol for what is not seen but always there', just like the oppressed women in Noah's patriarchal society.[28]

Mrs Munde, who has been working with Noah for many years, shares his beliefs. She cleaves to a simple life and traditional ways of preparing food, cooking afresh for every meal, declaiming from her soap-box: 'join me in the garden. Go back to the humble larder, the innocent marble slab; teach your children the value of fresh food.'[29] Both she and Noah would concur with MacClancy's description of the expected self-denial of women in food preparation in a patriarchal society:

> A dutiful wife is meant to cook what others want, not what she herself desires. And if all that is left after serving a roast are the burnt and crusty bits, then that's all the meat she is going to eat. She is not supposed to enjoy the meal, but to take pleasure from watching others tuck in. Her job is to prepare dishes that will be savoured, both as good food and as a sign of her love for them. Of course it is men, not women, who define what good food is.[30]

In this context, Noah represents male dominance in a patriarchal society, while Mrs Munde represents the traditional woman, who takes instructions from and obeys people like Noah. On the other hand, Bunny Mix, through her status as a woman writer, uses her novels to portray romance and, indirectly, women's position in society. However, similar to Mrs Munde, she still believes in 'the purity of love between men and women' and 'the importance of courtship and the absolute taboo of sex before marriage'.[31] Thus, these three characters represent the majority group or the normative view in terms of gender, sexuality and identity in the novel; the views of Noah, Mrs Munde and Bunny Mix on gender and sexuality are those sanctioned by societal norms. To these characters, such views appear to be essential rather than constructed and performed. By contrast, Gloria comes to represent an opposing, non-normative view of gender, sexuality and identity when she begins to think more independently and question the society around her.

The relationship with Marlene is a key component to understanding Gloria's character. Marlene, when the reader is first introduced to her, is a post-operative transgender woman, and Gloria is fascinated by her. Their relationship has a sexual undercurrent, hinted at by the innuendo of the narration: '[Gloria] was thirsty for new experiences, she had a hunch that drinking with Marlene might leave her speechless. [. . .] Gloria and Marlene were getting to know each other better'.[32] Though Marlene is mostly delighted with her sex-reassignment surgery, especially her new breasts, she misses having a penis and wants it reattached. Marlene suffers psychologically from the physical removal of her penis, even though she called it her 'sleeping snake', suggesting it was rarely used for sexual purposes. It signifies as more of a comforting item than a phallus but, in any case, its absence is fetishized by Marlene to the extent that any replacement penis will suffice, regardless of size, skin tone and functionality: 'I only want it for decoration'.[33] Marlene's original penis has been processed into sausage meat for the chain store 'Meaty Big and Bouncy', which implies a link between industrial food and alternative gender and sexuality.[34] Thus, in the novel, industrial food can act metaphorically for fluid and alternative gender, sexuality and identity and so oppose conventional ideas on these subjects; as Barthes puts it, food has a 'value of power'.[35] Winterson reconceptualizes the normative perceptions of society by – not unlike the manufacture of industrial food – processes of dismantling, destabilizing, and stabilizing. In food's various guises as replacement and substitute for lost objects and repressed emotions, alternative acts of food fetishism occur.

Other examples in the novel show how industrial food is perceived as evil and capable of changing a person's personality. Food is able to affect a person's identity; for example, those who 'drink instant coffee' are, in Mrs Munde's view, transformed from a good to a bad human being.[36] More obviously capable of causing permanent change is the hamburger machine, which is considered disastrous because of the dangers inherent in using it, as exemplified by the loss of Mrs Munde's arm: 'It had all happened very suddenly. One minute she was funnelling away singing a little song about love and the lack of it, and the next –

whoosh, the thing had scooped her up.'[37] Another example of the representation of conventional and contemporary ideas of gender, sexuality and identity is the connection of food and religion in cultural perception. In *Boating for Beginners*, industrial food is used as central image of how an alternative idea can be perceived as evil and against what has been previously taught in religion. There is a well-established link between organized religion and food, for example, kosher or halal practices, which prescribe a set of rules for the types of food to be eaten and its preparation. However, in *Boating for Beginners*, the relationship between gastronomy and faith is satirically subversive and transgressive, such as Mrs Munde's belief that she lost her arm to the 'hamburger machine for the glory of the Lord', even as 'six neat quarterpounders' were made out of it.[38] The connection between God and food is made most prominently by Noah, who creates the Almighty 'by accident out of a piece of gâteau and a giant electric toaster'.[39] This is an extreme and comedic use of the association between religion and food, but one which still aligns with MacClancy's view that food is 'an intimate medium for conversing with the other-worldly beings and for carrying out supernatural acts', such as, in this case, the creation of a deity.[40] This is because many communities believe that 'food is religion. From the sacred cow to the host of Holy Communion, we venerate the hallowed and commune with the Lord and other spirits through the medium of food.'[41] Furthermore, Noah feels that industrial food has pushed him into insanity:

> I am coming to hate the sight of a refrigerator. Last night, sleep-walking, I bumped into my deepfreeze and awoke crying for mercy. My eyes rolled wild in my head; I took an axe and tried to cut the vile thing down, but its enamel proved the defeater of me. I will never again eat frozen food.[42]

In Noah's increasingly troubled mind, women, especially mothers, feel, or are made to feel, unworthy in the house if they are not preparing or serving what is needed by their families. Thus, if all their work is done easily or by a machine, for instance, as presented in the novel, women can believe that their life is over because they no longer serve a domestic function. As Counihan writes:

> The woman who doesn't have anything to do for another person finds herself dead and lost because she has nothing to do for another person. And for herself she does nothing. For her whole life she does nothing. For her whole life she does things for her husband and children.[43]

Hence, Mrs Munde, Bunny Mix and all at NAFF represent what Counihan describes as 'the prominent power of women in feeding', which is 'a cultural universal, a major component of female identity and an important source of female connection to and influence over others'.⁴⁴ Thus, for NAFF, 'there is now every reason to believe that frozen food has contributed to the rise of feminism, premarital sex and premature hair loss'.⁴⁵ The fear of Noah, Mrs Munde, Bunny Mix and NAFF is that the easy life enabled by prepared foods will destroy the meaning of the old traditions they hold so close to their hearts. For them, technology is destroying things like home-cooked food and the aroma of fresh-ground coffee. They believe that in the modern, globalized world, where technology rules, people have become too reliant on machines instead of their own physical and psychological capabilities. Technology has converted and perverted young people, who are now 'craving for frozen food, particularly the sticky sweet variety'.⁴⁶ The idea that you are what you eat is shown clearly in the novel by depicting traditional and modern ideas of gender and sexuality through the different preparation and consumption of food.

We have seen that Winterson uses food as a fetish object to represent the fluid pleasures and desires of the self and the other in society. In *Sexing the Cherry*, the use of fruit iconography serves to complicate gender expectations of the social norm. In *The Passion*, the representation of meat demonstrates the power of the patriarchal society. The use of meat as the representation of the orthodox view of the subject makes it seem as if it is normal to police the unfortunate other's gender and sexual identity in society. However, Winterson gives her characters the choice of their desired gender and the ability to float fluidly in both the masculine and feminine world in order to survive in a patriarchal society. Similarly, in *Written on the Body*, foods are used to represent the fluidity of pleasure and desire. Food and sex are interrelated with one another but exist independent of restricted gender roles. Thus, when it comes to diverse pleasure and desire, given sex is blurred and fluid, and even fluctuates at times; instead, a person submits their pleasure and desire to the adventure and exploration of their body. In *Boating for Beginners*, traditional food and industrial food are used to represent the different schools of thought on the subject of gender and sexuality. In *Frankissstein*, the representation of dietary choices and culinary lifestyles, as meat-eating and vegetarianism are set in contrast with each other, produces a world in which patriarchal values, gender fixity, and sexual orientation are all subject to challenge. The use of food as alternative fetish objects indicates how the act of substitution and replacement can benefit the individual, particularly in a struggle against transphobia, homophobia and sexism.

As illustrated above, food in Winterson's texts represent both traditional and unorthodox perspectives, as it endorses and subverts patriarchal ideology through polarized imagery that encodes conventional and contemporary features of femininity and masculinity. Her version of alternative fetishism has a recognizable political, moral and cultural purpose, which allows for open-ended interpretations in the face of subjective insistence. Thus, fluid gender and sexuality can be seen as available and affirmed in Winterson's fiction and, consequently, the central characters in the above novels are frequently fluid and subversive. Further, as Probyn observes, 'thinking through food to sex may make us "infinitely more susceptible to pleasure"'.[47] Hence, fluid characteristics allow Winterson's men and women to have both feminine and masculine aspects, which aid them, especially in desperate situations. They can choose to wear their chosen gender, sexuality and identity, either temporarily or permanently, and this can make it easier for them to express their internal desires and accept external expectations. Winterson destabilizes and stabilizes the subject of gender and sexuality by fluidly floating between normative and contemporary positions to produce alternative views of the subject. Winterson's use of food and other daily products in her novels is an important fetishist element in interpreting the fetish object of desires and pleasures of the self and the other. In each community, food helps to reveal cultural practices and religious beliefs. In short, food is one of the significant components of our life in general, whether it is necessary for the development of the body or as a weapon to manipulate and control others.

An individual desire for someone or something often acts as a substitute, either temporary or permanent, in order for a person to survive accordingly in a certain society. This gives one a chance to escape from the normative views or orthodox practices of daily life, which are usually a mirror of expectations from those who hold the power to choose. In Winterson's novels, the escape is often from conventional definitions of gender, sexuality and identity. Derived from the conceptual models of both first-wave and second-wave analyses of fetishism, the idea of alternative fetishism, as applied in the above discussion, affirms that her texts represent fluid ideas of fetishism that reveal the ethical values of each character in everyday life, regardless of their gender and sexuality. We have seen that food and sex are connected; consequently, gender, sexuality and identity are shaped by each individual's choices and preferences. Therefore, 'food is the opportunity to explore the tangible links between what we are becoming'.[48] Food and its consumption shape the body, the self and the other through the various connections and disconnections of normative practices in society. Gamman and Makinen argue that 'reading about food [. . .] is almost comparable with reading about sex', and this leads on to the discussion of sexual fetishism in the next section, which examines how Winterson's overriding obsession with language creates an alternative form of fetishization in relation to the diverse desires and pleasures of the self and the other.[49]

Part III

Sexual fetishism

This section shows how Winterson's multiple narrative voices create an alternative discourse on sexual fetishism, achieved through the description of pathological and transgressive sexual practices that combine elements from first-wave and second-wave fetishism. The lens of sexual fetishism can examine potentially taboo scenarios to assess whether the actions constitute extreme negative behaviour or not. The concept of alternative fetishism also offers further insight into how the body and its parts are worshipped in the diverse sexual desires and pleasures of the self and the other. There are three key terms in relation to alternative sexual fetishism: 'perversity', 'deviance' and 'dissidence'. These concepts are related by their variance from social norms and their abhorrence by the moral majority; however, whereas perversity and deviance have a long history of negative associations and criminalized activity, dissidence offers the possibility of behaviour and actions that, though still in opposition to heteronormative practice, have less pejorative connotations and can positively embrace alternative lifestyles.[1]

In this section as a whole, I argue that to appreciate Winterson's thinking on gender and sexuality is to accept sexual differences and to challenge and strip away taboo perceptions and conventional notions of sexual desire and pleasure. The importance of sex to Winterson's work can be encapsulated by Desi's statement in *Boating for Beginners*: 'Sex is the only thing in life worth getting emotional about. It's the only thing in life you should pursue with all your resources. Work is fine, friends are valuable, but sex is dynamite. It stops you going mad.'[2] Winterson's representations of sexuality confront heteronormative and patriarchal structures and are capable of speaking to all individuals regardless of sexual orientation. She believes writing like hers should try to 'get to some truths about people's lives, which by their very nature are myriad, fragmentary and kaleidoscopic'.[3] The discussion here shows, first, how Winterson's female characters are more than capable of practising sexual fetishism and, second, how sexual deviance and dissidence can be considered normal depending on the situations faced and the influences of external and internal forces. Hence, sexual preferences and choices, including fetishistic behaviour, are mobile and fluid, and do not belong to any specific gender or sexuality in Winterson's texts.

With particular reference to *The Passion*, *Sexing the Cherry*, *Written on the Body* and *The Daylight Gate*, I argue that a distinctive Wintersonian model of sexual fetishism emerges in her work from the complex sexual struggles between conventional external expectations and the body's idiosyncratic internal desires. Winterson maintains a certain ambiguity in the language she uses to describe the plural nature of gender, sexuality and identity. Similarly, even in her representation of sexual repression, she extends this ambiguity and fluidity as if to admonish against a reductive codification of a person's sexual orientation or sexual behaviour in relation to their sexual choices. Winterson's characters endure and enact the processes of disavowal and avowal to fashion safe spaces to express their fluid desires. The disavowal for the lost object becomes an avowal for its substitute, and so the sexually fetishized replacement produces a beneficial effect for the subject. This in turn allows an individual to view and assess their sexual desires and activities from a more ethically and politically aware position. Rather than a pathological symptom and practice, alternative fetishism enables positive actions that transform negative aspects of extreme sexual obsession into potential benefits for the subject.

Winterson's characters regularly create and perform fetishistic rituals that are fluid and adaptable, yet replicable. The alternative sexual fetishism they practise through substitution incorporates first-wave, second-wave and contemporary notions of sexual fetishism. The originating psychoanalytical view saw fetishism as an exclusively masculine action practised only by men. Later views argued for the equal possibility of male and female fetishism; as Schor writes, 'the little girl's ego can be split along the very same fault lines as the little boy's.'[4] This shows that, though it may be difficult, it is possible and desirable to move away from Freudian notions of sexual fetishism. An amalgamation of first-wave and second-wave models help provide the basis for a contemporary rethinking of fetishism – in which, practices are not tethered to one gendered position – that offers productive analysis of the sexual themes and actions in Winterson's works. Sadism and masochism can be seen as potential and normal actions in a person's sexual life. Gilles Deleuze, who believed the works of de Sade and Sacher-Masoch had to be viewed in conjunction, stated, 'the word "disease" is clearly inappropriate' when discussing sadism and masochism.[5] In contrast, older theorists such as Richard Von Krafft-Ebing (who coined both 'masochism' and 'sadism'), Freud and Havelock Ellis regarded sadism and masochism as psychopathological phenomena which required treatment. These views will be considered later in the discussion of Winterson's works.

Through her characters, Winterson is able to show that some people see fetishism as a normal practice, while others feel uncomfortable with it. Judith Butler, responding to Foucault's work on sexuality and pleasure, suggests that understanding sexual difference requires the body, desire and pleasure to be considered equally and in relation to each other.[6] For Foucault, one vital element in sexuality is to understand and realize the significance of sex and to acknowledge sexual differences among individuals; this would allow us to

> counter the grips of power with the claims of bodies, pleasures, and knowledge, in their multiplicity and their possibility of resistance. The rallying point for the counterattack against the deployment of sexuality ought not to be sex-desire, but bodies and pleasures.[7]

Winterson's work responds and contributes to Foucault's plurality of 'rallying point' of 'bodies and pleasures', rather than the confines and restrictions of the singular 'sex-desire'. Foucault further argues that sex

> has become more important than our soul, more important almost than our life, and so it is that all the world's enigmas appear frivolous to us compared to this secret, minuscule in each of us, but of a density that makes it more serious than any other. [...] Sex is worth dying for.[8]

This is an argument that Winterson would have much sympathy with, and there follows here a brief introduction to the sexual fetishism in her texts. Her language of fluid pleasures and desires, especially regarding the deconstructed body and the concomitant remapping of gender and sexuality, has contributed to a new understanding of sexual fetishism as a whole, and non-binary fetishism in particular.

Winterson has her own style of capturing the various aspects of sensuous and sensual engagements. For her, sexuality is not constructed exclusively by any one biological, physical or cultural factor. Instead, she amalgamates all these facets in her conceptualization of sexuality and sexual fetishism that advances beyond the first and second waves of fetishism studies to posit an alternative mode of fetishism. Her writing depicts a fluid world where both conventional and contemporary ideas of gender and sexuality are combined, allowing more flexible interpretations of bodies, pleasures and desires. Sexual fetishism is a vital element in the way her work depicts and unpicks sexuality, but it has on the whole been overlooked by critics and scholars. In *The Lesbian Postmodern*, Laura Doan traces the development of lesbianism, the aesthetics of postmodernism and the politics of feminism in Winterson's writing. Doan believes that Winterson's work normalizes homosexuality, arguing that in *Oranges*, and other novels, Winterson's 'reconceptualization of the normal makes lesbian existence possible by, in effect, reversing the dominant culture's definition of natural and unnatural'.[9] This is a valid argument but the level to which it extends the structures of postmodernism needs to be considered further, and such analysis would function better with a focus more on fluidity, rather than solely lesbianism. Doan's arguments move towards the fluidity of Winterson's work, saying it displays 'a sexual politics of heterogeneity and a vision of hybridized gender constructions outside an either/or proposition, at once political and postmodern', but the overall argument predominantly relies on a fixed lesbian premise.[10]

The central characteristic of the sexuality portrayed in Winterson's writing is fluidity, which can be captured by Eve Sedgwick's definition of 'queer': '[a]n open mesh of possibilities, gaps, overlaps, dissonance and resonances, lapses and excesses of meaning when the constituent elements of anyone's gender, of anyone's sexuality, aren't made (or can't be made) to signify monolithically.'[11] Heather Nunn sees Winterson as a writer who explores and extends sexual categories by inverting and confounding gender roles and sexual identity. Talking of *Written on the Body*, Nunn says, 'The force and challenge of Winterson's fiction is in its offering up an erotic experience that contests the conventional fixity of identity.'[12] Lesbianism, which requires fixed identities for female subjects to be able to recognize and respond to each other, is unsettled by the way *Written on the Body* 'troubles this binary divide and arguably proliferates it to the point where it no longer makes sense.'[13] At this point, a more fluid reading of gender and sexuality is required to escape a rigid and redundant homo/hetero binary. Thus, I argue here that Winterson's novels engage with gender and sexuality by addressing sexual differences, challenging taboos and questioning conventional notions of sexual desire and pleasure. The alternative fetishism in her work challenges the categorization and restriction of practitioners of sexual fetishism, as many of her characters manifest diverse desires and seek atypical pleasures, regardless of their gender and sexuality.

This section is divided into three chapters, each discussing from a different angle how characters in Winterson's texts strive for the freedom to choose the object of their pleasures and desires. However, damaging sexual acts also often occur in her fiction, as many characters navigate difficult and dangerous situations. Whether the sexual activity is consensual and beneficial or forced and deleterious, alternative fetishism allows a greater insight into an individual's behaviour and psyche. Chapter 8, 'The extended boundaries: Pleasure and pain', looks at sadomasochistic practices across Winterson's novels, as well as how incidents of unintended pain can be addressed and ameliorated through a fetishistic mindset. This is followed by Chapter 9, 'The fetishistic phallus: Elongated objects', which investigates the significance of the distinctive and diverse phallus replacements in Winterson's fiction. The section ends with Chapter 10, 'Soft fetishes: Membranes and senses', which considers the fetishistic portrayal of the soft membranes of the body and the senses in Winterson's writing.

8

The extended boundaries

Pleasure and pain

The body and its parts in Winterson's novels become substitute objects in the fetishizing of sexual experience. This section explores diverse pleasure and pain, in particular acts of extreme sadism, masochism, bestiality and paedophilia. The external environment plays an important role in shaping any individual's life, and this applies to the sexual behaviour of the characters in Winterson's works, as they each have their own unique fetishistic fixations. The sexual fetishism in *The Passion* includes the Meat Man's violent treatment of others and Villanelle's cross-dressing. Fetishistic images exist in the imagination as visual erotica and are then transferred externally to the body. When Villanelle is dressed like a soldier, the Queen of Spades immediately comprehends the significance of the fetishistic act she is performing for both their benefit and pleasure. Villanelle's versatility in switching between masculine and feminine roles stems from her early childhood, which is often the case in the selection of a fetish. This is a perverse act relating to the concept of an early sexuality, as relayed by Lacan's notion of the phallus that contains the desire for the Other. In the village Villanelle comes from, males have webbed feet. However, Villanelle, seemingly female in all other respects, was also born with this condition, so her parents made her wear heavy boots from a young age to hide these masculine signifiers and conceal this transgression of gender boundaries. Villanelle's feet mean she is, in relation to her community, an intersex person, living between biological and cultural classifications yet attempting to pass as female.

Even though her true nature is initially suppressed, she converts the negative experiences of her youth into positive characteristics in later life, gaining self-confidence by embracing her liminal sexual status. For example, when Villanelle wears men's clothes it is called 'fancy dress' and triggers internal desires (the source of a fetish) and compels the body to act in certain ways.[1] Villanelle's external identity, her external appearance and clothing, is as fluid and changeable as her sexual preferences are; her physical and emotional desires respond to the situations she face: 'I am pragmatic about love and have taken pleasure with both men and women.'[2] Villanelle's sexual choices challenge any sense of a fixed, normative identity and instead show alternative ways – through perversity, deviance and dissidence – of embracing her fluid sexuality. She cross-dresses and feels comfortable with her chameleonic nature that mirrors her diverse physical make-up and sexual preferences. Winterson's characters are driven by a host of difficult, contradictory emotions, such as when Villanelle is looking for the Queen of Spades: 'More than eight years had passed, but when I knocked on her door I didn't feel like an heiress who had walked from Moscow and seen her husband murdered. I felt like a Casino girl in a borrowed uniform.'[3] In terms of her internal desire, even though Villanelle has various experiences in life, the feeling of uncertainty is still present.

Winterson weaves depth and meaning into her narrative by paying attention to the ways in which language is capable of bringing forth more textured, nuanced interpretations of her characters' interior sexual life. She regularly uses metaphorical language, which is essentially a semiotic system of substitution in which the object and subject in question are not described straightforwardly but are replaced with a tangential reference. Winterson teases her readers by making the language of sex and seduction implicit rather than explicit; the Queen of Spades, for example, tells Villanelle, 'I can't make love to you [. . .]. But I can kiss you.'[4] This suggests that a kiss may be more intimate and effective as a tool of desire, but it also suggests that although penile penetration is physically impossible between the two, their love-making might involve cunnilingus. Rather than unambiguously expressing her intent, the Queen of Spades arguably uses euphemisms to arrive at what she wants. Thus, when she desires to see Villanelle naked, she uses the excuse of Villanelle's well-being to tease around the subject of her imminent unclothing: 'In this inhospitable weather it would not be wise. Everyone has catarrh.'[5] The sexual ambiguity deployed by Villanelle's cross-dressing is further heightened by her application of feminine cosmetics overlaid by an artificial signifier of masculinity:

> I made up my lips with vermilion and overlaid my face with white powder. I had no need to add a beauty spot, having one of my own in just the right place. I wore my yellow Casino breeches with the stripe down each side of the leg and a pirate's shirt that concealed my breasts. This was required, but the moustache I added was for my own amusement.[6]

Villanelle's cross-dressing is an act of alternative fetishism, in which her fluid sexual desires turn the negative aspects of her upbringing into beneficial practices in her adulthood. Villanelle's transvestism is not only appreciated by the Queen of Spades, but it is also fetishized by the Meat Man, contributing to his sadistic behaviour towards Villanelle. The Meat Man enjoys Villanelle's performance of transvestite acts, and her sexual ambiguity indicates the Meat Man's barely supressed desire for a young man. A woman dressing up as a member of the opposite sex is a disruptive form of bisexuality; thus, when the Meat Man takes pleasure in watching Villanelle mask herself as a man to stimulate his sexual drive, an act of fetishism occurs that transforms an imaginative obsession into physical expression. This example of alternative fetishism – negative connotations of normative fetishism becoming positive through consensual conduct – is illustrated by the realization of the Meat Man's fantasies, thanks to Villanelle's willingness to participate:

> I go on dressing as a young man in the comfort of our own home. He likes that. He says he'll get me moustaches and codpieces specially made and a rare old time we'll have of it, playing games and getting drunk.[7]

Winterson deploys figurative language to convey the deeper, sexually fetishistic meanings of her texts. The use of metaphor and symbolism is prominent in her works and serves to challenge the boundaries of sexual desire and pleasure through her deconstruction of the bodily self and the other. Certain objects act emotionally and psychologically as substitute mechanisms for temporary or permanent sexual satisfaction for the body. For example, the codpiece, seen by Marjorie Garber as, 'bizarrely a sign of gender undecidability', is an object of fetishism in *The Passion*.[8] The Meat Man says he will supply Villanelle with bespoke moustaches and codpieces so that, wearing them, she can stoke his sexual desire. The Meat Man is proud and demanding, both psychologically and physically, and imposes his desire upon Villanelle. Villanelle treats the Meat Man like an adversary, but she is in charge of his eroticism and enjoys degrading herself and being dominated by his tyrannical will. She is sexually stimulated by the voluntary abnegation of control in their erotic relationship and derives pleasure from the Meat Man's dominating and sadistic tendencies. Thus, the codpiece is a sexual ornament to trigger the Meat Man's desire and give him pleasure, but, at the same time, it gives Villanelle the authority to act out her transgender fantasy. Hence, the codpiece can occupy either male or female fantasy because 'the codpiece is the thinking man's (or woman's) bubble, the ultimate detachable part'.[9] Thus, the use of a substitute object to initiate sexual pleasure for the self and the other illustrates the existence of female fetishism. Both the Meat Man and Villanelle create a symbolic space of having and being the phallus to double their sexual stimulation. Villanelle follows the demands of the Meat Man's desires in her desperation to survive in a patriarchal world, indicating that the three of them share in the relationship: 'He, me and my codpiece.'[10] Villanelle naturalizes her sexual desire as both man and woman, which is Winterson showing an eroticism from the perspective of both male and female fetishism. She indicates an emerging bisexual hunger between these two characters. For Villanelle, having to act as a male makes her feel satisfied with having and being the other (the penis) and in control (having the phallus) of the other (man); thus she can display and enact her sexual desire towards both the Meat Man and the Queen of Spades.

The Meat Man's authoritative acts are the metonymic equivalent of male power over others, especially women. Thus, through the Meat Man and Villanelle, Winterson illustrates that fetishism is not only possible but that both females and males can be practitioners. The moustache is another object used to construct the Meat Man's transvestite fantasy of a young man in a woman's body. Sadism and masochism coexist in the Meat Man's psyche, and his brutal behaviour towards others becomes his passion. This shows that in meeting sexual needs, violence can emerge, whether willingly or unwillingly. Sadism and masochism are extreme forms through which intricate sexual desire can be manifested. Sex and passion are not simple and transparent acts; instead, they are complicated choices made over the course of one's life or at a particular stage of life.

The Meat Man is similar to Villanelle in that he develops his sexual identity through a negotiation with the environment. He demonstrates his evil conduct towards others around him, especially in sexual contact. As a result, he develops exaggerated choices in his sexual life in acts of sadism. In the previous section, I examined the Meat Man's external environment, in which poor and inhuman working conditions contributed to his immoral behaviour, especially his sexual behaviour. Therefore, some of the Meat Man's sexual desires and actions result from the repressive effects of his confining and entrapping working conditions as a cook in a military camp. He is forced to contain himself in a limited space, which denies him freedom: 'The space from the ground to the dome of the canvas was racked with rough wooden cages about a foot square with tiny corridors running in between, hardly the width of a man.'[11] The birds in the cages there can be seen as representative of the Meat Man's psyche, malformed and restricted: '[i]n each cage there were two or three birds, beaks and claws cut off.'[12] The Meat Man suffers internally due to the war; the abuse of power and ill-treatment of women leads him to be malicious in his sexual endeavours, as is evident in his sadistic obsessions. He desires to cause pain to his sexual objects and abuses women, forcing them into sexual relations with him; he enjoys having sex with women after he has insulted and physically assaulted them, doing this both with passing prostitutes and Villanelle.

His sadistic characteristics are introduced early in the novel, when he is shown treating the prostitutes in the brothel cruelly and his behaviour reflects back to his repression and his claustrophobic working conditions. He diverts his repression into sexual violence and takes pleasure in it, for example, 'slapping a woman on the rump and making some joke about her corset'.[13] His violence against women escalates quickly and easily, and in the same scene he progresses to striking the unfortunate prostitute in her face, where a 'red mark on her cheek glowed despite her rough skin'.[14] The pain of others pleases and excites him. This sadistic behaviour continues towards his future wife, Villanelle:

> He hit me then [. . .] I hit him back. Hard. He started to laugh and coming towards me squashed me flat against the wall. It was like being under a pile of fish. I didn't try to move, he was twice my weight at least [. . .]. He left a stain on my shirt and threw a coin at me by way of goodbye.[15]

For Freud, sadism and masochism are interrelated concepts that provide an instance of complex sexual intent and conduct.[16] For example, when the Meat Man treats her terribly, Villanelle repays him with the same treatment: she hits him and spits in his face. Her retaliation is paired with the violent treatment she is receiving, and it seems to be enjoyed by both Villanelle and the Meat Man to a certain degree. Sadomasochism is a paradoxical condition since its two dissimilar traits exist within one person. The Meat Man takes his bodily pleasures by abusing other bodies and then using them for his sexual needs. He manipulates his masculine power for selfish sexual needs, which stems from the wartime repression of freedom. However, there is also another causal factor in the relationship between the Meat Man and the prostitutes: the prostitutes are forced to allow the Meat Man to abuse them due to economic and social necessity. This reflects Foucault's arguments on the deployment of sexuality, in which he posits that, rather than being repressed by society en masse, 'sexuality is tied to recent devices of power' and is 'repressed for economic reasons'.[17] The prostitutes' physical, emotional and sexual health are endangered by the desperate financial circumstances that drive them to the military camps in a desperate bid to survive. Thus, the workings of power in these sexual relationships demonstrate the sadism and masochism that underpin them, made physically evident in the social construction of sexual labour.

As the characters in *The Passion* are confronted by various aspects and levels of the power structures in their society, they are often forced to contain and supress their own desires. In turn this results in the channelling of these drives into deviant sexual activities. In this way, perversity, deviance and dissidence coincide as alternative sexual fetishism offers a substitute replacement for the lost or prohibited object. In *The Passion*, Winterson shows how her characters' lives depend just as much on external factors as on internal ones. External factors sometimes precede the onset of internal desires, which have the ability to turn into extreme obsessions. The contest between external forces and internal desires often leads to obligatory performances of good behaviour, the process of which represses thoughts and feelings deemed unsuitable in 'decent' society. A challenge to the social norms can be found through perversity, deviance and dissidence, which are revealed in Winterson's work by her character's sexual behaviour and choices.

When discussing *Written on the Body*, psychoanalytical concepts of sexuality offer great assistance in unpacking the sexual deviation, perversity and defiance in the novel. The discussion here primarily focuses on the two main characters, the Unnamed Narrator and Louise. Louise is a married woman who emotionally represses her responses to her husband's sexual obsession with masochism and prostitutes. At the root, if not indeed the heart, of Winterson's alternative depiction of fetishism is language, and while the body plays a necessary and vital role in physically reflecting the complexity of excitement, language, with its limits, becomes intertwined with desire and pleasure. Words gain strength in these charged situations because they try 'to fill the gap left by unconscious and unanswered desires and ward off our fear of the other', even if 'they do so only imperfectly'.[18] This linguistic gap results from invisible desires that can create disturbances in a person's psyche. The immateriality of language is translated into a corporeal expression, materialized by the body as the need to feel pain, either towards the self or the other. Violent or extreme erotic desires that are incapable of being voiced cause the body to react to their demands for pleasure and pain by the splitting of language. As Deleuze claims:

> In Sade the imperative and descriptive function of language transcends itself toward a pure demonstrative, instituting function, and in Masoch toward a dialectical, mythical and persuasive function. These two transcendent functions essentially characterize the two perversions, they are twin ways in which the monstrous exhibits itself in reflection.[19]

From phantasy in the sadism stage, the sadistic person then renounces that phantasy for masochistic action through the process of desexualization and sexualization between peculiar pain and sexual pleasure. The acts of sadism and masochism performed by Winterson's characters stem from such processes, as well as from fears of loss and feelings of guilt.

The language of pleasure and pain can also be seen in *Frankissstein*. In the book's near-future world, sexual possibilities are increased thanks to technology. However, much of this proliferation, such as Ron Lord's 'XX-BOTs', threatens to entrench established heterosexual hegemony, rather than create genuinely new paradigms. Ron's sex-bots are female figures, sexualized stereotypes and clichés made of synthetic flesh for a male market. Ron says he is performing a 'public service' for men, regardless of their age or socioeconomic status, because he believes 'sex is a democracy' and his sex-bots give his customers the opportunity to fulfil their chosen sexual preferences.[20] Despite the language of socialism being deployed by Ron to describe the services offered by his business (he does, after all, come from South Wales, traditionally a stronghold of trade union organization and left-leaning politics), this 'public service' that supports sexual 'democracy' is, in reality, a neo-liberal model of capitalist consumption that targets profits by renting out sex-bots for fixed periods of time. Ron calls these robotic inventions his 'girls', and pleasure is at the forefront of the services they provide, from their padded breasts and silicon nipples, to the in-built heating elements that ensure the 'girls are not clammy underneath'.[21] His business offers men the possibility of temporary ownership of, not partnership with, a range of models, including 'Cruiser': 'the fuller figure'; 'Racy': 'little waist, double-G-cup'; and the only sex-bot with a name, 'Germaine': 'a 70s feminist version with no bra, messy hair and a dildo for anal play'.[22]

The not-so-subtle reference to Germaine Greer raises some intriguing ideas about the psychological motives of the men who would choose this model. On the one hand, it may be imagined that by having sex with this avatar of the Women's Lib movement they would feel themselves reasserting male power and status over women who would fight for equality. On the other hand, the dildo is to be used *by* the Germaine bot, not on it: 'She gets to fuck you!'[23] Ron's inviolable sense of the correctness of his heteronormative and patriarchal views of the world, shown by his cheerfully delivered stream of sexist and transphobic remarks, means it is little surprise that this is the only sex-bot in his range he hasn't personally tried, but the demand to be penetrated by Germaine and her dildo must be sufficient to maintain her existence. This indicates that pain and non-normative sexual practices are also options in this neo-liberal, dehumanized sexual marketplace, as long as profit can be made; the answer of who rents Germaine is 'some masochists. And a few university professors.'[24]

Jokes aside, Ron hopes to capitalize on the demand for pain-related sexual activity in this new technological marketplace by making a tougher model, 'for the fetish market. Dominatrix. Spanking. That sorta thing. [. . .] Brits will like it'.[25] The term 'Dominatrix' suggests that the 'female' sex-bot would be spanking its submissive male renter, but how the mechanics of this would work are not established. More likely, Ron imagines a market for men who want to engage in dominant sexual activity but who have not found a submissive human partner. Enacting fantasies of domination and sadism on a machine built to resemble a woman creates an alternative act of fetishism if the substitute object replaces the original completely in the subject's psychosexual functioning. That is, if the sex-bot does away with the desire for a human partner, then the practice will be beneficial to the subject. The advanced frontiers of sexual activity opened up by sex-bots raise new ethical queries and new variations on existing concerns. In this instance, questions about Ron's business model might include: If domination/submission relies on consent, how would this work with a robotic sex slave hired for this purpose? If the sex-bots cannot feel actually pain or humiliation, how satisfying would domination/submission sex games be with them? Such issues are not directly discussed in *Frankissstein* as the fetish sex-bot market is only a future possibility, but the importance of free will to consensual (and thus non-pathological) sadomasochism would need to be addressed if the use of sex-bots in this area of sexual activity were to remain beneficial.

Melanie Klein argues that sadism begins in the period of Oedipal conflict, which indicates that a practitioner of fetishism can be male or female. She observed from her work with children that there is

> [a]n early stage of mental development at which sadism becomes active at all the various sources of libidinal pleasure. In my experience sadism reaches its zenith in this phase, which is ushered in by the oral-sadistic desire to devour the mother's breast (or the mother herself) and passes away with the earlier anal stage.[26]

In other words, the body and its parts become the site of language to answer the unspoken desire of the child to be the mother's body and imaginatively destroy organs such as the penis, vagina and breast through acts of sadism. Klein does not specify the gender of the child whose 'sadistic attacks have for their object both father and mother, who are in phantasy bitten, torn, cut or stamped to bits'.[27] These phantasies cause the objects to later become objects of anxiety, because the child owning the organs becomes confused, 'which form[s] the basis of interest in the new objects and symbolism'.[28] The love and loss that engender new symbols and act as a foundation for all phantasy and sublimation can result in perverse acts through which inexplicable desires and passions are achieved by acts of sadism. It is in this way that Elizabeth Grosz believes, 'the mind/body relation is frequently correlated with the distinctions between reason and passion, sense and sensibility'.[29] This anxiety and repression is brought forward by the child into their adulthood and continues their perversion, especially in sexual encounters. If human beings function in response to the demands and pressures of both external and internal environments, the fetishism performed needs to be alternative – fluid and adaptable, not static and linear – to navigate the transitions between the exterior and the interior.

As discussed earlier, pleasure and pain have a mutual relationship. For the Unnamed Narrator and their lovers in *Written on the Body*, sexual and instinctual desire occasionally lead to internal and external pain, but due to their mutually intense passions, pain is ignored and instead the pleasure of the experience is foregrounded. In fact, pain is often transmuted into pleasure by the alchemy of desire. The Unnamed Narrator knows that they will get hurt at the end of their relationships and consciously questions this: 'Why is the measure of love loss?'[30] However, unconsciously, the pain corresponds to the obtaining of pleasure for them, which is why the Unnamed Narrator is trapped in an unhealthy cycle of choosing tantalizing and tormenting objects of desire, such as 'another married woman'.[31] Perhaps a reason for this is that a stable relation could make an adventurous person, like the Unnamed Narrator, seem boringly static to married women, such as Louise. The Unnamed Narrator's adventurous acts are internally denounced but externally pursued due to the masochistic desire to punish themselves mentally and/or physically. In terms of the choice of sexual objects, the Unnamed Narrator has had both female and male lovers. Krafft-Ebing, at the end of the nineteenth century, called bisexual behaviour 'psychosexual hermaphroditism', as these individuals were thought to have male and female psyches, driving gay and straight desires. It was not seen as a balanced split though, as the 'traces' of heterosexuality were contrasted with the 'predominating homosexual instinct'.[32] To Freud, this bisexuality was a 'deviation in respect of the sexual aim' as non-normative behaviour outside a heterosexual and reproductive system.[33] Freud states that:

> It is well known that at all periods there have been, as there still are, people who can take as their sexual objects members of their own sex as well as of the opposite one, without the one interfering with the other.[34]

In this relation, the Unnamed Narrator's relationships move fluidly from one sex to another, following their desire to satisfy the pleasures of the body. The unorthodox behaviour of the Unnamed Narrator is similar to that of Villanelle's in *The Passion*: both of them have the capacity to take pleasure from either sex. The Unnamed Narrator has had numerous failed relationships with men and women so their all-embracing sexuality, if anything, just offers more opportunity for heartbreak. Through the Unnamed Narrator, Winterson presents an ungendered account of the body, sex, love and loss, depicting the fluid pleasures and desires a person can face in life. In the quest for love, which involves pleasure, desire and sex intertwined with internal and external needs, the Unnamed Narrator is 'looking for the perfect coupling; the never-sleep non-stop mighty orgasm. Ecstasy without end.'[35] Thus, through the character of the Unnamed Narrator, Winterson illustrates sexual differences outside the norm. For example, her language evokes the borderlessness and liminality of the sea to suggest a passionate sex that is enveloped in fluid desires and pleasures:

> She smells of the sea. She smells of rock pools when I was a child. She keeps a starfish in there. I crouch down to taste the salt, to run my fingers around the rim. She opens and shuts like a sea anemone. She's refilled each day with fresh tides of longing.[36]

Bodies in *Written on the Body* substitute for other phenomena, including memories, and at times other things are fetishized as sexual replacements for bodies, such as food and medical textbooks. The consistent feature is an act of substitution that seeks love in a tangible and beneficial presence, in response to the extreme desires and pleasures demanded by the body. These occurrences are often presented through the peculiar language of sexual perversion and deviation, the subject and object willing to undergo pain for the sake of extreme pleasure. Therefore, the other object is an important element as a substitute in satisfying the body's diverse desire, which is 'eternally stretching towards the desire of something else'.[37] In other words, a person needs an object of, at least temporary, substitution in the process of acquiring a sexual life; this is repeatedly demonstrated in characters across Winterson's works, such as Elgin, the Unnamed Narrator, Louise, Villanelle and Henri. As mentioned earlier, this substitution is formed by symbolism in the child's mental development, and this acts as a foundation for sublimation and phantasy. Sometimes these substitutes can be a peculiar object or subject and different from the usual sexual choice or preference. Thus, this act may well be considered wrong from the perspective of social norms. Therefore, this study reveals through Winterson's works that sexual differences and choices exist in everyone's sexual life, depending on how far a person wants to challenge the boundaries of desire and pleasure. What

Winterson's Unnamed Narrator illustrates is that fetishizing the body and its parts is an element of a diverse sexual performance found in both heterosexuality and homosexuality.

Winterson's use of certain words and metaphoric phrases are one way to affirm further her claim to the fluidity of diverse pleasures and desires. The human partner may be completely replaced by a sexual fetish, which relates to Paul Gebhard's schema of the intensities of sexual fetishism, and Freud's notion of sexuality, in particular fetishism.[38] More recent psychoanalysis has moved away from the Freudian model of sexual fetishism, while Gebhard's work can be used to understand the stages of sexual fetishism in the novels discussed here; Gebhard claims that sexual fetishism is divided into four stages, along 'a continuum of intensities'.[39] His studies developed from Freudian concepts of fetishism, but Gebhard's writing challenges orthodox psychoanalytical theory because he does not view the stages of sexual fetishism as a pathological phenomenon; rather, he considers every level of fetishist intensity to be a manifestation of human sexuality. Gebhard describes four levels of fetishism intensity: level one is a slight preference; level two is a strong preference, but still of comparatively low intensity; level three is a specific stimulus, exerting moderate intensity; and level four is the highest degree of preferential intensity. Levels one to three represent commonly seen modes of sexual fetishism, while level four defines the highest level of fetishism, in which a 'specific stimuli takes the place of a sex partner'.[40] Thus, while the first three levels represent orthodox sexual fetishism, level four refers to contemporary concepts of sexual fetishism. The stages can also be distinguished by the contrast between the passive appreciation of a fetish object in the first three levels and the active utilization of a fetish object that occurs in the fourth stage. Therefore, Gebhard's concept of sexual fetishism is important in understanding the heterogeneous levels of sexual difference in Winterson's characters

In *Written on the Body*, the Unnamed Narrator and Louise build their arousal by fetishizing each other's physical features. For Louise, her sexual objects and sexual aims are changeable over time – sometimes fluid, sometimes static. The Unnamed Narrator portrays their lover as a sexual object and aim, displaying an intense obsession with her body and its parts in order to accommodate their diverse desires. The Unnamed Narrator achieves sexual pleasure by appreciating the other body and their own: 'she held out her arms, her face softening with love, I took her two hands to my mouth.'[41] The hands and the mouth become substitute objects for temporary pleasures. The imagination plays a significant role in the Unnamed Narrator's subconscious belief that they and Louise are one person: 'You are still the colour of my blood. You are my blood.'[42] This brings to mind the consanguinity of Klein's notion of mother–child relationships, where the child feels safe in the mother's arms if it senses love and the life instinct from the good breast. In this case Louise makes the Unnamed Narrator feel protected when they are wrapped in her arms, and so Louise represents the good breast and the secured phallus symbol to the Unnamed Narrator, rather than arousing feelings of hatred or insecurity like a Kleinian bad breast.

As Winterson writes with a deep knowledge of critical theory, it is not surprising to see these things directly satirized in her work. In *The Gap of Time*, Leo goes to a Kleinian analyst who tells him, in his stereotypical analyst's Eastern European accent, it is 'a metter ov the gud brist and the bad brist'.[43] Leo's facetious response is to bring a men's magazine to the next session so the doctor can circle the good breasts for him, to which the doctor's calm response is to note Leo's 'objectification of the simultaneously loathed and loved object'.[44] To return to the Unnamed Narrator, fetishism can be seen in Lacanian terms as a desire for the other as the signifier; that is, a desire and demand in the subject of having the phallus and being the phallus. As mentioned earlier, Lacan believed all children desire to be the phallus for their mother; at a later stage of development, women, because they do not own a penis, turn their body into a symbolic phallic signifier. Whereas, men, who possess a penis, are able to move on from being to having the phallus. Thus, the Unnamed Narrator represents the child, Louise the mother, and both act as the phallus for the other.

The body is not only used to present the quest of love in the journey of pleasure and desire, but it is also used to portray the significance of the fetishistic element to convey the meaning of sexual differences and choices. Foucault writes of the moral aspect of sexual conduct in ancient Greece, in which, he says, rather than the act, the desire, or the pleasure in themselves, it was more the dynamics that joined all three in a circular fashion: 'the desire that leads to the act, the act that is linked to pleasure, and the pleasure that occasions desire'.[45] This cyclical relationship is repeatedly present in Winterson's novels as a representation of love, loss and passion, and it is also reflected in the circular nature of her writing style, in which repetition is used to encapsulate the self-replicating essence of her characters' romances. Her characters often possess diverse characteristics of gender and sexuality and have triangular love relationships. When pushed to an extreme, the demands for desire and pleasure a person feels internally forces them to act, regardless of the consequences.

The chemistry of desire and pleasure are potent enough to continue seeking sexual arousal and engagement, despite the triangle of loss and love between

Louise, her husband and the Unnamed Narrator. As Sedgwick notes: '[t]he triangles function thus as registers of bonds of power and meaning and of the play of desire and identification by which individuals negotiate with their societies for empowerment.'[46] In this way, the love triangle between these protagonists reveals the power relationships and dynamics of desire that form integral parts of their characters. Louise and the Unnamed Narrator's affair is full of lust and danger, and they feel satisfied in pleasuring themselves even though it hurts, because the pain evokes seemingly unexplainable desire. The Unnamed Narrator foresees the pain from the start, as he begins to fall in love with Louise despite knowing she is married: 'I told myself. Whenever you think you are falling remember that ring is molten hot and will burn you through and through.'[47] Thus, Winterson seems to be saying, to strive for sexual satisfaction, a person must go beyond normal social and sexual parameters and challenge the inner desire of the self and the others.

The Unnamed Narrator's actions in changing sexual partners and having sexual relations with married women symbolize the stages they face in the journey of knowing the self through the other. As Freud says, 'an experience of pleasure can give rise to a need for greater pleasure' until a climactic 'discharge' is reached, although the 'tension of the libido' is only temporarily 'extinguished'.[48] Through Winterson's language, cycles of pleasurable and painful sexual tensions are depicted, becoming alternative acts of sadomasochism as libidos and lust are raised, satisfied or denied, and the process repeated. Thus, torturing the self in order to release inner repressions is one of the paths the subject may take. In other words, the Unnamed Narrator releases their repression through sexual relations with either married women or single men, in which they are aware they will probably be hurt, but their compelling desire to attain sexual satisfaction becomes pivotal, above and beyond love and reason.

The Unnamed Narrator exhibits satyric behaviour with his extreme appetite for sex, though this intense passion only stimulates further his sexual excitement for the self and the other.[49] An ex-boyfriend of theirs liked to have sexual relations with different people and was very open-minded on the subject: 'his ambition was to find a hole in every port. He wasn't fussy about the precise location.'[50] He also believed in sex and friendship, rather than love: 'Don't people always behave better towards their friends than their lovers?'[51] He had body piercings to generate sexual arousal for himself and his sexual partners, 'wearing great gold hoops through his nipples'.[52] These piercings can be seen in relation to Freud's notion of pleasure and pain, in which he writes that pain is a necessary element in obtaining pleasure: 'erotogenic effect attaches even to intensely painful feelings.'[53]

In relation to Freud's notion of sadism, Klein observes that from an early stage of mental development, sadism becomes active and violent to the sexual object and/or subject, which later becomes an anxiety and gets repressed. Sadism that is repressed and cannot recognize the difference between fantasy and actual life will return through physical and mental means to the subject's own self. The masochistic act of inflicting pain on one's own self is accompanied by an extreme feeling of pleasure. Thus, the subject aligns pain with acts of perversion, and this usually takes place during the child's early development, concurrent with the pre-genital stage and the Oedipal stage. As Freud states of the fetish, 'the horror of castration sets up a sort of permanent memorial to itself by creating this substitute', which helps to overcome current, and future, traumatic events.[54]

While the Unnamed Narrator and Louise's sexual desires and pleasures play a central role in tracing the elements of alternative fetishism in the novel, Louise's husband, Elgin, is also a practitioner, and his sexual habits provide further examples of masochistic pleasure in pain. He is sexually submissive and passive as he enjoys having pain inflicted on himself: 'he lay on his single bed, legs apart', asking Louise 'to scaffold his penis with bulldog clips'.[55] Louise understands that Elgin is deviant and perverse in terms of his sexual practices, but she still marries him. She took pleasure in her married life because she thought that Elgin was a safe choice that she 'could control, and that she would be in charge.[56] Louise chooses to remain in the marriage even though she knows Elgin visits prostitutes to engage in fetishistic acts; it becomes his hobby to fly 'up to Scotland and be sunk in a bath of porridge while a couple of Celtic geishas rubber-gloved his prick'.[57] His fetishist choices and preferences impact upon his wife; Louise knows that she will get hurt eventually by his extramarital liaisons, but she weighs this future pain against the safety she feels from being married. However, as a human being, she finds it necessary to take refuge in an affair to feel sexually and emotionally satisfied.

In Winterson's novels, pleasure and pain are fluid and changeable, depending on the situations encountered. They are linked to the cultural, psychological and physical world by extreme internal desires and external influences, resulting in acts of alternative fetishism. In relation to the moral problematization of pleasures, Foucault states that 'there could not be desire without privation, without the want of the thing desired and without a certain amount of suffering mixed in'.[58] In each relationship there is, on the one hand, the performer of the activity and, on the other, the receiver of the performance. But Foucault argues, through the philosophy of Plato, that sexual desire, from either party, relies on the soul and not the body, and hence it 'can be aroused only by the representation, the image or the memory of the thing that gives pleasure.'[59] This can be seen in the Unnamed Narrator as they cannot erase their intense sexual memories of Louise, even after resorting to heavy drinking and sex with Gail. Louise remains a strong sexual focal point in their mind as they play back the time they shared together: 'I was holding Louise's hand, conscious of it, but sensing too that a further intimacy might begin, the recognition of another person that is deeper than consciousness, lodged in the body more than held in the mind.'[60] By repeatedly remembering the time they had spent together, they keep their intimacy alive and act in denial of the fact that the object (Louise) is lost. In this way, the substitute object of memory replaces the lost object to give some fetishistic relief and pleasure to the body.

The given, conventional scripts of the body, and all its sexual pleasures, are challenged by Winterson's texts again and again. In *The Passion*, social and interpersonal boundaries are negotiated in diverse ways, temporally and spatially, by characters such as Villanelle and the Queen of Spades. Villanelle's dual identity enables her to either be passive, and submit to the demands of social norms, or be active, and challenge them. Even though her relationship with the Queen of Spades seems unlikely to last, she accepts the consequences and enjoys the moment with her lover. Later, in order to survive, she is willing to marry the Meat Man, even after he has raped her. It is possible that Villanelle's behaviour is in direct response to her affair with the Queen of Spades, linking her experiences of sexual pleasure and pain. The dynamics of her same-sex affair, which is fraught with intensity, passion and jealousy, has the capacity to influence her subsequent life choices. Thus, when the Queen of Spades tells Villanelle she is leaving, Villanelle feels a sense of rejection, which throws her into the arms of a man who is socially acceptable, because he represents heterosexual love, but who is entirely wrong for her. However, with her fluid sexual preferences and choices, Villanelle's seemingly passive actions do not erase her determination entirely. She engages in sexual activity with the Meat Man for her own pleasure and uses his work to travel around and see the world. She converts her victimhood into a source of subversive sexual and physical power.

Winterson uses her characters' sexual behaviour to reveal their personalities. Despite Villanelle's proclamation, 'You see, I am no stranger to love', the beautiful, mysterious Queen of Spades unexpectedly steals her heart.[61] Their initial meeting is riddled with intense, passionate elements:

> Still she did not speak, but watched me through the crystal and suddenly draining her glass stroked the side of my face. Only for a second she touched me

and then she was gone and I was left with my heart smashing at my chest and three-quarters of a bottle of the best champagne. I was careful to conceal both.[62]

Villanelle's vacillation between dressing as a man and as a woman might confuse the choice of her sexual object and sexual aim, but instead of depressing her, this ambiguity allows her to take pleasure in both personalities. Her cross-dressing is a fetishistic act she plays with herself and the other, as she revels in disguising her sexuality. When visitors at the gambling den are asked to guess whether she is a man or a woman, it is a game, with all its elements of mystery and open-endedness, that thrills and arouses her. She extends this game to a sexually fetishized act with the Queen of Spades, 'When we met again I had borrowed an officer's uniform', and with her husband, the Meat Man, who already enjoys sadistic acts.[63]

Villanelle still suffers from some emotional repression, but alternative fetishism enables her to divert this pain by enjoying what she desires: sexual pleasure. At times she performs sadomasochistic acts with both men and women, letting her body speak in the fluid expression of sexual pleasures and changeable desires, to the extent that conscious personhood dissipates: 'I content myself with this: that where I will be will not be where I am.'[64] This idea of fetishism is changeable and mobile, governed by her capability to substitute dual identities. She is not positioned in any single form of identity and is thus, paradoxically, both where she is and where she is not. In this, Villanelle pre-empts Lacan's adaptation of the Cartesian *Cogito* by some one hundred and fifty years, though, of course, for Winterson, it comes thirty years after Lacan's first talk on the matter in 1957. In 'The Instance of the Letter in the Unconscious', Lacan inverts Descartes' axiom of 'I think, therefore I am' into its opposite: 'I am thinking where I am not, therefore I am where I am not thinking.'[65] For Lacan, 'the self's radical eccentricity with respect to itself' that is revealed by this formula decentres the subject's consciousness and positions the unconscious as the prime factor in defining the human subject, resulting in the impossibility of complete self-knowledge.[66] For Villanelle, her words suggest both an internal split on these lines, where her unconscious assumes ascendancy over her being, and a conscious attempt to separate her mind and from her body, which she hopes will free herself from the restrictions of her reality and release her psychical self from any dependency on her physical location. She seals off her emotions, making herself numb, and pretends she is emotionally invulnerable; by this, she creates a shield in her mind and lets her body play a defensive part in her daily life. Villanelle changes identities instead of repressing her behaviour; thus, instead of feeling sorry for her situation, such as being born with webbed feet, which leads to her parents making her wear boots all the time, she diverts her confusion and repression into sexual pain and pleasure. She comforts herself with the idea of gratification and practises peculiar pain and pleasure in her sexual encounters. She enjoys sadistic acts by her husband but also tender moments with the Queen of Spades, while enjoying displaying her bisexual characteristics to both. Her sexual fetishism is fluid through substitute identities, and she reconciles pleasure and pain as fluid and adaptable modes of alternative living.

In *The Daylight Gate*, fluid desire, sexual deviance, perversity and dissidence also play important roles. For Elizabeth Southern and Alice Nutter, the pleasure and pain they experience transform their identities and sexualities. These women represent opposite ends of the feminine ideal, with Alice as the ageless, alluring sexual being, and Elizabeth, previously similar, lately a wizened old crone. Elizabeth, the most significantly monstrous figure in the novel, is hybrid and mysterious, deviant and dissident, and, when younger, confusingly attractive to Alice:

> I have never seen a more beautiful body on a man or a woman. She was slender, full, creamy, dark, rich, open, luxurious. In her clothes she was like any other well-formed woman, but naked she seemed like something other than, or more than, human.[67]

Elizabeth's body eschews conventional ideas of feminine beauty, creating a physical appearance that somehow exceeds gender categorizations. It is a body that is seen as possessing hermaphroditic and animalistic attributes, constructed through the force of internal and external desires; to Alice it did not look 'like a goddess but like an animal and a spirit combined into human form'.[68] This is not only opposed to traditional notions of feminine passivity, beauty and purity, but it is also a corruption of the human form and being in general. Further to the concept of deviation, Elizabeth's body functions as a signpost of a greater difference from physical norms than can be culturally and biologically accepted. Her hybrid body contains a mixture of female and male desires and characteristics, just like Dog-Woman's in *Sexing the Cherry*. However, there is a marked difference in their sexual choices and preferences. Elizabeth likes both male and female partners for her sexual gratification, unlike Dog-Woman, who wishes only for male partners, even though her physical size is too large for any normal-sized man. Winterson's hybrid characters can be linked to Mary Russo's notion of the divine grotesque and Grosz's notion of the freak.[69] Elizabeth's freak body in the novel crosses 'the borders which divide the subject off from all ambiguities, interconnections and reciprocal classifications'.[70] Elizabeth, for example, suffers internally and externally in her choices of, and preferences for, sexual partners. She is in love with Alice, but, at the same time, enjoys male company sexually. She has sexual encounters with men and women and challenges the given norms of gender and sexuality. This is an exemplification of deviant and dissident desires, the struggle between pleasure and pain creating an alternative mode of fetishism.

Winterson presents Elizabeth as different not only in physical appearance but also psychologically, emotionally and culturally. Elizabeth is seen as monstrous by others due to her diverse demands in her peculiar sexual play. She enjoys having others watch her naked and she couples with both men and women to satisfy her sexual pleasure and aggression. Her sadistic actions mirror her as a mother figure, in control over her child's hunger. Her desire to have sex with both John Dee and Edward Kelley at the same time is an act of deviance from strict normality in the eyes of society and it is emotionally and psychologically different – a fluid combination of deviance, perversity and dissidence.[71] In a similar vein, her sexual desire for Alice Nutter would be deemed irregular in the eyes of heteronormative society. Elizabeth's and Alice's bodies are freakish in Grosz's definition, as both are 'beautiful and delicate like that of a woman, but [with] the masculine quality and vigour of a man'.[72] Both women have diverse sexual appetites, enjoying sexual relations with men and women. Thus, Winterson challenges orthodox notions of sexuality, gender and identity, especially in terms of sexual differences and preferences. Her characters shed new light on sexual choices and preferences made for the sake of satisfying the sexual appetite of the self and the other, to give new meaning to pleasure and desire.

Sexual excitement in Winterson's novels is furnished not only by the body and its parts as sexual substitutes but also by all aspects of the physical being and the mind. As Grosz argues: 'the body has been regarded as a source of interference in, and a danger to, the operations of reason'.[73] Thus, Winterson presents the body and its parts as elements that belong to human sexuality in all its diverse intensity, where they are at once physical objects that serve practical functions, which sometimes stimulate disgust, and yet are also sources of inexplicable pleasure. The alternative fetishism of sexuality, desire and pleasure offers a way for an individual to transform suppression into expression. The theme of pleasure and pain continues in *The Daylight Gate* through characters such as Christopher Southworth, Alice Nutter and Tom Peeper; each of these has their own way of experiencing their erotogenic moral desires that represent an alternative mode of perversity, deviance and dissidence. For example, Christopher accepts torture of his body because of his dissident obsession for the other. Likewise, Alice surrenders her body to torment in the name of love, while Tom Peeper enjoys sexual pleasure through the pain of others. Each character's fetishistic acts regarding pleasure and pain are linked to love and loss in their psychological, physical, emotional and cultural relation to the self and the other. The sadistic behaviour of the prison guards and Tom Peeper, for instance, is due to their strong superego, which becomes identified with their id. Hence, they can only find their ego through the external world, and therefore they treat others cruelly to get pleasure from their misery. As Deleuze argues, sadomasochism has its roots in the parental relationship: 'aggression against the father and mother may be turned around upon the self either under the effect of "fear of loss of love" or as the result of guilt-feelings'; in *The Daylight Gate* , this internalized anger is the effect of both fear and guilt.[74]

Christopher Southworth is Alice Nutter's lover, a handsome man with eyes like 'crystals'.[75] He is captured and tortured by the authorities for his part in the Gunpowder Plot. In addition to the crystalline eyes, Christopher's body also refracts when exposed to the light; the torture it has endured means it throws back a distorted reflection of masculinity. During his interrogation, the idea of the sealed masculine body is challenged and violated: 'The men were excited by him. They turned him over and buggered him.'[76] The prison guards enjoy performing sadistic acts on unfortunate others like Christopher, the acts of torture substituting for sexual acts until their desires can be contained no longer. Thus, the link between pleasure and pain achieved by sadism is supplemented by aggression against the subject's own self (Christopher allows himself to be tortured by refusing to confess his guilt or denounce his co-conspirators), and actual sadism is also projected during the torture to gain sexual pleasure. That is, the desires to punish and be punished are concurrent, as each plays a role of transformation between Christopher and the prison guards.

Christopher feels guilty about his capture, fearing he will lose the trust and love from the Catholic order he worships. Accordingly, he desires to protect his religion, even if it means exposing himself to humiliation and transforming his superego into becoming a willing recipient of torture. Hence, through his torture, Christopher substitutes the feeling of guilt with pain to gain back the love of his Catholic brethren. Further, the act of 'buggering' is not only monstrous but also taboo for the male body and considered uncivilized because it offends against the 'sealed-off' male body.[77] Teresa de Lauretis claims, 'when a man is raped, he too is raped as a woman', and Christopher's body is presented as passive and easily penetrated, either willingly or forcefully, due to his desire to save others.[78]

As a result, he acts monstrously towards himself, accepting pain as pleasure for his obsession.

Christopher's masculine identity is further stripped when they cut off his penis and testicles, burning the latter.[79] The torturers mean to leave Christopher passive and weak through this emasculation, but his escape and evasion of recapture proves otherwise, as does the substitution of his tongue for his penis when in bed with Alice. Similarly, Alice Nutter surrenders herself to the authorities rather than betray Christopher. As a result, she is tortured in prison: 'They had her naked, on her feet, her hands strapped above her head, her back towards them. [. . .] The first man rammed the metal spike of the awl into Alice's back. He twisted it out.'[80] She refuses to reveal Christopher's location due to her emotional, physical and psychological desire for his safety, which replaces her own instinct for self-preservation. By accepting the burden of this torment, Alice repudiates conventional notions of femininity, and the substitution of Christopher's well-being for her own shows an alternative fetishism that benefits the other. The prison guards enjoy arousing their sexual desire through the suffering and pain they inflict upon others. Their superegos run wild and act sadistically upon the ego, thus turning themselves into torturers as their superegos come from the external world and gain sexual pleasure from the torture and sodomy of their victims.

The bodies in Winterson's fiction make renegotiations possible between the sexes, in keeping with Catherine Waldby's observation about 'certain shared fantasies about the receptive erotic potentials of the male body, fantasies which find their cultural correlate in the proliferation of images of the phallic woman'.[81] Christopher and Alice can be viewed in relation to the orthodox treatment of male and female bodies, which, according to Waldby, is that 'the male body is understood as phallic and impenetrable', whereas 'the female body is its opposite, permeable and receptive, able to absorb all this violence'.[82] Winterson, however, inverts this view of male impenetrability and female permeability: the violence of the bodily self or the other occurs regardless of gender and constitutes an example of alternative fetishistic action. This violence affects not only the body, physically and sexually, but also the mind, psychologically and emotionally. For example, the acts of sadism and masochism illustrated above are practised by both males and females, and the victim and the performer can be either male or female. Thus, in the relationship between torturer and victim, the superego and ego of the self and the other enter into negotiation and are altered by the extreme nature of the interactions. This also relates to the theory that the sadomasochism stage starts from phantasy and then translates into action – to punish and be punished, first as a sexual pleasure, then as a sexual act. Violence to the body, either willingly or forcefully, is a harmful deed. Winterson presents examples of the hegemonic power relations between the female body and the male body but complicates their functioning through indicating the similar natures of Christopher and Alice's fetishistic embracing of erotic masochism. Regardless of their biological sex, both express their love for and loss of the desired object in masochistic acts of disavowal. For Christopher, the brutal physical effects of his torture and castration are disavowed by his continuing Catholic faith and the recommencement of his sexual activity with Alice. As such, these acts transform the loss of a desired object into a positive avowal that reveals the alternative fetishism in Winterson's writing. For Alice, the loss of the loved object of Christopher's penis – representing not only a penis or a phallus, but also by synecdoche suggesting the potential removal of Christopher as a whole from her life – is transformed by the substitution of his tongue for his penis in the act of love, and her enjoyment of this completes the process of disavowal to avowal that again constitutes the alternative fetishism so characteristic of Winterson's fiction.

In *Sexing the Cherry*, Dog-Woman witnesses the extreme pleasure and pain practised by the clientele of her local brothel. She describes it as a 'place of great skilfulness', which the reader might reasonably expect to refer to practices of satisfying sexual desires and pleasures.[83] The peculiar sexual desires, demands and practices of the customers, supposedly Puritans, revolve around extreme acts of pain. Rather than the more conventional sounds of sex are 'noises of pain and misery'.[84] For example, there are acts of masochism and bestiality being practised in one of the chambers in the house by a human being who relishes pain and enjoys sexual intercourse with animals: 'a man, naked', wearing a mask, 'being branded on the buttocks with a hot iron' by a woman who looks like a child.[85] 'The man is a farmer of pigs. He loves pigs, but his wife no longer allows him to creep into their hindparts with his member.'[86] Thus, he diverts his desires to the brothel and seeks his sexual gratification there:

> He was groaning with pain, but when the dwarf woman turned him over with her still-hot prong his member was swollen and hard out in front of him with lust. I heard a snorting, and a pig was driven into the room, wild with fright. The man leaped at it and, holding it fast between his legs, continued his pleasures with deep thrusts while the dwarf heated up the iron again.[87]

The extreme sadomasochism being practised here is also present in many of Winterson's other novels, although not often to the same degree as what Dog-

Woman witnesses in *Sexing the Cherry*. For instance, Jeanette in *Oranges* wants someone 'who will destroy and be destroyed' for love and in this case the mutual aspects of a sadomasochistic mindset can stimulate renegotiation and promote equality in the sexual relationships between bodies.[88] However, in a culture that privileges masculinity and male power, certain acts of violence towards the other, women in particular, are not deemed as actual violence because women's bodies are 'already damaged'.[89] In this view of the world, penetration does not require permission. Waldby states that 'destruction' seems the appropriate term for the damage done to individual autonomy and ego-status by the 'tender violence and the terrors involved in sexual practice and relationships'.[90] In other words, erotic pleasure presupposes a certain amount of loss or pain before the 'little death of orgasm' can be possible.[91]

In relation to penetration without permission, a particularly iniquitous form of sexual fetishism in *The Daylight Gate* is paedophilia. The full mechanisms of perversity, deviance and dissidence are deployed in the sexualizing and rape of Jennet Device by Tom Peeper. Jennet is a young girl, fetishized by Tom as a replacement object for a sexually mature woman, and Tom's control over her shows how females of any age can be commoditized as goods in a remorseless barter economy. Tom represents the hypocritical and hegemonic patriarchal community. Even though he is closer to the bottom of society than the top, as a man and an agent of the law, he wields more power than almost any woman in the novel. Alice may have the upper hand in their first encounter, but she is ultimately unable to resist the combined actions of Tom, Potts and Roger Nowell.

When it comes to satisfying his own sexual pleasures, Tom's abuse of power results in his paedophilia, which becomes even more perverse and taboo when the discovery that he is Jennet's father fails to change his desires and actions. His pathological behaviour is displayed throughout the novel, such as raping Jennet 'on a Saturday night and stand[ing] in Church on Sunday morning'.[92] For Tom, Jennet is an object of sexual desire even though she is just a child: 'Tom Peeper opening the door of the tower, calling for her. She kept quiet. She didn't want the hard thing tonight. She was sore. [. . .] He found her. [. . .] He was undoing his breeches. She didn't want it in her mouth.'[93] Despite being a child (and his child, at that) Jennet's female body positions her as a desirable object to Tom. Waldby argues that if female bodies are perceived as 'already damaged', they are also 'already transgressed'.[94] This can partly explain why Jennet is so readily an object of Tom's sexual desire and why learning of his paternity changes nothing: if the pathway of transgression is pre-existing and established, then little or no psychic resistance would be encountered. That is, if females are always already damaged and transgressed, there is no new, difficult psychic territory to traverse from their abuse. Waldby also invokes the language of commodification to describe 'an economy of sexual violence' in such circumstances, and such a system in *The Daylight Gate* is shown by how Elizabeth and James Device, Jennet's mother and brother, essentially sell her to Tom.[95] As Luce Irigaray puts it,

> women's bodies – through their use, consumption, and circulation – provide for the condition making social life and culture possible. [. . .] The exploitation of the matter that has been sexualised female is so integral a part of our sociocultural horizon that there is no way to interpret it except within this horizon.[96]

Tom is sadistic in his abuse of all defenceless women; early in the novel, he physically and sexually assaults Sarah Device:

> Tom hit her across the mouth. [. . .] Tom Peeper ripped her dress away from her shoulder and down to her waist. [...] Tom undid his breeches. He had an erection. 'Do you miss your broomstick? Here's one'. [. . .] Tom Peeper raped Sarah Device.[97]

Female bodies have no right to reject the needs of the male body, especially in sexual terms, because 'intercourse appears as just another example of the monotonous insistence on the male body as naturally penetrative, and on women's bodies as naturally penetrable'.[98] Therefore, sexual violence and daily sexual intercourse are categorized in the same way: as sexual intercourse. As Waldby argues, a patriarchal society sees nothing wrong in the sexual abuse of these women, 'in the phallic imagination at least. Sexual penetration without the woman's agreement does not count as violence'.[99] This is because the female body is fetishized as an object of penetration and domination. However, Winterson undoes this dominant, orthodox fetishism in *The Daylight Gate* in two ways: first, by having Christopher, the male, raped in prison but not Alice, the female, and second, by deploying an alternative fetishism, typified by Christopher's and Alice's positive embrace of love and loss in their acceptance of pain, which converts the disavowal of a lost loved object into an avowal of its substitute.

Similarly, in *Sexing the Cherry*, many characters perform acts of pleasure and pain in their lives. Whereas Villanelle in *The Passion* and Louise in *Written on the Body* have extremely appealing female beauty, Dog-Woman describes herself as an ugly creature, in complete contradiction of social norms and expectations of the feminine form. Her grotesque form and immense strength create an ambiguity around her gender as her masculine strength deviates from a feminine norm. However, she is still expected to display conventional female behaviour, emotionally and sexually, by the society in which she lives.

Her knowledge of sex is limited due to a lack of information from her mother, who held traditional perceptions about it. All she can tell her daughter is: 'Men take pleasure and women give it.'[100] This is consonant with the orthodox school of thought that women and passivity are equivalent. Dog-Woman's physical appearance opposes normal expectations of female beauty, and her knowledge of men and sex is clouded by her misconceptions of them. When she does get a sexual opportunity, it turns out to be a disaster. Winterson's works oppose any conventional view of female sexuality; despite Dog-Woman's ignorance of sex, she embodies a subversive strength and an erotically peculiar appetite in sexual encounters, instead of being femininely passive. For example, when a stranger asks her to perform fellatio, she is confused by the instructions she is given by the man: '"Put it in your mouth," he said. "Yes. As you would delicious things to eat."'[101] She ends up swallowing 'it up entirely and biting it off with a snap'.[102] Her ignorance leads her to believe that a penis can regrow, even if this 'still seems ridiculous as it must take some time to grow again'.[103] In her second sexual encounter, she engulfs the whole genitalia of a man with her vagina:

> He complained that he could not find the sides of my cunt and felt like a tadpole in a pot. [. . .] I took a great breath and squeezed with all my might and heard something like a rush of air through a tunnel, and when I strained up on my elbows and looked down I saw I had pulled him in, balls and everything.[104]

Dog-Woman's sexual strength is in excess of the weak and limited female body that Grosz says is projected by patriarchal culture:

> bodily cycles – menstruation, pregnancy, maternity, lactation, etc. – are in one case regarded as a limitation on women's access to the rights and privileges patriarchal culture accords to men [. . .] On the negative view, women's bodies are regarded as an inherent limitation on women's capacity for equality, while on the positive side, women's bodies and experiences are seen to provide women with a special insight, something that men lack. Both sides seem to have accepted patriarchal and misogynist assumptions about the female body as somehow more natural, less detached, more engaged with and directly related to its 'objects' than male bodies.[105]

In this connection, Winterson's women are versatile and unique creatures – they are an amalgamation of negative and positive views of women's bodies. The fluid sexuality of the characters represents the experience of both the feminine and the masculine worlds. Dog-Woman is too large a woman for any man's penis to penetrate her vagina sufficiently or satisfyingly. However, one aspiring lover's desire to pleasure her as a woman leads him to attempt oral sex: 'he burrowed down the way ferrets do.'[106] Even so, the man asks her forgiveness as her clitoris is too big and he cannot manage the task: 'I cannot take that orange in my mouth. It will not fit. Neither can I run my tongue over it. You are too big, madam.'[107] Dog-Woman, however, is not disheartened by her deviance and dissidence; instead, she is confident in speaking about her own appearance and emotionally happy with the condition of her body and her sexual ability. She views her own body as 'all in proportion', even though her sexual partner describes her clitoris as grotesquely oversized.[108] She takes pain as pleasure, as she is a strong woman and proud to utilize her body in any way, although her physicality prevents her from ever gaining sexual satisfaction. She is an example of Winterson's female characters who celebrate their diverse presentation to challenge and deconstruct oppressive sexual binaries. Dog-Woman's diverse sexuality, encompassing her prodigious strength, oversized genitalia and insatiable drives, serves as an example of the alternative fetishization in Winterson's works. This functions through positive avowal of her physical being, in opposition to orthodox narratives of the feminine female body as the only object worthy of sexualization.

The body and its parts in Winterson's novels become substitute objects in the fetishizing of sexual experience, and Winterson explores the capability of alternative fetishism to convert potentially negative acts into positive practices. For example, in a traditional, heteronormative view of sexual relationships, the male is seen as the holder of the 'key of pleasures' because the penis is the source of sexual satisfaction for the female.[109] However, in *The Daylight Gate* it is the castrated Christopher Southworth's tongue that performs as a phallic substitute, replacing the lost penis. The beneficial practice of substitution that underpins alternative fetishism means penises are not always necessary – either as a 'key of pleasures' or as the desired object. Winterson uses sexual substitutes to form imaginative references to the phallus, showing it is not the only object (or subject) of pleasure. Rather, it can be replaced by other items, such as body parts or objects associated with the self and other, to satisfy the needs of the sexual drive. The next chapter will analyse how elongated objects in Winterson's fiction can be used as replacements for the penis and how a phallus can also be seen as the object and subject of desire.

9

The fetishistic phallus
Elongated objects

Winterson creates fetishistic texts by utilizing different parts of the body to make up a language of diverse physical desire and pleasure. The lexis of flesh – including fingers, hands, lips and feet – describes a quest to fulfil these desires and attain such pleasures through sexual dissidence. Winterson's repeated sexualizing of the body and its parts reveals a unique relationship with fetishism, indicating it to be a common practice in the process of acquiring the other body. Therefore, everyone, regardless of gender and sexuality, can encounter and perform alternative sexual fetishism.

In *The Passion*, sexual obsession is not limited to any one part of the body. Many body parts of the self and the other substitute for the primary sex organs and become fetish objects of sexual fantasy. Sexual overvaluation, Freud's concept of the idealization of the sexual object of desire, is not restricted to one or two parts of the body. Instead, many body parts are focused upon as recipients of sexual aims. Villanelle's affair with the Queen of Spades relates to the concept of the imaginary penis (penis envy) and her relationship to having and being the phallus. In Lacan's paradoxical signification of the phallus and penis, the phallus is a signifier of power over the other that one fabricates in phantasy for the substitution of an actual object or organ. Instead of an act of repression, the desire for the phallus is a replacement or substitute and a form of cure for the repression and absence of the desired object, whereas the penis and the clitoris symbolize the other object, or part of the body, as an actual organ. The phallus is only a signifier in the phantasy, 'that it be in the place of the *Other* that the subject have access to it', an otherness that 'confirm[s] the phallus' signifying function'.[1] For example, both Villanelle and the Queen of Spades experience the imaginary penis, the demand to have the other as having the phallus, which thus symbolizes the other object as a substitute of the real.

The Queen of Spades's neck is the site of Villanelle's first erotic contact with her when she kisses it, and the neck can be seen as a penis substitute; as Freud points out, 'all elongated objects such as sticks, tree-trunks and umbrellas (the opening of these last being comparable to an erection) may stand for the male organ – as well as all long, sharp weapons, such as knives, daggers and pikes.'[2] These substitutes for the male organ reflect 'an assumption that all human beings have the same (male) form of genital', and they substitute the 'real' penis for the 'woman's penis' and act as a replacement for being the phallus.[3] The Queen of Spades, in her turn, treats Villanelle's feet as a penis substitute when she asks to stroke them as her first desired sexual contact with Villanelle's body.[4] Villanelle and the Queen of Spades constitutively take on their roles in pleasuring each other through their fluid and changeable sexual acts. The replacement of the object and subject of their desires, a movement from absence to presence via substitution, leads to consensual and non-pathological pleasure. Essentially, desire is neither the longing for pleasure nor the demand for love, but instead the desire to have and be the other.

The difference between the demand and the desire for love results in what Lacan calls the 'unconditionality of demand', in which 'desire substitutes the "absolute" condition: this condition, in fact, dissolves the element in the proof of love that rebels against the satisfaction of need.'[5] Thus, to have the other is to be the other, which is phallically having the power of the other. In *The Passion*, this power stems, at least in part, from the fluid and transgressive nature of the fetish objects. In Butlerian terms, Villanelle plays the feminine male with the Queen of Spades by 'fabricating', 'manufacturing' and 'constituting' a male gender performance with her.[6] In Lacanian terms, this means Villanelle plays at being the phallus, a fantasy that the Queen of Spades willingly embraces. In Lacan's analysis of the phallus in relation to language, a woman can fetishize and channel her desire by turning away from her feminine side and towards the penis substitute of the fetishized phallus:

> Paradoxical as this formulation might seem, it is in order to be the phallus, that is, the signifier of the desire of the Other, that the woman will reject an essential part of her femininity, notably all its attributes through masquerade. It is for what she is not that she expects to be desired as well as loved. But she finds the signifier of her own desire in the body of the one to whom she addresses her demand for love. Certainly we should not forget that the organ invested with this signifying function takes on the value of a fetish.[7]

Clearly, the 'Other' that a person desires can be of either sex, as a form of fantasy through the imaginary, and the phallus can be replaced with another object.

Hence, I argue that in Winterson's novels, elongated objects often act as penis replacements, taking on the function of the fetish. For instance, the feet and the neck are the object and subject of such a fetish for both the Queen of Spades and Villanelle and, therefore, they act as substitutes for the phallus in their sexual relationship. The imaginary penis (a woman's penis is a symbol of a phallus) is a symbol of the real object, and the desire to be the phallus and having the power of the phallus are reflected first in Villanelle's manner of dressing and acting like a man, and second in her choice of jobs. For example, she shows her masculine behaviour when she runs away from her husband and performs itinerant labour: 'I got odd jobs on ships and in grand houses.'[8] Thus, through her fetishistic language of obsession, Winterson's characters regularly focus on suggestive body parts, and the Unnamed Narrator in *Written on the Body*, just like Villanelle in *The Passion*, substitutes fingers, neck and feet for a penis. Winterson borrows the Freudian symbolism of elongated objects as penis symbols and depicts other objects such as the neck, hand, fingers, tongue and feet as penis substitutes that can provide the body and the other the desired pleasure. Winterson's novels envelop sexual desire in circuitous elements, suggesting that the very concept and language of sexuality is far from clear-cut and obvious. Rather, it is shown to be replete with insinuations, subtlety and a certain fluidity that flourishes in the intimacy between two sexual beings.

Throughout Winterson's fiction, sexual fetishization is not limited to one part of the body, and it is possible for almost any part of the self and the other to become an object in relation to sexual fantasy. In this connection, pleasuring the body of the self or the other is not necessarily related to, or directed towards, penile penetration. For example, in *The Daylight Gate*, Christopher gives Alice pleasure by using his tongue as a substitute for his castrated penis, and the Unnamed Narrator in *Written on the Body* makes love without any tell-tale reference to their genitals. Another object can represent the lost penis in penetration, and the relationship between the penetrable and penetrative does not simply derive from penetration by the penis. Instead, the lost penis can be substituted for any object, and so, without a penis, a subject is still capable of giving the self and the other sexual pleasure. Thus, the masculine characteristics both Villanelle and the Queen of Spades display in *The Passion* mean they can both act as the subject and the object of sexual desire and pleasure.

In addition to the imaginary penis, Louise and the Unnamed Narrator write their love story through the imagination, which they can revisit in their memory, the fingers functioning as a substitute for a pen: 'your fingers have become printing blocks, you tap a message on to my skin, tap meaning into my body.'⁹ The body itself substitutes for paper and is used to write the stories of their life together. The body also acts as a substitute for the phallus which has been desired and which desires. The Unnamed Narrator experiences the deviant body and their lovers' bodies in various ways to express their fluid erotic desires as a fetish object and subject. Fingers in *Written on the Body* act not only as tools of communication but also as means of expression: 'Articulacy of fingers, the language of the deaf and dumb, signing on the body body longing.'[10] The sexual and physical relationships in this novel are written as stories on bodies, and fingers act as pens to provide a metaphor for the objects of desire and pleasure, with or without penetration. In relation to fluid pleasure and desire, the fingers are seen as a subject and an object that are capable of expressing an invisible desire of the bodily self and the other. As the Unnamed Narrator's sex is never stated for the reader, sexual relations between the Unnamed Narrator and Louise utilize the imaginary to substitute parts of the other's body in order to initiate sexual engagement. For example, the Unnamed Narrator studies Louise intently as her hair 'warm[s] her neck and shoulders'.[11] These body parts become phallic symbols and temporary substitutes for the actual object, while the Unnamed Narrator maintains their lingering gaze to attain arousal.

The Queen of Spades and Villanelle represent those who face a particular set of difficulties in society: they have to hide their affair, which results in repression for both. For example, her impending confession at the church is complicated by her inability to stay fixed in one identity: 'If I went to confession, what would I confess? That I cross-dress?'[12] Villanelle paints a bold picture of her lover: 'for nine days and nights, we stayed in her house, never opening the door, never looking out the window. We were naked and not ashamed. And we were happy.'[13] They know that the kind of love they share is impossible to announce, being what Lord Alfred Douglas termed 'the love that dare not speak its name'.[14] However, Villanelle also follows social norms when she engages in heterosexual relationships and marriage. She enjoys this deviation from her previous sexual experiences, first, for the pleasure of her body and, second, in order to be accepted in the culture in which she finds herself. Due to this, Villanelle's chameleonic character changes all the time, depending on the situation. This suggests that she exercises the choice to fluidly veer between conventional and deviant sexual objects and sexual aims: 'I flirt with waiters and gamblers and remember that I enjoy that.'[15] She can love a man just to survive, or a woman to satisfy her body and desire.

She is conscious of her sexual deviance and willingly participates in many situations in order to survive in a patriarchal world. In the eyes of heteronormative society, Villanelle's sexual predilections for both women and men are considered perverse, but for her it is a choice that can be made easily. She shows her masculine behaviour not only by dressing and acting like a man but also by being capable of having sexual relations and intimate physical contact with a man or a woman, as she deems convenient in a particular situation. It seems she can just as easily satisfy her sexual needs with Henri as with the Queen of Spades, and her fluid gender and sexuality provide her with a certain mode of independence. For instance, she carries Henri's unborn child but refuses to marry him, as her heart, although rescued from the Meat Man, is still attached to the Queen of Spades. She combines her passive feminine and active masculine personae and lives alone with her child, without a man beside her, just as earlier, she ran away from her husband to work at sea. The freedom she manages to achieve reflects the struggles of many women in patriarchal society: her freedom is won by effort, rather than naturally accompanying her biological sex, and she has had to take possession of the penis and become the phallus, as a subject and an object, in society. She opposes any orthodox school of thought that sees the inherent differences between man and woman as non-exchangeable. In this way, Winterson, whose fetishism of language powers the depictions of her characters' sexual fetishes, manages to challenge the different roles and expectations of men and women in society.

Another example of fluid sexuality and survival in *The Passion* is the soldiers in the Grande Armée, who have little alternative but to be sexually attracted to one another due to the overwhelmingly male circumstances of war. When an officer sees Henri, for instance, he is violently aroused by him: 'He lifted his foot and, as I scrambled up, kicked me hard and still looking straight ahead said, "Firm buttocks, that's something."'[16] The officer's foot could be an elongated object, a penis replacement, in which case, Henri is sodomized by the officer. This alternative sexuality could be situational or permanent, and it can also be based on phantasy and reality from one's own experiences or the environment. Even marine animals can be elongated objects that function as phallic symbols and serve to represent the domination inherent in a patriarchal society. The Meat Man, who is a brutal and sexually aggressive man, refers to his own penis as an eel. He shouts at a prostitute: 'Put your hand in, can't you, or are you afraid of eels?'[17] It is apt that Winterson chooses an eel to represent the Meat Man's penis because eels, like the Meat Man himself, are slimy and considered repulsive. Villanelle later refers to the Meat Man's hands as a squid: 'I hardly felt his hand along my leg, his fingers on my belly. Then I was reminded vividly of squid and their suckers.'[18] She metaphorically presents the female sexual predicament in a patriarchal society inhabited by men like the Meat Man, who are more interested in selfish sexual gratification than in the needs of the other. Violence seems inevitable for an eel-like man such as the Meat Man, who takes pleasure in physical abuse as a route to sexual gratification. Women in the novel have little power against the cruelty of men like the Meat Man or Napoleon.

In the unusual relationships between Villanelle and the Queen of Spades, and the Unnamed Narrator and Louise, substitute objects such as the neck, shoulder, hands, fingers and feet take on a peculiar function where they transcend their role as a mere replacement of the penis into an extreme desire of the whole, these parts moving from signifying the phallus to actually becoming it. Therefore, the penetration of the other body is not dependent on just the penetration of the penis; in a world of fluid pleasures and desires, penetration of the other body can be replaced by any elongated object. This redefinition is important because Winterson is giving validation to the homoerotic and allowing a choice to those who are sexually different in terms of substitute tools for sexual desire and pleasure.

In connection to Freud's theory of infantile sexuality and its effects in later life, adult sexual dissidents may re-enact, alone or with a partner, several components of their childhood sexuality in order to achieve sexual arousal and satisfaction. If one component of pre-genitality is over-emphasized, the repression of the Oedipal complex is maintained, along with a fear of castration and feelings of guilt that would block sexual pleasure. However, the 'perverse' fantasy may serve as the source of sexual arousal leading to orgasm. When the Meat Man asks the prostitute to perform fellatio on him, a concentrated obsession referring to the pre-Oedipal stages is shown. The infantile action of sucking is obvious when the Meat Man forces the prostitute to put his penis in her mouth. Feeding from the mother satisfies a child's first experience of hunger, which denotes the biological processes of the oral drive and erotogenic zones, linking the sensual act of sucking and the desire to urinate or defecate.[19] However, in the Meat Man's adult life, his sexual gratification turns into cruelty as he performs sadistic acts toward his sexual partners, and roles are switched as he becomes the one who is sucked.

As might be expected from a book that takes *Frankenstein* as its inspiration, *Frankissstein* features many scenes of body parts; through Winterson's fetishistic reinterpretation, these often act as elongated objects of phallic substitution. Hands and fingers play an important role in the text as substitute objects of sexual desire and pleasure, and perhaps this is understandable, given Ry's transgender status. Ry presents as male following transitional procedures – a double mastectomy and hormone therapy – which have given them a flat chest and facial hair.[20] As Ron Lord says, 'You look like a bloke. [. . .] Not a serious bloke, but a bloke.'[21] Ry has had no surgery on their genitals, so they still have a vagina; as Ry says to Polly, 'I'm fully female, I am also partly male.'[22] This line is key to how Winterson wishes to present Ry's transness, that it makes them more of a person, rather than less (or even the same). However, despite the masculine sexual signifiers of the muscular chest and stubble, the absent penis means Ry still, in Lacanian terms, reflects the woman's position of being the phallus rather than having it. In this way, Ry's hybrid body reflects many of Winterson's female characters, such as Villanelle in *The Passion*, Dog-Woman in *Sexing the Cherry* and Elizabeth Southern in *The Daylight Gate*, rather than her male characters.

Ry has had sexual relationships with men and women, but there is little detail in the novel of their relationships with women, beyond confiding to Polly that one 'didn't work out', for reasons of love, not sex.[23] In contrast, their relationship with Victor forms a crucial component of *Frankissstein*, and their sexual activity is recorded by Ry in some detail. Ry and Victor's sex is, despite Ry's transgender situation, a distinctly heteronormative flavour of vanilla, and so Victor is the penetrator and Ry the penetrated. Hands and fingers are Ry's fetish objects, penis referents and substitutes that excite them more than the penis itself. They are one of the first things Ry notices about Victor, who clearly shares some of Ry's interest in this body part: 'His hands on the wheel are long, well-kept and clean. [. . .] He wears a gold signet ring on his little finger.'[24] Ry and Victor's first sexual encounter is instigated by Ry asking Victor to touch them, and again Victor's 'long fingers' are highlighted.[25] Victor touches Ry all over their body, including their face, throat and shoulders, before digitally penetrating their vagina.[26] Later in the novel, Victor needs Ry to procure body parts for his work, for which Ry's job as an Accident & Emergency doctor provides ample supply. Ry brings Victor a selection, from which an amputated leg is briefly discussed as being 'well-shaped', but the main object of interest for the pair is the 'bag of hands' Ry has secured.[27] Victor says, 'Hands fascinate me. [. . .] Hands are a huge challenge. It's the test of a good artist – can she draw hands?'[28] Ry mentions that Ron Lord is working on a 'wank hand', despite robotics companies facing difficulties similar to artists in capturing the complexities of the hand, and this topic is enough to arouse Victor:

> It won't be as good as you, he said.
> Am I good?
> Very good.
> He was moving my hand towards his crotch.

> Is this what I am to you? I said.
> A hand? No.
> A sex object. [...] (I spat in my palm.) [...] (He takes four minutes this way.)[29]

Victor's obsession with masturbation takes a bizarre and fetishistic turn when he fantasizes about being so small that his whole body could fit in Ry's hand. Victor talks of a trans- or post-human world, in which digital brains can be uploaded into new bodies of any size and shape:

> He took my fingers and kissed them. I love your big hands, he said. If I could choose another body, perhaps I would live in miniature and stand on your hand like one of those magical creatures caught in a nutshell.[30]

Victor imagines his whole body in Ry's hands, in the way his penis has been so often. In this way, his entire being would be a phallus, an elongated object enjoying stimulation all over. Victor's fetishism of Ry's hands offers him a way of distancing the reality of Ry's transgender status. It seems that Victor telling Ry (and himself) twice that he is not gay is insufficient heterosexual reinforcement for Victor and his troubled psychosexual identification, so he also states that if Ry had completed their transitioning with lower surgery, they would not have become sexually and romantically involved:

> Listen, I have said this before but I will say it again – if you did have a penis, then what happened between us in the shower in Arizona . . .
> And after the shower when you fucked me . . .
> He puts his finger to my lips to shush me. Would never have happened.[31]

The finger now becomes a physical manifestation of Victor's patriarchal dominance in the relationship, silencing Ry's voice and prohibiting their further contribution to this discussion. As such, Victor's finger now acts as a phallus in Lacan's concept of the Law of the Father – the law of language – and by silencing Ry and prohibiting their linguistic contributions, Victor maintains his masculine authority. It is fitting that when Victor disappears, or is uploaded, his signet ring is all that Ry can find of him. His fingers, for all their sexual substitution and phallic signification, no longer exist as a result of his transition to a post-human existence, but a metonymic symbol endures. Signet rings, in their original use of sealing the wax on correspondence, were an early form of wearable technology for the purposes of identity verification; the paradigm shift to digital consciousness Victor has achieved means this material object must now be left behind, but its symbolic power still resonates for Ry and leaves them with an alternative fetish object of their own that substitutes for Victor's fingers.

10

Soft fetishes

Membranes and senses

Moving away from the phallus, I argue here that the soft membranes of the body, such as the lips, the mouth and the skin, also become objects and subjects of alternative sexual fetishism in Winterson's work, as do the senses of touch, taste, smell and sight. As borders between interior and exterior, between subject and object, the soft membranes have important biological purposes and, thus, deep cultural and sexual symbolism. For example, the Unnamed Narrator in *Written on the Body* regularly fixates on Louise's mouth: 'The lining of your mouth I know through tongue and spit. Its ridges, valleys, the corrugated roof, the fortress of teeth. The glossy smoothness of the inside of your upper lip.'[1] Their desire, which is intensified by staring at Louise's lips, necessarily precedes physical touch. The Unnamed Narrator's mouth also becomes a site where intimations of sexual pleasure are linked with orality, even when they are not in Louise's presence: 'my lips were sealed and my cheeks must have been swelling out like a gerbil's because my mouth was full of Louise.'[2] The actions of the Unnamed Narrator relate to Freud's conceptualization of looking and touching as movements towards achieving sexual aims. Thus, observation of the mouth, lips and other similar soft membranes encourages their comprehension by the subject as substitute objects for desire and pleasure.

The focus on such specific and intimate body parts in Winterson's texts results in the whole, and therefore gendered, body being blurred from view; hence, desires and pleasures in her fiction are ungendered and refuse to follow the rules of conventional or traditional norms. In psychoanalytical thinking, the lips and the anus are the first parts of the body with which we identify ourselves as existing – these entrances and exits to the body that relate to gratification of hunger, the expulsion of excreta and other physical necessities. The biological links between them are indicated by the Unnamed Narrator's statement that the 'tissues of the mouth and anus heal faster', but it is with the mouth that they are primarily obsessed.[3] The Unnamed Narrator creates a fantasy in their mind and stimulates it from the unconscious to the conscious and finally gives in to the sexual impulse: 'You kissed me and I tasted the relish of your skin.'[4] The mouth and lips are often essential adjuncts to the genitals in the act of love-making, such as in Elgin's adolescent memories of his private school, where the other boys would engage in homosexual activity with 'mouths open, cocks hard'.[5] In Winterson's sensual language, references to the mouth are often suggestive of oral sex; when Louise is finishing her breakfast, 'she pops [it] into her mouth from the end of her knife'.[6] The knife (another elongated object) suggests a penis and so the mouth becomes a means of administering sexual desire and pleasure. A kiss involving the mouth, lips and tongue is capable of incarnating the intimacy and intricacy of sex: 'She kissed me and in her kisses lay the complexity of passion.'[7] Thus, not only are the mouth, lips and tongue objects and subjects of fetishes but so are the senses, such as touching, smelling and tasting. This gives rise to chapter headings in *Written on the Body* such as 'Taste' and 'The Nose'.[8]

In *The Passion*, Villanelle cannot provide her lover with a penis, and so she diverts her sexual objective and sexual aim by utilizing the soft membranes of her lips and her mouth: 'We stayed thus for a moment until I had courage enough to kiss her neck very lightly. She did not pull away. I grew bolder and kissed her mouth, biting a little at the lower lip.'[9] This employment of the mouth might be considered in Freudian terms as a replacement for a sex organ, in this case the penis, as the lips and tongue are brought into contact with those of the other as a substitute for penetrative intercourse. In this case, this is not least because Villanelle, though dressed as a man, has no penis and so requires an alternative process: 'kissing in this way is the strangest of distractions. [. . .] so the mouth becomes the focus of love and all things pass through it and are redefined. It is a sweet and precise torture.'[10] Winterson's fiction avoids reductive categorizations of desire, bodies and pleasure. Instead, for her, they are all fluid and mobile. Thus, sexual fetishism is a tool that can be a substitute for the lack or loss of a desired object.

Skin, the largest organ in the human body, plays many roles in sexual attraction, obsession and fetishistic substitution. In *Written on the Body*, the Unnamed Narrator's fetishism about skin includes a magnifying focus and a microscopic examination: 'The cells on the surface of your skin are thin and flat without blood vessels or nerve endings.'[11] At a slightly larger scale, it has its major function of covering the flesh of other organs, such as the breasts. Breasts are what a child hungers for when it first enters the world. Beyond their primary biological purpose of providing sustenance to the newly born, breasts are, of course, also secondary sexual characteristics that evoke arousal, and so they are doubly powered as fetish objects. In the Freudian and Kleinian psychoanalytical schools, breasts are the first pleasure a baby experiences with its mother, and the pleasure of sucking at the mother's breasts is a substitute for pleasuring the self. For the Unnamed Narrator, breasts are a perpetual sexual obsession, and Louise's are remembered and celebrated right from the start of the narration: 'You turned your back and your nipples grazed the surface of the river.'[12] They are invariably the first body part that comes to the Unnamed Narrator's mind when picturing their lovers, which makes them feel comforted and secure – they act as a substitute for a mother's love, replete with the associated ideas of protection and nourishment. Consequently, the breast can become a fetish object as part of a maternal substitution, as it is a significant object in male and female lives from a very young age. For example, the Unnamed Narrator looks at and imagines the breasts of their lover in the process of gaining pleasure: 'The flesh was brown, the aureoles browner still, nipples bead black.'[13] Even in an unhappy relationship, the Unnamed Narrator cannot resist continuing with the affair because of their lover's breasts: 'Why didn't I dump Inge and head for a Singles Bar? The answer is her breasts.'[14] The Unnamed Narrator's obsession with breasts also relates to Klein's concept of the mother–child relationship, in which the child searches for herself/himself in the other body, with 'the breast as being the model for the transitional object used by the child to bridge the gap between the "I" with the external world'.[15] The Unnamed Narrator, acting in a child-like manner, returns to their safe haven when they feel the danger of love. Breasts act as a refuge to which they can return if they can claim for their own. But they also link the subject with the world outside their own body and so the 'bridge' Klein invokes is certainly two way. Thus, breasts have the twin function of offering security as well as being the objects of the desire for sexual pleasure of the self and the other.

The Unnamed Narrator returns to their minute examination of skin when describing Louise's breasts: 'When I run my tongue in a long wet line across your breasts I can feel the tiny hairs, the puckering of the aureole, the cone of your nipples.'[16] At this level of magnification, the image of the breast as a whole breaks down, and the individual components gain their own position at the expense of a unified appearance. This offers a further level of fetishism as the breast itself is now subject to replacement and substitution by its constituent parts. The Unnamed Narrator attempts to forestall psychoanalytical readings of their breast fetishism by saying of Inge's breasts, 'I had idolised them simply and unequivocally, not as a mother substitute nor as a womb trauma, but for themselves. Freud didn't always get it right. Sometimes a breast is a breast is a breast.'¹⁷ However, I suspect neither the reader nor the Unnamed Narrator is particularly convinced by this denial, which itself suggests a psychic suppression, particularly in the repetition of 'breast'. They need to gain confidence in the self through the other, and the fetish object of the breasts helps this procedure. The Unnamed Narrator engages in many relationships in an attempt to find a comforting space in which they can feel strong; each relationship teaches them something new in the process of knowing their body, offering a different way to transform their sexual constraints and repressions into sexual freedom and appreciation.

Desire and pleasure recognize no name, gender or sexuality in the world of alternative fetishism. However, there is a sense of imprisonment, a positive claustrophobia, that contains the lust and loss experienced by Winterson's characters. The lust comes from looking and gazing at the other through the mirror of the bodily self, and any loss regularly leads to replacement. The acts of looking and gazing play important roles in the notion of fetishism, regardless of whether it is bodily, food or sexual fetishism. The interface between voyeuristic behaviour and physical contact provides a further source of alternative fetishism in Winterson's writing. Looking signifies the attempt to see and takes in those things caught by the corner of the eye on the periphery of vision and consciousness. Gazing, by comparison, is the deliberate application of sight onto an object of scrutiny. Looking and gazing are to the eyes what hearing and listening are to the ears. Looking and gazing are acts that can initiate sexual stimulation, while touching the sexual object can cause pleasure and produce sexual excitement. The scrutiny of individual body parts and their sensuous associations in Winterson's fiction has profound and significant connections to the realization or frustration of sexual desires and affects the performance of alternative fetishism. In *Written on the Body*, the Unnamed Narrator studies Louise intently:

> The naked eye. How many times have I enjoyed you with my lascivious naked eye. [. . .] I have had you beneath me for examination [. . .] My eyes are brown; they have fluttered across your body like butterflies. [. . .] I have mapped you with my naked eye and stored you out of sight. The millions of cells that make up your tissues are plotted on my retina.¹⁸

Libidinous excitement is frequently awakened by optical impressions, which permit the perceiving of the sexual object as a thing of beauty, and the Unnamed Narrator and Louise first use their eyes to show their sexual desire by gazing at each other with meticulous intensity: 'she wore a simple dress of moss green silk, a pair of jade earrings, and a wedding ring.'[19] The eyes are used to gauge how jewellery or accessories enhance the beauty of the lover and how they complement the sensitive areas of the body. The Unnamed Narrator notices more about Louise's appearance because it is enhanced by jewellery. Therefore, the eyes act as a temporary bridge towards a sexual object, and they are parts of the body that play a significant role in sensual and sensuous acts.

The intricacies of colour are also used in *Written on the Body* to project a more detailed, specific and corporeal representation of the body and its parts: 'Marrow where the blood cells are formed red and white. Red and white, the colours of Louise.'[20] The Unnamed Narrator continues:

> I scanned the row of industrious heads. Dark, blonde, grey, bald, wig. A long way round was a bright red flame. I knew it wasn't Louise but I couldn't take my eyes off the colour. It soothed me the way any bear will soothe a child not at home. It wasn't mine but it was like mine. If I made my eyes narrow slits the red took up the whole room. The dome was lit with red. I felt like a seed in a pomegranate.[21]

The red hair of a stranger is capable of reminding the Unnamed Narrator of Louise's body and its parts. The colour red and the word 'flame' symbolize the passionate desire that the Unnamed Narrator substitutes for the actual object in response to the intense feelings they associate with Louise. Winterson shows how one's inner desires connect with the outer environment through looking and, more particularly, gazing, and how one can be obsessed with an object that replaces or substitutes for another. The Unnamed Narrator is 'soothed' and feels secure, like a child in the womb, just by looking at an object that reminds them of Louise. The Unnamed Narrator, recalling their coupling, relishes oral sex in particular. They cannot take their eyes off Louise's vagina while stroking it, and so the act of oral sex is an intense form of sexual pleasure of the self (the Unnamed Narrator, through their sense of sight and touch) and the other (Louise, through vaginal and clitoral stimulation).

According to Freud, the libido serves 'as a measure of process and transformation occurring in the field of sexual excitation'; in Winterson's work this is shown through an appropriate excitement of erogenous zones such as the soft membranes of the vagina, anus, clitoris, lips and the tongue.[22] Thus, an extreme pleasure through contact with membranes corresponds to the stimulation of other body parts of the body, especially those connected to sexual penetration and excitement: 'Your sepulchral body, offered to me in the past tense, protects your soft centre from intrusion of the outside world. I am one such intrusion.'[23] The source of the instinctual drive is a stimulus arising from a somatic process, such as touching a certain part of the body, like the skin, mouth or lips. The instinctual feeling is a close precursor to sexual merging:

> Sleeping beside Louise had been a pleasure that often led to sex but which was separate from it. The delicious temperate warmth of the body, skin temperature perfect with mine. Moving away from her only to turn over again hours later and mould myself into the curve of her back.[24]

Fetishism, in Lacan's tripartite model of the symbolic, the imaginary and the real, represents the unconscious substitute transcending into a conscious substitute for the actual object (other). It is mostly silent in the mind of the fetishist at first, as imaginary and symbolic, before these combine to manifest the fetishism in reality. In the imaginary, a male child assumes that both sexes have a phallus like he does, and he denies that females do not possess this sensually rewarding and narcissistically invested organ. When the symbolic order is entered, the absence of the penis in the female is imposed through language. As the originating force behind all the fetishism in Winterson's work, language thus creates and enforces the knowledge of sexual difference. Therefore, symbolism and the imaginary are important elements in the notion of fetishism. Individual body parts, along with their sensuous feelings, have a profound and significant function for sexual engagement because fetishistic images exist in the mind before being transferred to the body and its parts. Having established this, fetishism is applied to all bodies, regardless of whether male, female or elsewhere on the gender continuum. In other words, sexual passion and fantasy are not static entities and should not be classified as gendered because sexual orientation itself is fluid and of less importance. The Unnamed Narrator fetishizes the lover's body in multiple ways, creating a substitute through the fantasy of a female phallus. Nonetheless, imagination and symbolism are essential in fetishism, while the sex of the person who practises it is irrelevant. The act of looking from top to toe is pleasurable to the eyes: 'I have seen you unclothed, bent to wash, the curve of your back, the concurve of your belly.'[25] From eyes down to the neck, the eyes move down to the shoulders, and eventually reach the breasts, which are considered a prominent element for the object and subject in the act of sexual fetishism.

As discussed in the previous chapter, by using phallic symbols, Winterson shows through language that, first, the object is a substitute for sexual oneness and, second, the object is a substitute for the penis or the imaginary penis. For example, the nose, fingers, thumbs, neck and feet can be seen as phallic objects. However, the nose is not just a phallic symbol, as the olfactory system is capable of greatly arousing sexual instincts:

> The smells of my lover's body are still strong in my nostrils. The yeast smell of her sex [. . .] From beyond the front door my nose is twitching, I can smell her coming down the hall towards me. She is a perfumier of sandalwood and hops. I want to uncork her. I want to push my head against the open wall of her loins. She is firm and ripe, a dark compound of sweet cattle straw and Madonna of the Incense. She is frankincense and myrrh, bitter cousin smells of death and faith. When she bleeds the smells I know change colour. There is iron in her soul on those days. She smells like a gun.[26]

In the above excerpt, smell plays a significant role in pleasuring the self and the other. Through the nose comes aroma capable of arousing sexual instincts: 'It was your smell I was after.'[27] Smell seduces the body physically and acts psychologically to enhance the desire and pleasure of the body. Her smell makes the Unnamed Narrator want to explore Louise's body, heart and soul. The Unnamed Narrator at this point not only wants to make love to Louise, but to explore inside her, to witness what is going on, to be an x-ray to inspect her desire and her thirst. They compare Louise with the most sensual smells. The Unnamed Narrator sees her as a dream come true, something they imagined becoming a reality. The Unnamed Narrator's nostrils are sensitive to smells – even the smell of blood captures their attention. In *The Passion*, smell has similar functions of creating and reproducing emotional and sexual responses. For Villanelle, the idea of the Queen of Spades's smell becomes heightened enough to threaten her emotional balance and disturb the order of her life:

> If I smell her skin, find the mute curves of her nakedness, she will reach in her hand and withdraw my heart like a bird's egg. I have not had time to cover my heart in barnacles to elude her. If I give in to this passion, my real life, the most solid, the best known, will disappear and I will feed on shadows again like those sad spirits whom Orpheus fled.[28]

Villanelle senses the chains of memory and inevitability of future heartbreak which is tied to her diverse desire for the Queen of Spades.

This section has argued that the discourse around gender and sexuality in Winterson's texts challenges taboo perceptions and conventional notions of sexual pleasure and desire, creating a space where sexual difference can be appreciated. Winterson's fluid characters express a diverse range of sexual preferences and so her work is capable of speaking to all, regardless of sexuality. This study shows how her female characters can be counted as practitioners of sexual fetishism, and how sexual perversity, deviance and dissidence, at certain points, can be considered normal due to the situation and the influences of internal and external forces. Winterson presents in her texts contemporary and alternative practices of sexual fetishism, in which preferences and choices are fluid and mobile and not the reserve of any specific gender. Her fiction indicates how each individual in the society has the right to equality and the freedom to choose the object of their pleasures and desires. Often, consensual, but atypical, sexual practices are performed, and non-consensual acts endured, in order to survive in difficult, dangerous and even deadly situations. The discussion of the texts in this section, as throughout the book, has shown how Winterson's characters endure and enact the processes of disavowal and avowal in their search for replacements and substitutions for lost objects of desire. Alternative fetishism is shown to be a positive act that transforms the negative aspects of extreme sexual obsession, rather than a pathological symptom and practice; the disavowal of the lost object or unobtainable desire becomes an avowal for its substitute, and so the sexually fetishized replacement produces a beneficial effect for the subject. When the conditions are favourable, this procedure allows an individual to view and assess their sexual desires and activities from an ethically and politically aware position.

Conclusion

As discussed in each of the preceding sections, Winterson's work has contributed positive representations of an alternative fetishism in contemporary literature. Her distinctive notions of the body, gender and sexuality go beyond conventional boundaries and hetero/homo binaries. Winterson, in her correspondence with me, writes: 'I am proud to have been a part of the change in attitudes towards gender and sexuality.'[1] Winterson's overriding fetish is language, and it is through language that the fetish objects of the body, food and sex are revitalized and reconceptualized. Her character's relationships with the body, food and sex – sometimes simultaneously – reveal the fluid and changeable nature of gender, sexuality and identity in her texts, which are also capable of stimulating great emotions. The distinctive features of this study include its proposal of a new way at looking at fetishism and its contribution to current critical debates regarding the body, desire and pleasure. A central argument in this study is that Winterson's novels portray a mode of fetishism that cannot be explicated by the phallocentric notions of Freudian psychoanalysis and which resists the restrictive categorizing of later theories of female and lesbian fetishism. By reading her work in light of an alternative fetishism in which the focus on the substitute object offers real succour to the subject in response to lost or unobtainable objects of desire, and which operates without reliance on a fixed gender position, new pathways of understanding are opened into Winterson's work. Alternative fetishism becomes a daily practice of the individual to benefit the mind and body, while also relating to wider issues of community and society.

Winterson's texts create worlds that reflect and exaggerate reality, giving hope of acceptance to each individual by encouraging the expression and performance of their desires in society. The fetish objects discussed in each section have been shown to contain many layers of significance in respect to issues of gender, sexuality and identity, and these objects also demonstrate how contemporary perceptions of fetishism are fluid and contingent on the situations faced by each individual. The application of alternative fetishism as a critical method of enquiry in Winterson's texts is a vital approach in analysing the multiple meanings of her work. These significant fetish objects – the body, food and sex – have been used to examine the manifold metaphoric and symbolic meanings employed by Winterson to engage with culture, psychology and philosophy. She uses figurative language to convey deep, evocative meaning in her texts, and her technique of using fantasy and the imagination to consider and contest individual subjectivity serves to further complicate the connection between bodies, pleasures and desires. For example, many of Winterson's female characters are either androgynous or possess animalistic characteristics. Such unorthodox depictions of the body serve as metaphoric material for the remapping of social norms and the disputing of prevailing ideologies.

As this book has discussed, Winterson's fetishistic language of obsession provides the foundation for the fetishizing of the body, food and sex, illustrating that these objects and activities are not merely receptacles for compulsive habits; they are capable of relaying deeper messages about the behaviour, personality, beliefs and practices of individuals and communities in society. Therefore, it is clear that Winterson's work represents an alternative fetishism, as she fluidly intermingles the negative and positive connotations of substitution, disavowal and avowal. Each section of this book has stated that the object and subject of fetishism represent substitutions for the desired thing or person, and that at times the process can lead to insanity, either temporarily or permanently. The distinctive and beneficial aspect of this alternative fetishism is the way this negative potential can be transmuted into positive outcomes for the individual, offering them ways to survive, and even thrive, in society. In all of Winterson's novels, there is much fluidity in the realms of desire and pleasure, and the texts depict the way the fetish objects are connected with extremes of desire, mediated through the flux of shifting genders, sexualities and identities. The object of fetishism does not have a singular signification, rather it is an amalgamation of physical, cultural and ethical facets. Alternative fetishism reveals how language itself is capable of bringing to light this more textured and nuanced interpretation of internal and external human behaviours as it responds to political, economic and patriarchal power, as well as to primal passions.

A variety of forces affect the way in which Winterson's characters project their gender, sexuality and identity onto the other; for example, in Part I, 'Bodily fetishism', Villanelle's webbed feet, a unique biological feature, are objects and subjects of fetishism for the other, in this instance, the Queen of Spades. Also, Villanelle's cross-dressing and chameleonic nature originate from both an inbuilt desire for, and an obsession with, freedom. Her character is fluid and mobile from the need to survive in a male-dominated society. In a further example, external authority and inner desire influence Napoleon's political and sexual power. In order to effectively represent the multiple elements that contribute to the complexity of her characters, Winterson uses the inventive language of fetishism to generate a more nuanced, less simplistic understanding of peculiar acts. In the end, Winterson's characters are bound by a complex exchange of desire and pleasure in internal and external environments that complicate any easy understanding of their deeds, virtues and vices. The female and male body in her texts are equally capable of performing actions regarded as masculine and feminine. Fetishism of the body occurs when a person becomes fixated with its disjunctive physicality; the body consequently gains an excess value and becomes an object of excessive worship. This act of extreme obsession turns normative desire into diverse desire as a substitute for the actual object, and the rendering of the body into separate parts enables its fetishizing regardless of gender and sexuality.

As discussed in Part II, 'Food fetishism', Winterson's depiction of the political, cultural and sexual beliefs associated with food results in a further indication of the fluidity of gender, sexuality and identity. Winterson creates unorthodox presentations of the preparation and consumption of food, and through the discourse of alternative fetishism she shows different perspectives of each individual or community in society. By playfully using metaphoric language, the terminology in her novels makes manifest the fetish practices linked to the making and eating of meals. This not only reveals how fluid pleasures and desires embedded in the self and the other are challenged by political, cultural and sexual norms, but also how, in turn, the alternative fetishizing of these pleasures and desires creates a countering response to these normative challenges. Winterson's writing on food agrees with Probyn's statement: 'pleasure and ethics, sex and food are about breaking up the strict moralities which constrain us.'[2] Reading about the preparation and consumption of food in Winterson's novels is a way of understanding gender and sexuality within the complex relations of power, love, loss, quest, sex, pleasure, politics and religion. For instance, in *Boating for Beginners* the convenience of frozen food leads to societal schisms and fears of sexual anarchy. Thus, food is never simply subsistence but contains multiple significances connected to politics and the economy, as well as to culture and society as a whole.

Likewise, in Part III, 'Sexual fetishism', physical pleasure is linked with the psychological world through extreme internal desires and external influences. The subject of an alternative sexual fetishism becomes obsessed and reacts according to that obsession, and most of the time, it involves arduous consequences, as has been shown in the discussion. For instance, Villanelle in *The Passion* is accustomed to using both her masculine and feminine sexual characteristics to survive. Although Dog-Woman in *Sexing the Cherry* is the opposite of Villanelle in terms of conventional female perceptions of beauty, both women still enjoy their ability to perform in both feminine and masculine worlds, physically and sexually. In *Written on the Body*, Louise, following the extinction of passion in her culturally and socially sanctioned relationship with her husband, takes refuge in sexual pleasure with another person. Elizabeth Southern in *The Daylight Gate* is presented as a hermaphrodite sexually, physically and emotionally – she too enjoys her ability to exist simultaneously in two worlds. Christopher Southworth, despite the lack of a penis, manages to give pleasure to his lover, which shows that having a penis is not necessarily a symbol of masculinity in Winterson's invented worlds.

The sexual act is itself an object of fetishism for many of Winterson's characters and plays a vital role in the various practices and performances that drive an individual's behaviour. Winterson presents both the pathological practices of sexual fetishism, that is, those deemed immoral and psychologically damaging by society, and practices that can be perceived as beneficial, such as those founded on the need to survive, or performed solely for the satisfaction of the self and the other. Her characters engaged in beneficial acts of fetishism tend towards sexual ambiguity, either in their physical bodies or in their pursuit of diverse pleasures and desires, and this reclamation of the positive aspects of their sexuality encourages them to enjoy their existence. Their bodies and desires deconstruct any notion of stable physical identity and natural, gendered desire, encouraging the reader to accept difference. The body's seeking of pleasure is presented in Winterson's fiction through a language of sexual dissidence, which can be understood through Lacan's description of unbridled desire, which is 'eternally stretching towards the desire of something else'.[3] This dissidence, a refusal to be satisfied with what is immanent, challenges and extends the boundaries of orthodox views of the subject in modern society. Winterson presents both normative and contemporary ideas of sexual differences, giving her texts a powerful method of interpreting and presenting the subject.

Each fetish object forms a significant element in the multivalence of her writing and the portrayal of the individual in society. As a consequence, Winterson gives her characters opportunities to experience both masculine and feminine aspects of life, regardless of their gender and sexuality, through her distinctive use of fantasy and the imagination. Therefore, it is no overstatement to suggest Winterson's language is the driving energy behind her novels, their poetry and cadence capable of creating both psychological and emotional atmospheres – rarely literal, always lateral – that present both despair and satisfaction. Christy L. Burns says Winterson's 'repeated phrases work like musical motifs, associatively accruing different levels of meaning across [her] text'; they also function to complicate any attempt to conclusively comprehend the world and individual subjectivity.[4] Winterson refers to language as a 'tightrope', which invites the creation, as she puts it, of 'audaciousness and delicateness'.[5] A tightrope compels the walker (analogically, the writer) to simultaneously present a level of boldness in the very participation in such an act, as well as a gentleness or subtlety in the performance of balancing the body on the tightrope (in other words, the act of writing). This study has shown the counterpoise achieved by Winterson's writing through the analysis of its multi-layered meanings and multi-dimensional perceptions that still manage to relate closely with political, social and cultural specifics. Winterson stays true to her words, both philosophically and artistically; the use of metaphors and symbols in her works serve not only to reimagine historical, conventional and contemporary language of gender, sexuality and identity, but also, through the multiple meanings of the fetish objects of the body, food and sex, they challenge orthodox notions of subjectivity and thus produce diverse presentations of pleasures and desires in society.

I have proposed that Winterson's texts display an alternative fetishism that recasts the negative connotations of pathological fetishism by also depicting the positive associations of obsessive acts and granting the power of choice to the individual. The discussion in each section has affirmed that the mechanisms of a fluid and alternative fetishism emerge in Winterson's narratives, which portray a diversity of pleasures and desires through the deconstruction of the body and the remapping of gender, sexuality and identity. Hence, the concept of alternative fetishism allows the investigation of the various psychological, physical, social, sexual, cultural and political perceptions and meanings in Winterson's texts. As mentioned in the Introduction, Winterson's works reward an analysis through a wide range of critical thinkers and their theories; the views of Butler are especially fruitful when it comes to her depictions of language and the body. Butler regards the body's materiality as produced through a system of signs that translate the language of diverse acts of pleasures and desire into an ambiguity of gender and sexuality; she writes, 'Language and materiality are not opposed, for language both is and refers to that which is material, and what is material never fully escapes from the process by which it is signified.'[6] Winterson's living language presents her version of the body's pleasures through acts of fragmentation and re-imagination that refigure notions of gender and sexuality as they multiply and shift between normative and contemporary views, creating alternative perspectives in, and for, society.

Recurring themes of boundaries, loss, power, desire, love and history are presented through the prominent fetish objects of the body, food and sex; these objects in Winterson's invented realities are fluid and mobile, capable of communicating latent meanings of the inner pleasures and desires of the self and the other. Winterson's deconstruction of the body and her fluid remapping of gender and sexuality are also formed by the creative, significant and imaginative language of internal and external desires that revolve around the fetish objects. The alternative fetishism in Winterson's invented reality is always mobile and fluid, showing the relationships between normative and contemporary, as well as negative and positive aspects of fetishism. The significant fetish objects of the body, food and sex allow Winterson's writing to speculate on the diverse perceptions and meaning of the subject. Fetishism is often misunderstood as only the practice of a taboo sexual behaviour or an extreme obsession with something or someone that is unnatural or immoral. However, as discussed in this book, Winterson's versions of fetishism are alternative as they are not necessarily negative; at times the negative is transformed into a positive as the substitute replaces the lost object. The act of substitution, as demonstrated in the preceding sections, can help a person to manage the competing claims of the id, the ego and the superego, and to cope with the societal demands of biological, psychological and cultural recognition in the self and other. Therefore, fetishism in Winterson's texts is not limited to any outmoded and reductive view as only deriving from a sexual origin. Rather, alternative fetishism stretches beyond sex to involve culture, society and politics in extreme obsessions. The close relationship between anthropology and psychology in Winterson's novels is shown by how all her characters seek pleasure, either in reality or fantasy, through the object of alternative fetishism.

This study has affirmed that the wellspring of Winterson's literary creativity lies in the crucial, qualitative difference between the experiences that produce despair and the ones that spark satisfaction, and, as has been demonstrated in this study, Winterson plumbs the depths of her psyche to extract and present profound insights, at once intensely personal yet poignantly universal. Further, this study of alternative fetishism has offered an important insight, and an influential concept, for the reading of not only Winterson's works, but also other literature, and art in general, as it enables the psychological, anthropological and cultural study of human behaviours and practices. As continuously illustrated in this book, orthodox notions of fetishism are transformed into alternative forms that challenge the boundaries and desires of the self and the other. Studies of gender and sexuality tend to focus on these issues as narrowly twinned, often insufficiently engaging with the interconnectedness of other elements, such as religion and social class, in moulding the face and nature of gender, sexuality and identity. This book has shown that the creation of these subjects stems from a more complex mix, which in Winterson's works is the amalgamation of all such factors. While studies have been done on particular aspects of sex and sexuality, gender and identity, Winterson's alternative views and perceptions of these subjects are vital in this field as they show her notion of the fluid relationship between ethics, ideology and the individual. As such, new ideas about the body, gender and sexuality arise; Schabert observes, 'the body which reappears in contemporary art as in contemporary literature in order to break the cultural monopoly of disembodied intelligence, of abstraction, spirituality, and virtual reality, is not a body outside culture, it is the body of an alternative culture'.[7] In this context, Winterson is one of those authors who has created significant bodies and incarnated fluid pleasures and desires, regardless of gender and sexuality.

The recurring fetish objects of the body, food and sex in her work project an alternative approach to subjectivity in their multiple meanings. Winterson uses art to challenge and destabilize the normative views of the subject; she writes, '[it] is extraordinary what art can do'.[8] Therefore, the radical roots of Winterson's distinctive and heterodox approach to gender, sexuality and identity result in the alternative fetishism in her work. She presents a more open-ended and positive fetishism, which follows the pathways of adaptation and change. The essentialist and constructionist viewpoints in the study of gender, sexuality and identity have tended to obscure the actual convergence of innate desire and social convention, which can fluidly form new combinations amid interdependence. Gender, sexuality and identity are complex structures that simultaneously hold together physical, biological, cultural and social elements, and this study has shown that Winterson's works are sufficiently bold and unconventional to explore this expansive area through the lens of alternative fetishism. Moreover, her texts have their own perceptions of gender, sexuality and identity that bypass a merely gendered attitude towards the subject, as they capture a host of sexual, cultural, political and moral components. Hence, as this study has demonstrated, theories derived from Freud, Lacan, Foucault, Marx and Butler enable divergent approaches to the subjects of sexuality, identity and gender. This book has contended that these theories meet in Winterson's paradoxical notion of the individual in which the extreme behaviours and personalities of many of her characters are worked out in different circumstances. Regardless of the origins of gender and sexuality, whether essentialist or constructionist, Winterson's novels represent the fluid, the mobile and the multiple.

The concept of alternative fetishism can contribute to the further understanding of Winterson's works as she utilizes both normative and contemporary ideas of fetishism – embodied in the fetish objects of the body, food and sex – that are significant in the relationship between anthropology, philosophy and psychology in literature, and art as a whole. As examined in the preceding sections, Winterson's texts evince that it is important to understand the different choices and preference of gender, sexuality and identity in the everyday life of human behaviour. Her works display a desire to exceed historical, conventional and contemporary boundaries not only to illustrate the fluidity of the situations each individual faces in life, but also to relate the effects of culture, psychology and sexuality on the body. Through Winterson's characters, the multiple meanings of language reveal a diversity of ethical, ideological and political viewpoints each community or individual embodies. For example, in *Gut Symmetries*, Stella and Jove's maritime journey suggests a metaphor of new adventures and new visions. But this vision is marred when their boat becomes stranded at sea, suggesting that every journey has its obstacles and consequences that have to be surpassed before one can achieve what one desires, especially if these desires fall beyond societal norms. Similarly, in *Art & Lies*, Sappho, Handel and Picasso meet on the train, where all their stories commence; voicing their unfortunate situations in life, each of them has their own narrative to tell the reader. Jordan, in *Sexing the Cherry*, also willingly embarks upon voyages into the unknown – all of which reflect the search for self-knowledge in their worlds of fluid and shifting gender, sexuality and identity, and these journeys present the use of fetish objects to reveal the various motives behind human behaviour.

A distinguishing feature of this study is that it has combined attention to, and intervention in, current critical debates surrounding the body, sex, pleasure, desire and fetishism in contemporary literature. It has explored, through bodily, food and sexual fetishism, the implications of the recent critical turn to the deconstructed body, trans issues and the remapping of gender, sexuality and identity. In Winterson's writing, fluid pleasures and desires play a vital role in refiguring and interrogating the fetishized body, and the reconceptualization of fluid gender, sexuality and identity offer a new way to study fetishism as a quotidian and consensual practice in society today. The alternative fetishism in Winterson's texts is revealed by the destabilization of the normative framework of fetishism and the consequent combination of the historical and contemporary definitions of fetishism into her alternative version. The alternative fetishism shown to be present in Winterson's works functions through acts of disavowal and avowal and contests established notions of fetishism. Disavowal is a process of denial that both consciously suppresses and unconsciously represses the desire, whereas avowal is when this process becomes conscious, accepted and adapted. As this study has illustrated, Winterson's texts show that disavowal is not necessarily a negative or repressed act; instead she converts this repression into an expressed act or avowal. In other words, her characters make use of substitutes to continuing living and cherishing the situations they face. Therefore, the acts of disavowal and avowal that many of her characters effectuate embrace both the negative and the positive consequences of obsession to create an alternative fetishism. As such, these behaviours at times invert the either/or of desire as realized through objects and subjects of fetishism, defying any notion of it as prejudicial and pernicious to the mind and body. Therefore, the alternative fetishism in Winterson's writing can be an acceptable practice in society and performable in a subject's daily life. The study of alternative fetishism in her works makes a further contribution to revealing the performative character of aesthetic and cultural acts through both normative and contemporary ideas of fetishism.

Throughout the discussion, the main argument of this study shows that Winterson's work reveals an alternative fetishism, in which the negative and positive connotations of substitution, disavowal and avowal are fluidly mixed. Furthermore, while the subject's gender and sexuality may feed into the particular expression of the fetishistic practice, they do not form its defining and demarcating characteristics as alternative fetishism operates beyond restrictive and reductive identity formations. It is still difficult today to resist the norms of given gender and sexuality, and in many ways, the fight for equality is more pressing than ever as issues of power relations in respect to oppressed others seem to worsen. This study has illustrated how Winterson's work presents a person's choices and preferences of gender, sexuality and identity, and she refers to her participation, through the impact of her words, phrases and books – that is, her living language – when she writes, '[m]y work has been useful and powerful, and separate to my work, I continue to be a provocateur'.[9] Winterson's literary fiction, for its activity, critical thinking and popular reception, is vitally urgent today, and this study has identified and recognized its importance in relation to the fluidity of culture, psychology, physicality and sexuality, for each individual. Winterson's writing shows an enormous courage in the risks it takes, the belief it shows and the practices it offers to fight the oppression of social norms. Returning to the critical reception of her works discussed at the beginning of this book, it is now possible to state that her rigorous calls for acts of diversity are aligned with her refusal to be restricted to any one literary category, as she understands each individual to be unique and fluid. As illustrated, she urges readers, scholars and critics to grasp the wildness and freedom of meanings and interpretations in her works. Further, this study has claimed that, for Winterson, language is not merely a medium of communication – it is a living presence that naturally invites the amalgamation of form and content to enhance the understanding and acceptance of ambiguous ideas of politics, culture and ethics in society. Hence, the fetish objects act as a medium to convey the fluidity of each character in her novels through her alternative and non-judgemental depictions of individualism.

The fetishism in Winterson's work is distinctive when compared with other contemporary writers; for instance, in the work of Zadie Smith and Salman Rushdie the effects of race are more prominent, whereas for Winterson, the quotidian ubiquity of the body, food and sex, which means fetishism can be practised by all, sometimes seems to erase racial difference. As we have seen, Winterson avows herself a feminist but resists categorization by her sexuality. This stance increases the universality of her contributions to contemporary literature, as Winterson refuses to target solely a queer readership. However, having mentioned Smith and Rushdie, the comparative lack of racial diversity in Winterson's work is problematic and hinders a discussion of the links between intersectionality and the practice of alternative fetishism in her novels and indicates that this area is worthy of further investigation in a future study.

This book has shown that Winterson's writing conveys in its diversity a challenge to, and refutation of, the facile and the conventional and that espousing the complex and the alternative will aid understanding and acceptance. Her narrators observe and bring forth change in their internal and external lives in ways that force the reader to examine the reality of their world. Winterson's works represent political, economic and ethical difficulties that society perhaps finds too difficult to consider openly or directly. Hence, one of the effective tools to convey societal dissatisfaction is through the medium of literature. Her texts utilize alternative fetishism, altering the normative view, to allow a multiplicity of perceptions on humanity, which drastically alter the self and the other. Winterson's writing is a representation of psychological pluralism, as this study has demonstrated; she is a writer who creates narratives that are simultaneously aggressive and natural, sensitive and rigid, dominant and submissive, regardless of the gender and sexuality of the characters in them. Her protagonists invariably have a fluid and shifting repertoire of responses, and they interact with the world according to the muddied and varied spectrum of opportunities they encounter.

This book also suggests that Winterson's texts need to be viewed in light of developing trends discernible in this post-postmodern juncture. Transgender, transhumanist and post-humanist issues need to be analysed further to investigate the direction the contemporary world is taking and might go on to take. The notion that post-postmodernism could strengthen the bridge between literature and life, to the benefit of both, is expressed by Nealon: 'Within such a rethinking, even literature's seeming uselessness could be recoded from a stoic, prophylactic avoidance to a positive (maybe even joyful) form of critical engagement with contemporary biopolitical and economic life.'[10] In particular, the idea of New Sincerity offers a fruitful way to engage with Winterson's work since her writing reflects so deeply an intellectual movement that recentres faith and compassion in the human subject. As Timotheus Vermeulen writes, the end of postmodernism has rediscovered 'within the postmodern the modern, within apathy hope, within irony sincerity, within distrust (of grand narratives) belief, within the representative presence'.[11] All of which can be used to describe the features of Winterson's work, and to which I would add: 'within conventional fetishism the alternative'.

Appendix

Email from Jeanette Winterson

19 August 2017
Re: Interview questions

Hi Shareena,
Thanks for your questions. I don't think I can answer them as such, because I don't think about myself or my work in this way. I am a feminist – as is any sane woman. Feminism isn't a label, it is a political position, and I believe that writers need to be actively involved in the world, and yes, to make a difference where we can. I don't like labels though – and they are usually a way of reducing or confining a person or their work, and mostly unhelpful. I write for anyone who is interested in books, in thinking, in expanding their imagination, female or male, any sexual orientation etc. That said, I am proud to have been a part of the change in attitudes towards gender and sexuality. My work has been useful and powerful, and separate to my work, I continue to be a provocateur for change.

As for books – well I had plenty of books to read, in the library mainly, and I have written about that extensively in WBH, and I have been clear that the Bible is a great resource for any writer and was for me. Kids from poor working-class backgrounds didn't have access to much in the 1960s, but libraries were wonderful places – quiet cathedrals for the mind. And church was a community that taught me the power of collective action, and the capacity of individuals to change – and to experience life at a level beyond the daily impoverishment of circumstances.

How you are brought up will always influence you but biography and biology, any more than gender and sexuality, don't explain how we turn out the way we do. People are stranger than the facts about them.

Re food – I don't have a thing about food – and I don't think our diet was worse than most kids eating now – it was a lot better – no e numbers or additives or transfats or general crap. To me though, there is no body mind split. We are one. We work from who we are, and that includes the body – the body isn't a fragile vessel for our minds – and if we ever manage to upload consciousness from our bodies to a more durable state, we will find that our consciousness changes profoundly – because it no longer belongs to a body.

Best, JW

Questions for Jeanette Winterson

1. You have talked of 'being driven by a need to preach to people and convert them', these days for art's sake rather than for God's; why does this role of preacher appeal to you so much?
2. Fluid representations of gender and sexuality are critical components of your work; do you feel a responsibility to change perceptions involving these issues with your readers and those you address at your public talks?
3. It seems the mind and the body are equal partners in the search for sustenance in your work; is it fair to say the limited diet available in your youth led to a hunger for, and obsession with, food in your writing?
4. In your work, the body is a significant subject and object; how well do you think language is able to capture its processes when faced with the demands of love, sex and loss?
5. You refuse to be labelled or categorized as a feminist, lesbian-feminist, modernist, or postmodernist writer, but what do you think about post-postmodernism as a mode of art production that rejects the cynicism and ironic detachment of postmodernism? Is this description of an intellectual movement that reintroduces, among other positive qualities, faith and compassion to the human subject reflective of your writing?

Notes

Introduction

1 Jeanette Winterson, *Frankissstein* (London: Jonathan Cape, 2019), 2.
2 Dean Bakopoulos, '"The Gap of Time," by Jeanette Winterson', *New York Times*, 25 October 2015. Available online: http://www.nytimes.com/2015/10/25/books/review/the-gap-of-time-by-jeanette-winterson.html?_r=1 (accessed 29 June 2020).
3 Jeanette Winterson, *Art Objects: Essays on Ecstasy and Effrontery* (New York: Vintage International, 1997), 76.
4 Eleanor Wachtel, *Writers & Company: New Conversations with CBC Radio's Eleanor Wachtel* (Toronto: Vintage Canada, 1997), 139.
5 Jeanette Winterson interview with Jeremy Isaac, *The Late Show: Face to Face with Jeanette Winterson*, 28 June 1994. Available online: http://www.bbc.co.uk/iplayer/episode/p00nw1xh/the-late-show-face-to-face-jeanette-winterson (accessed 29 June 2020).
6 Andrew Dickson, '*The Gap of Time* by Jeanette Winterson – review', *Evening Standard*, 24 September 2015. Available online: https://www.standard.co.uk/lifestyle/books/the-gap-of-time-by-jeanette-winterson-review-a2955231.html (accessed 29 June 2020).
7 Melanie Klein, *The Selected Melanie Klein*, ed. by Juliet Mitchell (New York: The Free Press, 1986), 70.
8 Ibid., 72.
9 Nikki Sullivan, *A Critical Introduction to Queer Theory* (New York: NYU Press, 2003), 168.
10 Massimo Fusillo, *The Fetish: Literature, Cinema, Visual Art*, trans. by Thomas Haskell Simpson (London: Bloomsbury, 2017), 8.
11 Sigmund Freud, *Three Essays on the Theory of Sexuality*, ed. and trans. by James Strachey (New York: Basic Books, 2000). See also, Sigmund Freud, *General Psychological Theory: Papers on Metapsychology* (New York: Touchstone, 2008).
12 Naomi Schor, 'Female Fetishism: The Case of George Sand', *Poetics Today: The Female Body in Western Culture: Semiotic*, 6, no. 1/2 (1985): 301–10 (305).
13 Juliet Mitchell and Jacqueline Rose (eds), *Feminine Sexuality: Jacques Lacan and the École Freudienne*, trans. by Jacqueline Rose (London: Macmillan Press, 1982), 90.
14 Mitchell and Rose, *Feminine Sexuality*, 90.

15 Judith Butler, 'Revisiting Bodies and Pleasures', *Theory, Culture & Society*, 16, no. 2 (1999): 11–20 (11).
16 Alfred C. Kinsey, Wardell B. Pomeroy and Clyde E. Martin, *Sexual Behavior in the Human Male* (Philadelphia, PA: W.B. Saunders, 1948), 197.
17 Winterson, *Art Objects*, 58.
18 Sullivan, *Critical Introduction to Queer Theory*, 168.
19 Paul Gebhard, 'Fetishism and Sado-Masochism', *Science and Psychoanalysis*, 25, no. 15 (1969): 71–80.
20 Lorraine Gamman and Merja Makinen, *Female Fetishism: A New Look* (London: Lawrence & Wishart, 1994), 37–46.
21 Ibid., 15.
22 Teresa de Lauretis, *Practice of Love: Lesbian Sexuality and Perverse Desire* (Indianapolis: Indiana University Press, 1994), 266.
23 Winterson, *Art Objects*, 171.
24 Ibid., 166.
25 Ibid., 167.
26 Ibid., 27.
27 Ibid., 153.
28 Jeanette Winterson, *Why Be Happy When You Could Be Normal?* (London: Jonathan Cape, 2011), 33.
29 Winterson, *Art Objects,* 119; 153.
30 Winterson, *Why Be Happy?*, 37.
31 Winterson, *Art Objects*, 126.
32 Ibid., 156.
33 Ibid., 153.
34 Ibid., 93.
35 Winterson, *Why Be Happy?*, 40.
36 Winterson, *Art Objects*, 158.
37 Ibid., 131.
38 Ibid., 4.
39 Ibid., 187.
40 Ibid.
41 Roland Barthes, *The Pleasure of the Text*, trans. by Richard Miller (New York: Noonday, 1975), 31.
42 Ibid., 17.
43 Winterson, *Art Objects*, 44.
44 Barthes, *The Pleasure of the Text*, 51.
45 Ibid., 35.
46 Margaret Reynolds and Jonathan Noakes, *Jeanette Winterson: The Essential Guide* (London: Vintage, 2003), 22.

47 Winterson, *Art Objects*, 38.
48 Ursula K. Le Guin, 'Head Cases', *The Guardian*, 22 September 2007. Available online: https://www.theguardian.com/books/2007/sep/22/sciencefictionfantasyand horror.fiction (accessed 29 June 2020).
49 Winterson, *Art Objects*, 189.
50 Ibid., 26.
51 Judith Butler, *Gender Trouble: Feminism and the Subversion of Identity* (London: Routledge, 2006).
52 Ibid., 105.
53 Winterson, *Art Objects*, 167.
54 In correspondence with the author; see Appendix.
55 Winterson, *Art Objects*, 168.
56 Ibid., 169.
57 Barthes, *The Pleasure of the Text*, 35.
58 Sonya Andermahr, *Jeanette Winterson* (Basingstoke: Palgrave Macmillan, 2009), 128.
59 Winterson, *Art Objects*, 35.
60 In correspondence with the author; see Appendix.
61 Winterson, *Art Objects*, 37.
62 Winterson, *Art Objects*, 41.
63 Ibid., 165.
64 Lucasta Miller, '*The Gap of Time* by Jeanette Winterson, book review: A modern rewriting', *Independent*, 1 October 2015. Available online: http://www.independent.co.uk/arts-entertainment/books/reviews/the-gap-of-time-by-jeanette-winterson-book-review-a6675676.html (accessed 29 June 2020).
65 In correspondence with the author; see Appendix.
66 *The Late Show: Face to Face with Jeanette Winterson*; Wachtel, *Writers & Company*, 141.
67 Winterson, *Art Objects,* 157.
68 Susana Onega, *Jeanette Winterson: Contemporary British Novelists* (Manchester: Manchester University Press, 2006), 132.
69 Jeanette Winterson, *Gut Symmetries* (London: Granta Books, 1997), 13.
70 Peter Childs, *Contemporary Novelists: British Fiction Since 1970* (Basingstoke: Palgrave Macmillan, 2012), 275.
71 Joanna Kavenna, '*The Gap of Time* by Jeanette Winterson, review: "poignant"', *Telegraph*, 1 October 2015. Available online: http://www.telegraph.co.uk/books/what-to-read/the-gap-of-time-jeanette-winterson-review/ (accessed 29 June 2020).
72 *The Late Show: Face to Face with Jeanette Winterson*.
73 Winterson, *Art Objects*, 7–15.
74 Ibid., 72.

75 T. S. Eliot, 'Tradition and the individual talent', *The Sacred Wood: Essays on Poetry and Criticism*, 4th edn (London: The Fountain Library, 1934), 59 [italics in original].
76 Lucasta Miller, 'A Mind of One's Own', *The Guardian*, 22 October 2005. Available online: https://www.theguardian.com/books/2005/oct/22/fiction.jeanettewinterson (accessed 29 June 2020).
77 Bakopoulos, '*The Gap of Time*, by Jeanette Winterson', *New York Times* (2015).
78 Winterson, *Art Objects*, 113.
79 Reynolds and Noakes, *Jeanette Winterson*, 11.
80 Alexei Yurchak, cited in, Wolfgang Funk, *The Literature of Reconstruction: Authentic Fiction in the New Millennium* (London: Bloomsbury, 2015), 100.
81 Eliot, 'Traditional and the Individual Talent', *The Sacred Wood*, 53–4.
82 Winterson, *Art Objects*, 129–30.
83 Lisa Moore, 'Teledildonics: Virtual Lesbians in the Fiction of Jeanette Winterson', in *Sexy Bodies: Strange Carnalities of Feminism*, ed, by Elizabeth Grosz and Elspeth Probyn (Abingdon: Routledge, 1995), 104–27 (107).
84 *The Late Show: Face to Face with Jeanette Winterson*.
85 In correspondence with the author; see Appendix.
86 Gamman and Makinen, *Female Fetishism*, 44.
87 See Jacques Lacan and Wladimir Granoff, 'Fetishism: The Symbolic, the Imaginary and the Real', in *Perversions, Psychodynamics and Therapy*, ed. by Sándor Lorand (New York: Gramercy Books, 1956), 265–76.
88 Gamman and Makinen, *Female Fetishism*, 95.
89 Jon Stratton, *The Desirable Body: Cultural Fetishism and the Erotics of Consumption* (Manchester: Manchester University Press, 1996).
90 Stratton, *The Desirable Body*, 87–115.
91 Winterson, *Art Objects*, 123.
92 Jeffrey Nealon, *Post-Postmodernism: Or, the Cultural Logic of Just-In-Time Capitalism*, (Stanford, CA: Stanford University Press, 2012), 156.
93 Michael Foucault, *The History of Sexuality, Vol. 1: An Introduction*, trans. Robert Hurley (New York: Vintage, 1990), 157.
94 Judith Butler, *Bodies That Matter: On the Discursive Limits of 'Sex'* (London: Routledge, 1993), 9.
95 Butler, *Gender Trouble*, 33.
96 Ibid., 34.
97 Ibid., 22.
98 Ibid., xv.
99 Nealon, *Post-Postmodernism*, 170.
100 Elizabeth Grosz, *Volatile Bodies: Toward A Corporeal Feminism* (Indianapolis: Indiana University Press, 1994), 193.

101 Jeanette Winterson, 'Food 2', 1 September 2005. Available online: http://www.jeanettewinterson.com/journalism/food-2/ (accessed 29 June 2020).
102 For more information on the gendering of food, see Jeremy MacClancy, *Consuming Culture* (London: Chapmans, 1992), 146–7.
103 Jeanette Winterson, 'Once upon a Life', *The Guardian*, 13 June 2010. Available online: http://www.theguardian.com/lifeandstyle/2010/jun/13/once-upon-a-life-jeanette-winterson (accessed 29 June 2020).
104 Ibid.
105 Jeanette Winterson, 'Food', 10 January 2005. Available online: http://www.jeanettewinterson.com/journalism/food/ (accessed 29 June 2020).
106 Winterson, 'Once upon a Life', *The Guardian* (2010).
107 Elspeth Probyn, 'Beyond Food/Sex: Eating and an Ethics of Eating', *Theory, Culture & Society*, 16, no. 2 (1999): 215–28 (216); Arjun Appadurai, 'Gastro-Politics in Hindu South Asia', *American Ethnologist*, 8, no. 3 (1981): 494–511 (509).
108 Gamman and Makinen, *Female Fetishism*, 145.
109 Jeanette Winterson, *The Passion* (London: Vintage, 2001), 70.

Part I

1 Jeanette Winterson, *Written on the Body* (New York: Vintage International, 1994), 89.
2 Grosz, *Volatile Bodies*, 193.
3 Ina Schabert, 'Habeas Corpus 2000: The Return of the Body', *European Studies*, 16, no. 1 (2001), 87–115 (105).
4 Grosz, *Volatile Bodies*, xi.
5 Winterson, *Art Objects*, 36.
6 Grosz, *Volatile Bodies*, 146.
7 De Lauretis, *Practice of Love*, 229 [italics in original].

Chapter 1

1 Grosz, *Volatile Bodies*, 27.
2 Ibid., 85.
3 The pronouns 'they' and 'them' are used in this study when discussing the Unnamed Narrator.
4 Heather Nunn, '*Written on the Body*: An Anatomy of Horror, Melancholy and Love', *Women: A Cultural Review*, 7, no. 1 (1996): 16–27 (25).
5 Winterson, *Written on the Body*, 25.
6 Ibid., 113.

7 Jeanette Winterson, *Oranges Are Not the Only Fruit* (New York: Grove Press, 1985), 104.
8 Ibid., 134.
9 Ibid., 102.
10 Ibid., 127.
11 Ibid., 127.
12 Ibid., 11.
13 Ibid., 56.
14 Sidney Axinn, *The Logic of Hope: Extensions of Kant's View of Religion* (Amsterdam: Rodopi, 1994), 20.
15 Winterson, *Oranges*, 21–2.
16 Ibid., 23–4.
17 Ibid., 85.
18 Ibid., 30; 133; 131.
19 Winterson, *The Passion*, 17.
20 Ibid., 44.
21 Luce Irigaray, *This Sex Which is Not One*, trans. Catherine Porter (New York: Cornell University Press,1985), 81.
22 Winterson, *The Passion*, 101.
23 Ibid., 148.
24 Foucault, *The History of Sexuality, Vol. 1*, 48.
25 Winterson, *The Passion*, 38.
26 Ibid., 104.
27 Ibid., 20.
28 Grosz, *Volatile Bodies*, 146.
29 Winterson, *The Passion*, 24–5.
30 I use the pronouns 'they' and 'them' to refer to Ry.
31 Winterson, *Frankissstein*,73.
32 Ibid.
33 Ibid., 89.
34 Ibid.
35 Ibid., 157.
36 Ibid., 298.
37 Ibid., 159.
38 Grosz, *Volatile Bodies*, 187.
39 Gavin Keulks, 'Winterson's Recent Work: Navigating Realism and Postmodernism', in *Jeanette Winterson: A Contemporary Critical Guide*, ed. by Sonya Andermahr (London: Continuum International, 2007), 146–62.
40 Jeanette Winterson, *The PowerBook* (New York: Vintage, 2000), 39.
41 Ibid., 10–11.
42 Ibid., 3.

43 De Lauretis, *Practice of Love*, 262.
44 Ibid., 203.
45 Ibid., 70.
46 Andermahr, *Jeanette Winterson*, 104.
47 Jeanette Winterson, *Sexing the Cherry* (London: Vintage, 1996), 87–9.
48 Butler, *Gender Trouble*, 59.
49 Winterson, *Sexing the Cherry*, 32.
50 Grosz, *Volatile Bodies*, 119.
51 Winterson, *Sexing the Cherry*, 31.
52 Winterson, *The Passion*, 51.
53 Butler, *Gender Trouble*, 45.
54 Grosz, *Space, Time, and Perversion*, 33 [italics in original].

Chapter 2

1 Grosz, *Space, Time, and Perversion*, 84.
2 Ibid. [italics in original].
3 Winterson, *Art Objects*, 185.
4 Olu Jenzen, 'Reworking Linear Time: Queer Temporalities in Jeanette Winterson's *Sexing the Cherry* and *Art & Lies*', in *Winterson Narrating Time and Space*, ed. by Margaret J.-M. Sönmez and Mine Özyurt Kiliç (Newcastle: Cambridge Scholars Publishing, 2009), 48.
5 Grosz, *Space, Time, and Perversion*, 98.
6 Ibid., 99.
7 Jeanette Winterson, '*Gut Symmetries*'. Available online: http://www.jeanettewinterson.com/book/gut-symmetries/ (accessed 29 June 2020).
8 Winterson, *Written on the Body*, 29.
9 Ibid., 37.
10 Ibid., 82.
11 Jeanette Winterson, *Lighthousekeeping* (London: Fourth Estate, 2004), 150.
12 Winterson, *Written on the Body*, 91.
13 Ibid., 120.
14 Grosz, *Volatile Bodies*, 121.
15 Grosz, *Space, Time, and Perversion*, 86.
16 For more details, see Diana Gasparyan, 'Mirror for the Other: Problem of the Self in Continental Philosophy (From Hegel To Lacan)', *Integrative Psychological & Behavioural Science*, 48, no. 1 (2014): 1–17.
17 Winterson, *Written on the Body*, 20.
18 Ibid., 82.

19 Ibid., 119.
20 Grosz, *Space, Time, and Perversion*, 26.
21 Winterson, *Written on the Body*, 49.
22 Ibid.
23 Ibid., 95.
24 Ibid., 49.
25 Ibid., 117.
26 Ibid., 36.
27 Ibid., 89.
28 Grosz, *Volatile Bodies*, 117.
29 Winterson, *Written on the Body*, 89.
30 Ibid.
31 Butler, *Gender Trouble*, 176.
32 Winterson, *Written on the Body*, 9.
33 Ibid., 10–11.
34 Ibid., 12.
35 Winterson, *Written on the Body*, 76.
36 Ibid., 98.
37 Ibid., 156.
38 Winterson, *Written on the Body*, 20.
39 Grosz, *Space, Time, and Perversion*, 93.
40 Ibid., 150.
41 Ibid., 94.
42 Winterson, *Written on the Body*, 141.
43 Ibid.
44 Ibid.
45 T. S. Eliot, 'The Waste Land', *Collected Poems 1909–1962* (London: Faber and Faber, 1963), 63.
46 Winterson, *Written on the Body*, 111; 149.
47 Ibid., 111.
48 Grosz, *Volatile Bodies*, 117.
49 Winterson, *Written on the Body*, 48–9.
50 Ibid., 49.
51 Ibid., 190.
52 Winterson, *The Passion*, 102; 123.
53 Grosz, *Space, Time, and Perversion*, 104.
54 Winterson, *The PowerBook*, 108.
55 Winterson, *The Passion*, 54; 89.
56 Ibid., 98.
57 Ibid., 99.

58 Ibid.
59 Ibid.
60 Foucault, *The History of Sexuality, Vol. 1*, 78.
61 Winterson, *The Passion*, 19.
62 Grosz, *Space, Time, and Perversion*, 100.
63 Ibid., 109.
64 Ibid., 56.
65 Ibid., 67–8.
66 Kristeva, 'On the Melancholic Imaginary', 108.
67 Winterson, *The Passion*, 26.
68 Winterson, *Frankissstein*, 3.
69 Winterson, *Art Objects*, 146.
70 Ibid., 143.
71 Charlotte Trueman, '*Culture Crossover: Frankissstein: A Love Story*' (2019). Available online: https://www.techworld.com/tech-innovation/frankissstein-love-story-3701120/ (accessed 29 June 2020).
72 Winterson, *Frankissstein*, 43.
73 Ibid., 154.

Chapter 3

1 Michel Foucault, *Language, Counter-Memory, Practice: Selected Essays and Interviews*, ed. by Donald F. Bouchard (New York: Cornell University Press, 1980), 160.
2 Grosz, *Volatile Bodies*, 29.
3 Winterson, *Frankissstein*, 67.
4 Winterson, *The Passion*, 5; 13; 40; 69; 160.
5 Ibid., 43; 66; 73; 133.
6 Ibid., 160.
7 Ibid., 43.
8 Ibid., 103.
9 Ibid., 73.
10 Ibid., 86.
11 Ibid., 88.
12 Ibid., 88.
13 Ibid., 154.
14 Ibid., 134.
15 Ibid., 133.
16 Grosz, *Volatile Bodies*, 122

17 Winterson, *The Passion*, 157–8.
18 Kristeva, 'On the Melancholic Imaginary', 106 [italics in original].
19 Winterson, *The Passion*, 151.
20 Ibid., 86 [italics in original].
21 Winterson, *Written on the Body*, 13.
22 Ibid., 111.
23 Ibid.
24 Ibid.
25 Ibid., 280.
26 Winterson, *Sexing the Cherry*, 48.
27 Ibid.
28 Ibid.
29 Ibid.
30 Ibid., 52.
31 Winterson, *Oranges*, 108.
32 Ibid.
33 Winterson, *The PowerBook*, 5.
34 Sonya Andermahr, 'Cyberspace and the Body', in *British Fiction of the 1990s*, ed. by Nick Bentley (London: Routledge, 2005), 108.
35 Winterson, *The PowerBook*, 4.
36 Ibid., 203.
37 Ibid., 235–6.
38 Winterson, *Frankissstein*, 3.
39 Ibid., 81.
40 Ibid., 73.
41 Ibid., 36.
42 Ibid., 37.
43 Ibid., 38.
44 Ibid.
45 Ibid., 209.
46 Ibid., 153.
47 Jeanette Winterson, *Art Objects: Essays on Ecstasy and Effrontery* (New York: Vintage International, 1997), 171.
48 Grosz, *Space, Time, and Perversion*, 35.
49 Grosz, *Volatile Bodies*, xii.

Part II

1 Jeanette Winterson, 'Essay on Food for Nigella Issue of *Stylist* Magazine – December 2011'. Available online: http://www.jeanettewinterson.com/journalism

/essay-on-food-for-nigella-issue-of-stylist-magazine-december-2011/ (accessed 29 June 2020).
2. Schabert, 'Habeas Corpus 2000', 102.
3. Carole M. Counihan, *The Anthropology of Food and Body: Gender, Meaning, and Power* (London: Routledge, 1999), 47.
4. Gamman and Makinen, *Female Fetishism*, 28.
5. Ibid., 30.
6. Ibid., 33.
7. Anna Freud, 'The Psychoanalytic Study of Infantile Feeding Disturbances', in *Food and Culture: A Reader*, eds by Carole Counihan and Penny Van Esterik (London: Routledge, 1997), 108.
8. Counihan, *Anthropology of Food and Body*, 7.
9. Probyn, 'Beyond Food/Sex', 216.
10. MacClancy, *Consuming Culture*, 6.
11. Counihan, *Anthropology of Food and Body*, 9.
12. MacClancy, *Consuming Culture*, 74.

Chapter 4

1. Sarah Toulalan, *Imagining Sex: Pornography and Bodies in Seventeenth-Century England* (Oxford: Oxford University Press, 2007), 68.
2. Laura Doan, 'Jeanette Winterson's Sexing the Postmodern', in *The Lesbian Postmodern*, ed. by Laura Doan (New York: Columbia University Press, 1994), 150.
3. Elizabeth Langland, 'Sexing the Text: Narrative Drag as Feminist Poetics and Politics in Jeanette Winterson's *Sexing the Cherry*', *Narrative*, 5, no. 1 (1997): 99–107 (103).
4. Ibid., 99.
5. Winterson, *Sexing the Cherry*, 12.
6. Ibid., 11.
7. Ibid.
8. Ibid., 14.
9. Ibid., 17.
10. Ibid., 32.
11. Ibid.
12. MacClancy, *Consuming Culture*, 5.
13. Ibid., 2.
14. Pamela R. Frese, 'The Union of Nature and Culture: Gender Symbolism in the American Wedding Ritual', in *Transcending Boundaries: Multi-Disciplinary Approaches to the Study of Gender*, eds by Pamela R. Frese and John M. Congeshall (London: Bergin & Gravey, 1991), 76–8.

15 For more details on Lacan's concept of the mirror stage, see Jacques Lacan, 'The Mirror Stage as Formative of the Function of the I as Revealed in Psychoanalytic Experience', *Écrits: A Selection*, trans. by Alan Sheridan (London: Tavistock, 1977), 1–7.
16 Winterson, *Sexing the Cherry*, 114.
17 Ibid.
18 Ibid., 138.
19 John O. Wisdom, *Freud, Women, and Society* (London: Transaction Publishers, 1992), 71–87.

Chapter 5

1 Carol J. Adams, *The Sexual Politics of Meat* (London: Bloomsbury, 2015), 241.
2 Adams, *Sexual Politics of Meat*, 56–7.
3 Counihan, *Anthropology of Food and Body*, 8.
4 Adams, *Sexual Politics of Meat*, 48.
5 Ibid.
6 Winterson, *The Passion*, 3.
7 MacClancy, *Consuming Culture*, 145.
8 Winterson, *The Passion*, 3.
9 Ibid., 4.
10 Winterson, *The Passion*, 4.
11 Ibid.
12 Adams, *Sexual Politics of Meat*, 55.
13 Winterson, *The Passion*, 3.
14 Ibid., 38.
15 Ibid.
16 Ibid.
17 Winterson, *Passion*, 37–8.
18 Counihan, *Anthropology of Food and Body*, 7.
19 Adams, *Sexual Politics of Meat*, 55.
20 Winterson, *The Daylight Gate*, 14.
21 Counihan, *Anthropology of Food and Body*, 8.
22 Ibid.
23 Kate Millett, *Sexual Politics* (London: Virgo Press, 1971), 23.
24 Winterson, *The Passion*, 87.
25 Ibid.
26 MacClancy, *Consuming Culture*, 145.
27 Adams, *Sexual Politics of Meat*, 55.
28 Probyn, 'Beyond Food/Sex', 216–17.
29 Winterson, *The Passion*, 15.

30 Foucault, *History of Sexuality, Vol. 1*, 136.
31 MacClancy, *Consuming Culture*, 145.
32 Winterson, *Frankissstein*, 85.
33 Ibid., 88.
34 Ibid., 94.
35 Adams, *Sexual Politics of Meat*, 57.
36 Winterson, *Frankissstein*, 119.
37 Ibid., 119.
38 Ibid., 120.
39 Ibid., 112–13.
40 Ibid., 35.
41 Adams, *Sexual Politics of Meat*, 127.

Chapter 6

1 Counihan, *Anthropology of Food and Body*, 9.
2 Gilles Deleuze and Félix Guattari, *A Thousand Plateaus* (London: Bloomsbury, 2013), 104–5.
3 Cath Stowers, 'The Erupting Lesbian Body: Reading *Written on the Body* as a Lesbian Text', in *'I'm telling you stories': Jeanette Winterson and the Politics of Reading*, eds by Helena Grice and Tim Woods (Amsterdam: Rodopi, 1998), 89–102 (89).
4 Winterson, *Written on the Body*, 118.
5 Foucault, *History of Sexuality, Vol. 2*, 40.
6 Probyn, 'Beyond Food/Sex', 223.
7 Fusillo, *The Fetish*, ix.
8 Gamman and Makinen, *Female Fetishism*, 146–7.
9 MacClancy, *Consuming Culture*, 2.
10 Winterson, *Written on the Body*, 89.
11 Ibid., 90; 118.
12 Ibid., 53.
13 Freud, *Three Essays on the Theory of Sexuality*, 48.
14 MacClancy, *Consuming Culture*, 74.
15 Jeanette Winterson, *Art & Lies: A Piece for Three Voices and a Bawd* (New York: Vintage, 1996), 65.
16 Winterson, *Written on the Body*, 91.
17 Ibid., 89.
18 Ibid., 50.
19 MacClancy, *Consuming Culture*, 72.
20 Winterson, *Written on the Body*, 20.

21 Ibid., 137.
22 Ibid., 89.
23 Ibid., 39.
24 Ibid., 89.
25 Ibid., 37.
26 Gamman and Makinen, *Female Fetishism*, 145.
27 Winterson, *Written on the Body*, 35.
28 Ibid., 38.
29 Ibid., 39.
30 Gamman and Makinen, *Female Fetishism*, 145.
31 Winterson, *Written on the Body*, 39.
32 Ibid.
33 Ibid.
34 Ibid., 40.
35 Ibid., 56.
36 Ibid., 37.
37 Counihan, *Anthropology of Food and Body*, 48.
38 Gamman and Makinen. *Female Fetishism*, 145.
39 Foucault, *History of Sexuality, Vol. 2*, 110.
40 Probyn, 'Beyond Food/Sex', 226.
41 Ibid., 216.
42 Foucault, *History of Sexuality, Vol. 2*, 215–16.
43 MacClancy, *Consuming Culture*, 71.
44 Probyn, 'Beyond Food/Sex', 223.
45 Winterson, *Written on the Body*, 36.
46 Ibid., 136.
47 Ibid., 37.
48 Ibid., 72.
49 Ibid.
50 Ibid., 51; 106; 110; 129; 137.
51 Adams, *Sexual Politics of Meat*, 96.
52 Ibid., 62.
53 Winterson, *Gut Symmetries*, 195–6.

Chapter 7

1 Winterson, 'Food 2', (2005).
2 Counihan, *The Anthropology of Food and Body*, 48.
3 Winterson, 'Once Upon a Life', (2010).

4. Merja Makinen, *The Novels of Jeanette Winterson: A Reader's Guide to Essential Criticism* (New York: Palgrave Macmillan, 2005), 53.
5. Probyn, 'Beyond Food/Sex', 217.
6. Jeanette Winterson, 'Food 3', 10 December 2004. Available online: http://www.jeanettewinterson.com/journalism/food-3/ (accessed 29 June 2020).
7. Jeanette Winterson, '*The Shape We're in* review – Jeanette Winterson on Britain Getting Fatter', *The Guardian*, 2 July 2014. Available online: https://www.theguardian.com/books/2014/jul/02/shape-were-in-junk-food-sarah-boseley-review (accessed 29 June 2020).
8. Winterson, 'Food 3', (2004).
9. Andermahr, *Jeanette Winterson*, 127.
10. Counihan, *Anthropology of Food and Body*, 60.
11. Ibid., 57.
12. Jeanette Winterson, *Boating for Beginners* (London: Minerva, 1990), 12; 16.
13. Ibid., 13.
14. Appadurai, 'Gastro-Politics in Hindu South Asia', 509.
15. Ibid.
16. Winterson, *Boating for Beginners*, 87.
17. Ibid.
18. Ibid., 101.
19. Ibid., 105.
20. Ibid., 104.
21. Ibid., 88.
22. Ibid., 104.
23. Ibid., 38–9.
24. Ibid., 15.
25. Ibid.
26. Ibid., 50–1.
27. Ibid., 54.
28. Adams, *Sexual Politics of Meat*, 96.
29. Winterson, *Boating for Beginners*, 105.
30. MacClancy, *Consuming Culture*, 138.
31. Winterson, *Boating for Beginners*, 16.
32. Ibid., 79; 81.
33. Ibid., 37.
34. Ibid., 46.
35. Roland Barthes, 'Toward a Psychosociology of Contemporary Food Consumption', in *Food and Culture: A Reader*, ed. by Carole M. Counihan and Penny van Esterik (London: Routledge, 1997), 20–7.
36. Winterson, *Boating for Beginners*, 11.
37. Ibid., 86.

38 Ibid., 89; 86.
39 Ibid., 85.
40 MacClancy, *Consuming Culture*, 4–5.
41 Ibid., 3.
42 Winterson, *Boating for Beginners*, 84.
43 Counihan, *The Anthropology of Food and Body*, 52.
44 Ibid., 46.
45 Winterson, *Boating for Beginners*, 88.
46 Ibid.
47 Probyn, 'Beyond Food/Sex', 226.
48 Ibid.
49 Gamman and Makinen, *Female Fetishism*, 145.

Part III

1 Although Freud himself was not particularly condemnatory about perversion, saying, for instance, 'there is no difference between perverse and normal sexuality other than the fact that their dominating component instincts and consequently their sexual aims are different'. Sigmund Freud, *The Complete Psychological Works: Volume XVI*, ed. and trans. by James Strachey (London: Hogarth Press, 1964), 323.
2 Winterson, *Boating for Beginners*, 35.
3 Reynolds and Noakes, *Jeanette Winterson*, 19.
4 Schor, 'Female Fetishism: The Case of George Sand', 306.
5 Gilles Deleuze and Leopold Sacher-Masoch, *Masochism* (New York: Zone, 1991), 16.
6 Butler, 'Revisiting Bodies and Pleasures', 11–20.
7 Foucault, *History of Sexuality, Vol. 1*, 157.
8 Ibid., 156.
9 Doan, 'Jeanette Winterson's Sexing the Postmodern', 138.
10 Ibid., 150.
11 Eve Sedgwick, *Gender Asymmetry and Erotic Triangles* (New York: Columbia University Press, 1985), 527–8.
12 Heather Nunn, '*Written on the Body*: An Anatomy of Horror, Melancholy and Love', *Women: A Cultural Review*, 7, no. 1 (1996): 16–17.
13 Ibid.

Chapter 8

1 Winterson, *The Passion*, 70.
2 Ibid., 59–60.

3 Ibid., 143.
4 Ibid., 67.
5 Ibid., 70.
6 Ibid., 55.
7 Winterson, *The Passion*, 63.
8 Marjorie Garber, *Vested Interests: Cross-Dressing and Cultural Anxiety* (London: Routledge, 1992), 122.
9 Ibid.
10 Winterson, *The Passion*, 96.
11 Ibid., 5.
12 Ibid., 6.
13 Winterson, *The Passion*, 14.
14 Ibid.
15 Ibid., 64.
16 Freud, *Three Essays on the Theory of Sexuality*, 23–6.
17 Foucault, *History of Sexuality, Vol. 1*, 107; 114.
18 Jennifer Gustar, 'Language and the Limits of Desire', in *Jeanette Winterson: A Contemporary Critical Guide*, ed. by Andermahr, 66.
19 Deleuze, 'Coldness and Cruelty', in *Masochism*, 23.
20 Winterson, *Frankissstein*, 47.
21 Ibid., 43.
22 Ibid., 42–7.
23 Ibid., 47.
24 Ibid.
25 Ibid., 51.
26 Klein, *Selected Melanie Klein*, ed. by Mitchell, 95–6.
27 Ibid.
28 Ibid., 97.
29 Grosz, *Volatile Bodies*, 3.
30 Winterson, *Written on the Body*, 9.
31 Winterson, *The Passion*, 32.
32 Richard Von Krafft-Ebing, *Psychopathia Sexualis: A Medico-Forensic Study*, trans. by C. G. Chaddock (London: F. A. Davis, 1893), 222.
33 Freud, *Three Essays on the Theory of Sexuality*, 15.
34 Sigmund Freud, 'Analysis Terminable and Interminable', *The Complete Psychological Works: Volume XXIII*, ed. and trans. by James Strachey (London: Hogarth Press, 1964), 243–4.
35 Winterson, *Written on the Body*, 21.
36 Ibid., 73.
37 Gamman and Makinen, *Female Fetishism*, 45.
38 Freud, *Three Essays on the Theory of Sexuality*, 5–6. Freud states that 'in the case of many others, it is possible to point to external influences in their lives, whether

of a favourable or inhibiting character, which have led sooner or later to a fixation of their inversion. (Such influences are exclusive relations with persons of their own sex, comradeship in war, detention in prison, the dangers of heterosexual intercourse, celibacy, sexual weakness, etc.)' In other words, acts of perversion and deviance may or may not show up in adult life. In any case, if diverting and perverting acts were chosen in adult life, this would mean that sexual choices and preferences are expressed and exposed, and not repressed.

39 For more information, read Paul Gebhard, 'Fetishism and Sado-Masochism', *Science and Psychoanalysis*, 25, no. 15 (1969): 71–80; also, see Gamman and Makinen, *Female Fetishism*, 37–46.
40 Gebhard, 'Fetishism and Sado-Masochism', 71–80.
41 Winterson, *Written on the Body*, 51.
42 Ibid., 99.
43 Winterson, *Gap of Time*, 21.
44 Ibid., 22.
45 Foucault, *History of Sexuality, Vol. 2*, 43.
46 Sedgwick, *Gender Asymmetry and Erotic Triangles*, 527–8.
47 Winterson, *Written on the Body*, 32.
48 Freud, *Three Essays on the Theory of Sexuality*, 76
49 Satyriasis is a neurotic condition in men in which the symptoms are a compulsion to have sexual intercourse with as many women as possible and an inability to form lasting relationships with them. It denotes an enormous amount of excessive sexual passion in a man and can be classified as perverse behaviour.
50 Winterson, *Written on the Body*, 93.
51 Ibid.
52 Ibid.
53 Freud, *Three Essays on the Theory of Sexuality*, 204.
54 Sigmund Freud, *Sexuality and The Psychology of Love* (New York: Touchstone, 1997), 204–9.
55 Winterson, *Written on the Body*, 34.
56 Ibid.
57 Ibid., 68.
58 Foucault, *History of Sexuality, Vol. 2*, 43.
59 Ibid.
60 Winterson, *Written on the Body*, 82.
61 Winterson, *The Passion*, 59.
62 Ibid.
63 Ibid., 69.
64 Ibid., 150.
65 Lacan, *Écrits*, 430.

66 Ibid., 435.
67 Jeanette Winterson, *The Daylight Gate* (London: Arrow Books, 2012), 67.
68 Ibid.
69 See Mary Russo, *The Female Grotesque: Risk, Excess and Modernity* (New York/London: Routledge, 1994), 53–70.
70 Elizabeth Grosz, 'Freak', *Social Semiotic*, 1, no. 2 (1991): 22–38 (25).
71 Winterson, *The Daylight Gate*, 76.
72 Grosz, 'Freak', 27.
73 Grosz, *Volatile Bodies*, 5.
74 Deleuze, 'Coldness and Cruelty', in *Masochism*, 32.
75 Winterson, *The Daylight Gate*, 60.
76 Ibid., 84.
77 Catherine Waldby, 'Destruction: Boundary Erotics and Refigurations of the Heterosexual Male Body', in *Sexy Bodies: The Strange Carnalities of Feminism*, eds by Elizabeth Grosz and Elspeth Probyn (London: Routledge, 1995), 266–77.
78 Teresa de Lauretis, *Technologies of Gender: Essays on Theory, Film, and Fiction* (Bloomington/Indianapolis: Indiana University Press, 1987), 37.
79 Winterson, *The Daylight Gate*, 84.
80 Ibid., 192.
81 Waldby, 'Destruction', 267.
82 Ibid., 268.
83 Winterson, *Sexing the Cherry*, 86.
84 Ibid.
85 Ibid., 126.
86 Ibid., 86.
87 Ibid.
88 Winterson, *Oranges*, 170.
89 Waldby, 'Destruction', 269.
90 Ibid., 266.
91 Ibid.
92 Winterson, *The Daylight Gate*, 55.
93 Ibid., 207.
94 Waldby, 'Destruction', 269.
95 Ibid.
96 Luce Irigaray, *This Sex Which Is Not One* (New York: Cornell University Press, 1985), 171.
97 Winterson, *The Daylight Gate*, 11–2.
98 Waldby, 'Destruction', 269.
99 Ibid., 268.
100 Winterson, *Sexing the Cherry*, 107.

101 Ibid., 41.
102 Ibid.
103 Ibid., 106.
104 Ibid.
105 Grosz, *Volatile Bodies*, 15.
106 Winterson, *Sexing the Cherry*, 107.
107 Ibid.
108 Ibid.
109 Winterson, *The PowerBook*, 25.

Chapter 9

1   Lacan, *Écrits*, 581–2.
2   Winterson, *The Passion*, 70.
Sigmund Freud, *The Interpretation of Dreams*, ed. and trans. by James Strachey (New York: Basic Books, 2010), 367.
3   Freud, *Three Essays on the Theory of Sexuality*, 61.
4   Winterson, *The Passion*, 70.
5   Lacan, *Écrits*, 580.
6   Butler, *Gender Trouble*, 167.
7   Jacques Lacan, 'The Meaning of the Phallus', in *Feminine Sexuality: Jacques Lacan and the École Freudienne*, eds by Juliet Mitchell and Jacqueline Rose, trans. by Jacqueline Rose (New York: Norton, 1985), 84.
8   Winterson, *The Passion*, 98.
9   Ibid., 89.
10 Winterson, *Written on the Body*, 89.
11 Ibid., 49.
12 Ibid., 72.
13 Ibid., 95.
14 Lord Alfred Douglas, *'Two Loves' & Other Poems: A Selection* (Michigan: Bennett & Kitchel, 1990).
15 Winterson, *The Passion*, 73.
16 Ibid., 6.
17 Ibid., 14.
18 Ibid., 64.
19 Freud, *Three Essays on the Theory of Sexuality*, 182–3.
20 Winterson, *Frankissstein*, 89; 119.
21 Ibid., 84.
22 Ibid., 97.

23 Ibid.
24 Ibid., 109.
25 Ibid., 119.
26 Ibid., 119–21.
27 Ibid., 149.
28 Ibid.
29 Ibid., 153.
30 Ibid., 197.
31 Ibid., 156.

Chapter 10

1 Winterson, *Written on the Body*, 117.
2 Ibid., 41.
3 Ibid., 117.
4 Ibid., 51.
5 Ibid., 33.
6 Ibid., 49.
7 Ibid., 81.
8 Ibid., 136–7.
9 Winterson, *The Passion*, 67.
10 Ibid., 59.
11 Winterson, *Written on the Body*, 123.
12 Ibid., 11.
13 Ibid., 24.
14 Ibid.
15 Gamman and Makinen, *Female Fetishism*, 114.
16 Winterson, *Written on the Body*, 123.
17 Ibid., 24.
18 Ibid., 117.
19 Ibid., 32.
20 Ibid., 110.
21 Ibid., 91.
22 Freud, *Three Essays on the Theory of Sexuality*, 83.
23 Winterson, *Written on the Body*, 117; 123.
24 Ibid., 110.
25 Ibid., 117.
26 Ibid., 136.
27 Ibid., 62.
28 Ibid.

Conclusion

1. In correspondence with the author; see Appendix.
2. Probyn, 'Beyond Food/Sex', 226.
3. Gamman and Makinen, *Female Fetishism*, 45.
4. Christy L. Burns, 'Fantastic Language: Jeanette Winterson's Recovery of the Postmodern Word', *Contemporary Literature*, 37, no. 2 (Summer 1996), 279.
5. Winterson, *Art Objects*, 70.
6. Butler, *Bodies That Matter*, 68.
7. Schabert, 'Habeus Corpus 2000', 111.
8. Winterson, *Boating for Beginners*, 23.
9. In correspondence with the author; see Appendix.
10. Nealon, *Post-Postmodernism*, 154
11. Timotheus Vermeulen, 'Hard-boiled wonderland, blue velvet and the end of postmodernism' (2010). Available online: http://www.metamodernism.com/2010/09/23/hard-boiled-wonderland-from-pomo-to-metamo/ (accessed on 29 June 2020).

Bibliography

Adams, Carol J., *The Sexual Politics of Meat: A Feminist-Vegetarian Critical Theory*. New York: Continuum International, 2010.
Andermahr, Sonya, 'Cyberspace and the Body'. In *British Fiction of the 1990s*, edited by Nick Bentley, 108–22. London: Routledge, 2005.
Andermahr, Sonya, 'An Introduction to Time and Space in Jeanette Winterson's Short Fiction'. In *Winterson Narrating Time and Space*, edited by Margaret J.-M. Sönmez and Mine Özyurt Kiliç, 85–97. Newcastle: Cambridge Scholars Publishing, 2009.
Andermahr, Sonya, *Jeanette Winterson*. Basingstoke: Palgrave Macmillan, 2009.
Andermahr, Sonya, ed., *Jeanette Winterson: A Contemporary Critical Guide*. London: Continuum International, 2007.
Antakyahoglu, Zekiye, 'Telling the Temporary as Permanent: Winterson's Re-Working of Autobiography in *Oranges Are Not the Only Fruit* and *Weight*'. In *Winterson Narrating Time and Space*, edited by Margaret J.-M. Sönmez and Mine Özyurt Kiliç, 2–16. Newcastle: Cambridge Scholars Publishing, 2009.
Apter, Emily S., and William Pietz, eds, *Fetishism as Cultural Discourse*. London: Cornell University Press, 1993.
Armitt, Lucie, 'Storytelling and Feminism'. In *Jeanette Winterson: A Contemporary Critical Guide*, edited by Sonya Andermahr, 14–26. London: Continuum International, 2007.
Axinn, Sidney, *The Logic of Hope: Extensions of Kant's View of Religion*. Amsterdam: Rodopi, 1994.
Bachelard, Gaston, *The Poetics of Space*, trans. Maria Jolas. Boston, MA: Beacon Press, 1969.
Barthes, Roland, *A Lover's Discourse: Fragments*, trans. Richard Howard. Harmondsworth: Penguin, 1990.
Barthes, Roland, *The Pleasure of the Text*, trans. Richard Miller. Oxford: Blackwell, 1990.
Barthes, Roland, 'Toward a Psychosociology of Contemporary Food Consumption'. In *Food and Culture: A Reader*, edited by Carole Counihan and Penny Van Esterik, 20–7. London: Routledge, 1997.
Bell, Vikki, *Performativity & Belonging*. London: SAGE, 1999.
Braidotti, Rosi, *Metamorphoses: Towards a Materialist Theory of Becoming*. Cambridge: Polity, 2002.
Braidotti, Rosi, 'Signs of Wonder and Traces of Doubt: On Teratology and Embodied Differences'. In *Between Monsters, Goddesses and Cyborgs: Feminist Confrontations with Science, Medicine and Cyberspace*, edited by Nina Lykke and Rosi Braidotti, 135–51. London: Zed, 1996.

Bratton, Mary, 'Winterson, Bakhtin and the Chronotope of a Lesbian Hero', *Journal of Narrative Theory*, 32, no. 2 (Summer 2002): 207–26.

Burns, Christy L., 'Fantastic Language: Jeanette Winterson's Recovery of the Postmodern Word', *Contemporary Literature*, 37, no. 2 (Summer 1996): 278–306.

Burns, Christy L., 'Powerful Differences: Critique and Eros in Jeanette Winterson and Virginia Woolf', *Modern Fiction Studies*, 44, no. 2 (1998): 364–92.

Butler, Judith, *Bodies that Matter: On the Discursive Limits of 'Sex'*. London: Routledge, 1993.

Butler, Judith, *Gender Trouble: Feminism and the Subversion of Identity*. New York: Routledge, 1999.

Butler, Judith, 'Revisiting Bodies and Pleasures', *Theory, Culture & Society*, 16, no. 2 (1999): 11–20.

Childs, Peter, *Contemporary Novelists: British Fiction since 1970*, 2nd edn. Basingstoke: Palgrave Macmillan, 2012.

Counihan, Carole M., *The Anthropology of Food and Body: Gender, Meaning, and Power*. London: Routledge, 1999.

Counihan, Carole M., and Penny van Esterik, eds, *Food and Culture: A Reader*. London: Routledge, 1997.

Cox, Katherine, 'Knotting up the Cat's Cradle: Exploring Time and Space in Winterson's Novels'. In *Winterson Narrating Time and Space*, edited by Margaret J.-M. Sönmez and Mine Özyurt Kiliç, 50–64. Newcastle: Cambridge Scholars Publishing, 2009.

Davis, Lennard J., 'Visualizing the Disabled Body'. In *The Body: A Reader*, edited by Mariam Fraser and Monica Greco, 167–81. London: Routledge, 2005.

Deleuze, Gilles, *Masochism: Coldness and Cruelty*. New York: Zone, 1991.

Deleuze, Gilles, and Félix Guattari, *A Thousand Plateaus*. London: Bloomsbury, 2013.

de Lauretis, Teresa, *Technologies of Gender: Essays on Theory, Film, and Fiction* Bloomington: Indiana University Press, 1987.

Doan, Laura, 'Jeanette Winterson's Sexing the Postmodern'. In *The Lesbian Postmodern*, edited by Laura Doan, 137–55. New York: Columbia University Press, 1994.

Douglas, Lord Alfred, *'Two Loves' & Other Poems: A Selection*. Michigan: Bennett & Kitchel, 1990.

Elias, Amy J., *Sublime Desire: History and Post-1960s Fiction*. Baltimore, MD: Johns Hopkins University Press, 2003.

Eliot, T. S., *Collected Poems, 1909–1962*. London: Faber and Faber, 1963.

Eliot, T. S., *The Sacred Wood: Essays on Poetry and Criticism*, 4th edn. London: The Fountain Library, 1934.

Eliot, T. S., *Selected Poems*. London: Faber and Faber, 1961.

Foucault, Michel, *The History of Sexuality, Vol. 1: An Introduction*, trans. Robert Hurley. New York: Vintage Books, 1990.

Foucault, Michel, *The History of Sexuality, Vol. 2: The Use of Pleasure*, trans. Robert Hurley. London: Penguin, 1987.

Foucault, Michel, *The History of Sexuality, Vol. 3: The Care of the Self*, trans. Robert Hurley. London: Penguin, 1990.
Foucault, Michel, *Language, Counter-Memory, Practice: Selected Essays and Interviews*, ed. Donald F. Bouchard. New York: Cornell University Press, 1980.
Fraser, Mariam, and Monica Greco, eds, *The Body: A Reader*. London: Routledge, 2005.
Frese, Pamela R., 'The Union of Nature and Culture: Gender Symbolism in the American Wedding Ritual'. In *Transcending Boundaries: Multi-Disciplinary Approaches to the Study of Gender*, edited by Pamela R. Frese and John M. Congeshall, 97–112. London: Bergin & Gravey, 1991.
Freud, Anna, 'The Psychoanalytic Study of Infantile Feeding Disturbances'. In *Food and Culture: A Reader*, edited by Carole Counihan and Penny Van Esterik, 107–16. London: Routledge, 1997.
Freud, Sigmund, *The Complete Psychological Works: Volume XVI*, ed. and trans. James Strachey. London: Hogarth Press, 1964.
Freud, Sigmund, *The Complete Psychological Works: Volume XXIII*, ed. and trans. James Strachey. London: Hogarth Press, 1964.
Freud, Sigmund, *General Psychological Theory: Papers on Metapsychology*. New York: Touchstone, 2008.
Freud, Sigmund, *The Interpretation of Dreams*, ed. and trans. James Strachey. New York: Basic Books, 2010.
Freud, Sigmund, *Three Essays on the Theory of Sexuality*, ed. and trans. James Strachey. New York: Basic Books, 2000.
Front, Sonia, *Transgressing Boundaries in Jeanette Winterson's Fiction*. Frankfurt: Peter Lang GmbH, 2009.
Funk, Wolfgang, *The Literature of Reconstruction: Authentic Fiction in the New Millennium*. London: Bloomsbury, 2015.
Fusillo, Massimo, *The Fetish: Literature, Cinema, Visual Art*. London: Bloomsbury, 2017.
Gamman, Lorraine, and Merja Makinen, *Female Fetishism: A New Look*. London: Lawrence & Wishart, 1994.
Garber, Marjorie, *Vested Interests: Cross-Dressing and Cultural Anxiety*. London: Routledge, 1992.
Gasparyan, Diana, 'Mirror for the Other: Problem of the Self in Continental Philosophy (From Hegel To Lacan)', *Integrative Psychological & Behavioural Science*, 48, no. 1 (2014): 1–17.
Grice, Helena, and Tim Woods, eds, *'I'm telling you stories': Jeanette Winterson and the Politics of Reading*. Amsterdam: Rodopi, 1998.
Griffin, Gabrielle, 'Acts of Defiance: Celebrating Lesbians'. In *It's My Party: Reading Twentieth-Century Women's Writing*, edited by Gina Wisker, 80–103. London: Pluto, 1994.
Grosz, Elizabeth, 'Freak', *Social Semiotic*, 1, no. 2 (1991): 22–38.
Grosz, Elizabeth, 'Refiguring Bodies'. In *The Body: A Reader*, edited by Mariam Fraser and Monica Greco, 47–51. London: Routledge, 2005.

Grosz, Elizabeth, *Space, Time, and Perversion*. London: Routledge, 1995.
Grosz, Elizabeth, *Volatile Bodies: Toward A Corporeal Feminism*. Indianapolis: Indiana University Press, 1994.
Grosz, Elizabeth, and Elspeth Probyn, eds, *Sexy Bodies: Strange Carnalities of Feminism*. Abingdon: Routledge, 1995.
Gustar, Jennifer, 'Language and the Limits of Desire'. In *Jeanette Winterson: A Contemporary Critical Guide*, edited by Sonya Andermahr, 55–68. London: Continuum International, 2007.
Haslett, Jane, 'Winterson's Fabulous Bodies'. In *Jeanette Winterson: A Contemporary Critical Guide*, edited by Sonya Andermahr, 41–54. London: Continuum International, 2007.
Hinds, Hilary, '*Oranges Are Not the Only Fruit*: Reaching Audiences Other Lesbian Texts Cannot Reach'. In *New Lesbian Criticism: Literary and Cultural Readings*, edited by Sally Munt, 153–72. Hemel Hempstead: Harvest Wheatsheaf, 1992.
Hutcheon, Linda, *A Poetics of Postmodernism: History, Theory, Fiction*. London: Routledge, 1988).
Irigaray, Luce, *This Sex Which Is Not One*, trans. by Catherine Porter. New York: Cornell University Press, 1985.
Irigaray, Luce, *To Be Born: Genesis of a New Human Being*. Cham, Switzerland: Springer, 2017.
Jenzen, Olu, 'Reworking Linear Time: Queer Temporalities in Jeanette Winterson's *Sexing the Cherry* and *Art & Lies*'. In *Winterson Narrating Time and Space*, edited by Sönmez and Kiliç, 31–49.
Kauer, Ute, 'Narration and Gender: The Role of the First-Person Narrator in Jeanette Winterson's *Written on the Body*'. In *'I'm telling you stories': Jeanette Winterson and the Politics of Reading*, edited by Helena Grice and Tim Woods, 41–52. Amsterdam: Rodopi, 1998.
Keulks, Gavin, 'Winterson's Recent Work: Navigating Realism and Postmodernism'. In *Jeanette Winterson: A Contemporary Critical Guide*, edited by Sonya Andermahr, 146–62. London: Continuum International, 2007.
Kinsey, Alfred C., Wardell B. Pomeroy and Clyde E. Martin, *Sexual Behavior in the Human Male*. Philadelphia, PA: W.B. Saunders, 1948.
Krafft-Ebing, Richard Von, *Psychopathia Sexualis: A Medico-Forensic Study*. London: Heinemann, 1939.
Kristeva, Julia, 'On the Melancholic Imaginary'. In *Discourse in Psychoanalysis and Literature*, edited by Shlomith Rimmon-Kenan, 104–23. London: Methuen, 1987.
Lacan, Jacques, *Écrits: A Selection*, trans. Alan Sheridan. London: Tavistock, 1977.
Lacan, Jacques, *Écrits: The First Complete Edition in English*, trans. Bruce Fink. New York: Norton, 2006.
Lacan, Jacques, and Wladimir Granoff, 'Fetishism: The Symbolic, the Imaginary and the Real'. In *Perversions, Psychodynamics and Therapy*, edited by Sándor Lorand, 265–76. New York: Gramercy Books, 1956.

Langland, Elizabeth, 'Sexing the Text: Narrative Drag as Feminist Poetics and Politics in Jeanette Winterson's *Sexing the Cherry*', *Narrative*, 5, no. 1 (1997): 99–107.

Lewis, Lisa A., ed., *The Adoring Audience: Fan Culture and Popular Media*. London: Routledge, 1992.

Lyotard, Jean-François, *The Postmodern Condition: A Report on Knowledge*, trans. Brian Massumi. Manchester: Manchester University Press, 2004.

MacClancy, Jeremy, *Consuming Culture*. London: Chapmans, 1992.

Makinen, Merja, *The Novels of Jeanette Winterson: A Reader's Guide to Essential Criticism*. New York: Palgrave Macmillan, 2005.

Malinowski, Bronislaw, *Sex, Culture, and Myth*. London: Rupert Hart-Davis, 1963.

Marshall, Brenda K., *Teaching the Postmodern: Fiction and Theory*. New York: Routledge, 1992.

Millett, Kate, *Sexual Politics*. London: Virgo Press, 1971.

Mitchell, Juliet, ed., *The Selected Melanie Klein*. New York: The Free Press, 1986.

Mitchell, Juliet, and Jacqueline Rose, eds, *Feminine Sexuality: Jacques Lacan and the École Freudienne*, trans. Jacqueline Rose. London: Macmillan Press, 1982.

Moore, Lisa, 'Teledildonics: Virtual Lesbians in the Fiction of Jeanette Winterson'. In *Sexy Bodies: Strange Carnalities of Feminism*, edited by Elizabeth Grosz and Elspeth Probyn, 104–27. Abingdon: Routledge, 1995.

Munt, Sally, ed., *New Lesbian Criticism: Literary and Cultural Readings*. Hemel Hempstead: Harvest Wheatsheaf, 1992.

Nealon, Jeffrey, *Post-Postmodernism: Or, the Cultural Logic of Just-In-Time Capitalism*. Stanford, CA: Stanford University Press, 2012.

Nunn, Heather, '*Written on the Body*: An Anatomy of Horror, Melancholy and Love', *Women: A Cultural Review*, 7, no. 1 (1996): 16–27.

Onega, Susana, *Jeanette Winterson*. Manchester: Manchester University Press, 2006.

O'Rourke, Rebecca, 'Fingers in the Fruit Basket: A Feminist Reading of Jeanette Winterson's *Oranges Are Not the Only Fruit*'. In *Feminist Criticism: Theory and Practice*, edited by Susan Sellers, 57–70. Hemel Hempstead: Harvester Wheatsheaf, 1991.

Osborne, Thomas, 'Body Amnesia'. In *Sociology after Postmodernism*, edited by David Owen, 188–204. London: SAGE, 1996.

Palmer, Paulina, '*The Passion*: Storytelling, Fantasy, Desire'. In *'I'm telling you stories': Jeanette Winterson and the Politics of Reading*, edited by Helena Grice and Tim Woods, 103–16. Amsterdam: Rodopi, 1998.

Pearce, Lynne, 'The Emotional Politics of Reading Winterson'. In *'I'm telling you stories': Jeanette Winterson and the Politics of Reading*, edited by Helena Grice and Tim Woods, 29–40. Amsterdam: Rodopi, 1998.

Pearce, Lynne, *Reading Dialogics*. London: Edward Arnold, 1994.

Probyn, Elspeth, 'Beyond Food/Sex: Eating and an Ethics of Eating', *Theory, Culture & Society*, 16, no. 2 (1999): 215–28.

Reynolds, Margaret, and Jonathan Noakes, *Jeanette Winterson: The Essential Guide*. London: Vintage, 2003.

Rimmon-Kenan, Shlomith, ed., *Discourse in Psychoanalysis and Literature*. London: Methuen, 1987.

Russo, Mary, *The Female Grotesque: Risk, Excess and Modernity*. London: Routledge, 1994.

Schabert, Ina, 'Habeas Corpus 2000: The Return of The Body', *European Studies*, 16, no. 29 (2001): 87–115.

Schor, Naomi, 'Female Fetishism: The Case of George Sand'. In *The Female Body in Western Culture: Contemporary Perspectives*, edited by Susan Rubin Suleiman. Cambridge, MA: Harvard University Press, 1986, 363–72.

Seaboyer, Judith, 'Second Death in Venice: Romanticism and the Compulsion to Repeat in Jeanette Winterson's *The Passion*', *Contemporary Literature*, 38, no. 3 (1997): 483–509.

Sedgwick, Eve, *Gender Asymmetry and Erotic Triangles*. New York: Columbia University Press, 1985.

Simmel, Georg, 'The Sociology of the Meal', trans. M. Symons, *Food and Foodways*, 5, no. 4 (1994): 333–51.

Sönmez, Margaret J.-M., and Mine Özyurt Kiliç, eds, *Winterson Narrating Time and Space*. Newcastle: Cambridge Scholars Publishing, 2009.

Stoller, Robert J., *Perversion*. London: Karnac Books, 1986.

Stone, Lawrence, *The Family, Sex and Marriage in England, 1500–1800*. London: Weidenfeld & Nicolson, 1977.

Stowers, Cath, 'The Erupting Lesbian Body: Reading *Written on the Body* as a Lesbian Text'. In *'I'm telling you stories': Jeanette Winterson and the Politics of Reading*, edited by Helena Grice and Tim Woods, 89–102. Amsterdam: Rodopi, 1998.

Stowers, Cath, '"No Legitimate Place, No Land, No Fatherland": Communities of Women in the Fiction of Roberts and Winterson', *Critical Survey*, 8, no. 1 (1996): 69–79.

Stratton, Jon, *The Desirable Body: Cultural Fetishism and the Erotics of Consumption*. Manchester: Manchester University Press, 1996.

Sullivan, Nikki, *A Critical Introduction to Queer Theory*. New York: New York University Press, 2003.

Taylor, Clare L., *Women, Writing, and Fetishism, 1890–1950: Female Cross-Gendering*. Oxford: Oxford University Press, 2003.

Toulalan, Sarah, *Imagining Sex: Pornography and Bodies in Seventeenth-Century England*. Oxford: Oxford University Press, 2007.

Wachtel, Eleanor, *Writers & Company: New Conversations with CBC Radio's Eleanor Wachtel*. Toronto: Vintage Canada, 1997.

Wagner-Lawlor, Jennifer A., 'Lusting Toward Utopia: Winterson's Utopian Counter-spaces from *The Passion* to *The PowerBook*'. In *Winterson Narrating Time and Space*, edited by Sönmez, and Kiliç, 65–84.

Waldby, Catherine, 'Destruction: Boundary Erotics and Refigurations of the Heterosexual Male Body'. In *Sexy Bodies: Strange Carnalities of Feminism*, edited by Elizabeth Grosz and Elspeth Probyn 266–77. Abingdon: Routledge, 1995.

Wilchins, Riki, *Queer Theory, Gender Theory: An Instant Primer*. Los Angeles: Alyson books, 2004.

Wingfield, Rachel, 'Lesbian Writers in the Mainstream: Sara Maitland, Jeanette Winterson and Emma Donoghue'. In *Beyond Sex and Romance? The Politics of Contemporary Lesbian Fiction*, edited by Elaine Hutton, 60–80. London: Women's Press, 1998.

Winterson, Jeanette, *Art & Lies: A Piece for Three Voices and a Bawd*. New York: Vintage International, 1996.

Winterson, Jeanette, *Art Objects: Essays on Ecstasy and Effrontery*. New York: Vintage International, 1997.

Winterson, Jeanette, *Boating for Beginners*. London: Minerva, 1990.

Winterson, Jeanette, *The Daylight Gate*. London: Arrow Books, 2012.

Winterson, Jeanette, *Fit for the Future: The Guide for Women Who Want to Live Well*. London: Pandora Press, 1986.

Winterson, Jeanette, *Frankissstein*. London: Vintage, 2019.

Winterson, Jeanette, *The Gap of Time: The Winter's Tale Retold*. London: Hogarth, 2015.

Winterson, Jeanette, *Gut Symmetries*. London: Granta, 1997.

Winterson, Jeanette, *Lighthousekeeping*. London: Fourth Estate, 2004.

Winterson, Jeanette, *Oranges Are Not the Only Fruit*. New York: Grove Press, 1985.

Winterson, Jeanette, *The Passion*. London: Vintage, 2001.

Winterson, Jeanette, *The PowerBook*. New York: Vintage International, 2001.

Winterson, Jeanette, *Sexing the Cherry*. London: Vintage, 2001.

Winterson, Jeanette, *The Stone Gods*. London: Penguin, 2008.

Winterson, Jeanette, *Why Be Happy When You Could Be Normal?* London: Jonathan Cape, 2011.

Winterson, Jeanette, *Written on the Body*. New York: Vintage International, 1994.

Wisdom, John O., *Freud, Women, and Society*. London: Transaction Publishers, 1992.

Woolf, Virginia, *A Room of One's Own and Three Guineas*. Oxford: Oxford World's Classics, 2015.

Woolf, Virginia, *To the Lighthouse*. London: Penguin, 2000.

Wright, Terry R., *The Genesis of Fiction: Modern Novelists as Biblical Interpreters*. Aldershot: Ashgate, 2007.

Zimmerman, Bonnie, 'What Has Never Been: An Overview of Lesbian Feminist Literary Criticism', *Feminist Studies*, 7, no. 3 (Autumn 1981): 451–75.

Zimmerman, Bonnie, 'Lesbians Like This and That: Some Notes on Lesbian Criticism for the Nineties'. In *New Lesbian Criticism: Literary and Cultural Readings*, edited by Sally Munt, 1–15. Hemel Hempstead: Harvest Wheatsheaf, 1992.

Ziv, Amalia, *Explicit Utopias: Rewriting the Sexual in Women's Pornography*. New York: SUNY Press, 2015.

Websites

Alteroct, Alexandra, 'Novelists Reimagine and Update Shakespeare's Plays', https://www.nytimes.com/2015/10/06/books/novelists-reimagine-and-update-shakespeares-plays.html?_r=0 (accessed 29 June 2020).

Bakopoulosoct, Dean, '*The Gap of Time*, by Jeanette Winterson', http://www.nytimes.com/2015/10/25/books/review/the-gap-of-time-by-jeanette-winterson.html?_r=1 (accessed 29 June 2020).

Dickson, Andrew, '*The Gap of Time* by Jeanette Winterson – review', https://www.standard.co.uk/lifestyle/books/the-gap-of-time-by-jeanette-winterson-review-a2955231.html (accessed 29 June 2020).

Kavenna, Joanna, '*The Gap of Time* by Jeanette Winterson, review: "poignant"', http://www.telegraph.co.uk/books/what-to-read/the-gap-of-time-jeanette-winterson-review/ (accessed 29 June 2020).

Khomami, Nadia, 'Jeanette Winterson to close London shop due to business rates surge', https://www.theguardian.com/books/2017/jan/23/jeanette-winterson-close-london-shop-business-rates-tax (accessed 29 June 2020).

The Late Show: Face to Face with Jeanette Winterson, 28 June 1994, http://www.bbc.co.uk/iplayer/episode/p00nw1xh/the-late-show-face-to-face-jeanette-winterson (accessed 29 June 2020).

Le Guin, Ursula K., 'Head cases', Review of *The Stone Gods*, https://www.theguardian.com/books/2007/sep/22/sciencefictionfantasyandhorror.fiction (accessed 29 June 2020).

Levins, Hoag, 'Social History of the Pineapple', http://www.levins.com/pineapple.html (accessed 29 June 2020).

Miller, Lucasta, '*The Gap of Time* by Jeanette Winterson, book review: A modern rewriting', http://www.independent.co.uk/arts-entertainment/books/reviews/the-gap-of-time-by-jeanette-winterson-book-review-a6675676.html (accessed 29 June 2020).

Vermeulen, Timotheus, 'Hard-boiled wonderland, blue velvet and the end of postmodernism', http://www.metamodernism.com/2010/09/23/hard-boiled-wonderland-from-pomo-to-metamo/ (accessed 29 June 2020).

Williams, Holly, '*The Gap of Time*, by Jeanette Winterson – book review: Novel way to bring back the Bard … never mind the gap', *Independent*, 4 October 2015. Available online: http://www.independent.co.uk/arts-entertainment/books/reviews/the-gap-of-time-by-jeanette-winterson-book-review-novel-way-to-bring-back-the-bard-never-mind-the-a6677401.html (accessed 29 June 2020).

Winterson, Jeanette, 'Essay on Food for Nigella Issue of Stylist Magazine', http://www.jeanettewinterson.com/journalism/essay-on-food-for-nigella-issue-of-stylist-magazine-december-2011/ (accessed 29 June 2020).

Winterson, Jeanette, 'Food 2', http://www.jeanettewinterson.com/journalism/food-2/ (accessed 29 June 2020).

Winterson, Jeanette, 'Food 3', http://www.jeanettewinterson.com/journalism/food-3/ (accessed 29 June 2020).

Winterson, Jeanette, 'Once Upon a Life', http://www.theguardian.com/lifeandstyle/2010/jun/13/once-upon-a-life-jeanette-winterson (accessed 29 June 2020).

Winterson, Jeanette, 'The Shape We're In Review – Jeanette Winterson on Britain Getting Fatter', *The Guardian*, 2 July 2014, 'Health, Mind and Body', https://www.theguardian.com/books/2014/jul/02/shape-were-in-junk-food-sarah-boseley-review (accessed 29 June 2020).

Index

Adams, Carol J. 26
    meat and masculinity 98
    meat and patriarchy 90–6, 107–8, 115
    meat and visual pleasure 99
alternative fetishism 1–4, 9, 19–20, 22–5, 28, 168–78
    bodily 34–5, 41–3, 46–9, 53, 65, 75–6
    food 79–80, 86, 91, 93, 96–7, 118–19
    sexual 122–5, 128–9, 132, 144–51, 163, 167
anatomy 9, 30, 50, 71
Andermahr, Sonya 13, 43, 73
androgyny 40, 58, 74, 77, 95, 169
anthropology 4, 106, 173, 175
Appadurai, Arjun
    semiotics of food 26
    social contexts of 112–13
artificial intelligence 16, 62–3
avowal 3, 8, 169, 176
    and bodily fetishism 31
    and food fetishism 82, 86, 103
    and sexual fetishism 122, 147, 149, 151, 167

bananas 83–5, 87–9, 103
Barthes, Roland
    atopic writer 13
    and food 116
    The Pleasure of the Text 11–12
bestiality 147
Bible, The, *see* religion
bisexuality 135
bodily fetishism, *see under* fetishism
Brexit 65, 74
Burns, Christy 172
Butler, Judith 24, 26, 174
    and the body 7, 53, 64, 123
    and the Lacanian Phallus 44
    and language 172
    performativity 12, 22–3, 46, 84–5, 153

cancer 35, 51, 57
cannibalism 108
capitalism 80, 133
cartography 9, 30, 38, 50–1, 163
castration 43, 67, 146–7
castration anxiety, *see under* Freud, Sigmund
cherry 83
chicken 69, 92–3, 96, 130, *see also* meat
codpiece 129–30
Counihan, Carole 26
    food and female power 105, 112
    food and female subordination 95, 117–18
    food and symbolism 80–2, 100, 110
counter-memory, *see under* Foucault, Michel
cross-dressing 3, 42–6, 67, 84–5, 128–9, 142
cyberspace 16, 42, 61

de Lauretis, Teresa 8–9, 31, 145
Deleuze, Gilles 122–3, 132, 145
    and Felix Guattari 50, 100
depression 55–6, 62, 70
Descartes, René 142
desire 2, 6–8, 11, 13–15, 20–2, 26–8,
    see also sexual desire
deviance 27, 28, 121, 132, 143–4, 148
disavowal 3, 8, 20, 27, 169, 176
    and bodily fetishism 31, 42, 57
    and food fetishism 80, 82, 84, 86, 91, 103–4
    and sexual fetishism 122, 147, 149, 167
dissidence 27–8, 121, 132, 143–4, 148, 171
Doan, Laura 84, 124
Douglas, Lord Alfred 155

Eliot, T. S. 11, 17–18
    'The Waste Land' 57
Ellis, Havelock 123
eroticism 11, 21, 129–30, 132, 146–8, 155
    and food 26, 79, 90, 92, 100–1

and identity 124
visual 127

fairy tales 15, 48, 71–2, 83
female community 38, 45, 94
femininity 76–7, 88–9, 118–19, 146, 153
    and fruit 84–6
    and space 48, 73
    stereotypes 98–9
feminism 18, 19, 100, 113
fetishism
    alternative (see alternative fetishism)
    bodily 8–9, 24–5, 29–78, 169
    commodity 4–5, 8, 80–1, 105
    female 3–8, 20–1, 42, 103, 122, 129–30
    first-wave 2–3, 20–2, 76, 86, 119, 122–3
    food 8–9, 25–6, 79–125, 170
    lesbian 3, 42, 168
    original meaning 4
    second-wave 2–3, 22, 76, 86, 119, 122–3
    sexual 8–9, 27–8, 89, 121–67, 170–1, 175
fetish object 2, 20, 23, 171
    bodily 44, 68, 75–8
    food 79, 82, 93, 97, 104, 118–19
    sexual 137, 155, 159, 162–3
folk tales 12, 15
food fetishism, see under fetishism
Foucault, Michel
    and the body 69, 99
    and counter-memory 64–5, 73
    and food 101, 105
    and power 39, 97
    and sexuality 6–7, 22–3, 38, 123, 131, 138, 140–1
Frankenstein 40, 62, 74, 97, 157, see also Shelley, Mary
Freud, Anna 81, 104
Freud, Sigmund 10, 61, 160
    and castration anxiety 2–3, 5, 140, 157
    and fetishism 2–7, 19–20, 122, 137, 140, 168
    and food 102–3, 162
    and infantile sexuality 157
    and libido 139, 164
    and melancholy 31
    and memory 64
    and phallic substitutes 153, 161
    and sadomasochism 122–3, 131, 139–40
    and sexuality 22–3, 135
    and sexual overvaluation 150, 152
    Three Essays on the Theory of Sexuality 4, 102, 131, 135
    (see also Oedipal complex)
fruit 82–9, 102–3
Fusillo, Massimo 5, 101

Gamman, Lorraine, and Merja Makinen
    and commodity fetishism 80–1
    and female fetishism 3, 8, 21, 26
    and food fetishism 27, 101, 103, 119
    and language 20
Garber, Marjorie 129
gastronomy 8–9, 30, 52, 91, 102, 117
gaze 21, 34, 46, 52, 90, 99, 155
Gebhard, Paul 8, 27, 137
gender
    binary 3, 8, 87, 89
    dysphoria 40
    equality 62, 75
    hierarchy 91, 94
    norms 4, 7, 33, 46, 84–6, 109, 144, 176
    reassignment (see transgender)
    roles 2, 86, 89, 95, 112, 118, 124
    stereotypes 33, 44, 49, 63, 84–5, 97–9, 108, 133
    theory 22–3
gender fluidity 3, 9, 15–16, 25, 168–70, 173–5
    and body 30, 41, 45–6, 60–2, 71, 74–7
    and food 79–83, 89–91, 102, 109, 111, 119
    and sex 124, 156
gender performance 4, 12, 22–4, 28, 170–1
    and body 30, 44–5, 77
    and food 83–6, 88–9, 96, 109, 116
    and sex 153
Granoff, Wladimir 6, 20
Greer, Germaine 133
Grosz, Elizabeth
    and the body 22, 29–30, 33, 39, 41, 46–8, 50, 52, 77, 135, 150
    and the city 59
    and cyberspace 61
    and fetishism 3, 42
    and freak 143–4

and memory 64–5
and place 55–6

Henry VIII 92
hermaphrodite 135, 143, 171
heteronormativity 9
  and body 40, 63, 72
  and food 91, 101, 112, 114–15
  and sex 121, 133, 144, 151, 156, 158
heterosexuality 53, 99, 137
homophobia 113, 118
homosexuality 24, 53, 114, 124, 135, 137, 161
hybridity 74, 143, 158

Irigaray, Luce 5
  gendering of time and space 48
  and women as commodities 75, 149
  and women's movements 38

Jenzen, Olu 47

Kant, Immanuel 36
Keulks, Gavin 42
Kinsey, Alfred 7
Klein, Melanie 134, 140
  mother–child relationship 2–3, 138, 162
von Krafft-Ebing, Richard 123, 135
Kristeva, Julia 5, 29
  and melancholy imagination 62, 70

Lacan, Jacques
  and desire 171
  and fetishism 2, 6, 20, 142, 165
  and mirror stage 87–8
  and phallus 44, 127, 138, 152–3, 158–9, 165
  and symbolic, imaginary and real 6, 50, 165
Langland, Elizabeth 84
Lawrence, D. H. 10, 53
lesbian 3, 13, 18–19, 24, 47, 72, 124, *see also under* fetishism; lesbian

MacClancy, Jeremy 26, 106, 115
  food and sex 82, 101–3
  food and symbolism 86, 117
  food as identity 81

meat 92, 96
madness 24–5, 29, 34–7, 43, 55, 66–8, 71–2, 77
Makinen, Merja 110–11
Marxist theory 4–5, *see also under* fetishism; commodity
masculinity 171
  and body 40, 42, 76
  and food 84, 86, 88–9, 97–9, 115, 119
  and sex 128, 145, 148
masochism, *see* sadomasochism
meat 26, 87, 90–9, 102, 106–8, 115–18
melancholy 20, 24–5
  and bodily fetishism 29, 31, 34–7, 43, 66–72, 77
memory
  and bodily fetishism 49, 58, 62, 64–71, 73–4, 76
  and sexual fetishism 141, 154, 166
metaphor 8, 13, 17, 19–20, 26–7, 169–72
  body 30, 33, 48–9, 51, 53, 58
  food 79–80, 82, 90–2, 102, 112–13, 115–16
  sex 128–9, 137, 155–6
metonymy 3, 112–13, 130, 159
Miller, Henry 53
Miller, Lucasta 17
Millet, Kate 95
mirror stage, *see under* Lacan
misogyny 3, 150
monstrous 28, 34–5, 88, 95, 132, 143–5
Moore, Lisa 19
mourning 24
  and bodily fetishism 29, 31, 35, 57, 62, 66–7, 71, 77
myth 10, 69, 110, 132

narcissism 25, 30, 98, 165
narrative techniques
  multiple strands 12, 16, 65, 71–4, 76, 83, 175
  nonlinear 48–9, 66
  repetition 48, 59, 64–6
Nealon, Jeffrey 21, 23–4, 178
neurosis 4, 7
New Sincerity 18, 178
Nietzsche, Friedrich 69
Nunn, Heather 34, 124

Oedipal complex   6, 134, 140, 157
Onega, Susana   16
oral sex   151, 161, 164
orgasm   136, 148, 157

paedophilia   148
patriarchy   19, 41, 85, 90, 96, 108, 115, 150
penetration   154, 157, 164
   digital   51, 99, 155, 158
   penile   3, 128, 148–9
perversity   27, 28, 121, 132, 143, 148
phallocentrism   3, 87, 168
phallus, *see under* Lacan
phantasy   132–4, 136, 146, 152, 156
pineapples   83–9
Plato   140–1
post-humanism   62, 75, 87, 159, 178,
      see also transhumanism
postmodernism   18, 42, 61, 71, 124
post-postmodernism   18, 21, 23–4, 40, 178
Probyn, Elspeth   26, 81, 96, 101, 105–6,
      111, 119, 170
psychoanalysis   1–4, 6, 9–10, 16, 21–3,
   27, 168
   and sex   122, 132, 137, 160, 162

queer   8, 108, 124, 177

rape
   female   67, 141, 148–9
   male   145, 149
religion   4, 14, 36–7, 76, 102, 117, 170, 174
   Catholicism   145, 147
   evangelism   10, 14, 36, 73
Rushdie, Salman   175
Russo, Mary   143

sadomasochism   27, 122–3, 131–5,
      139–40, 143–5, 147–8
Schabert, Ina   29, 79, 174
School of Venus, The   83
Schor, Naomi   5, 122
seasons   53–8
Sedgwick, Eve Kosofsky   124, 139
semiotics   26, 86, 128
sex-bots   16, 62–3, 75, 133–4
sex laws   7
sexual aim   103, 135, 137, 142, 152, 155,
      160–1

sexual desire   5, 121–2, 124, 128–30,
      140, 146–8, 154, 157, 161–3,
      167
   and food   101, 103, 105
sexual fetishism, *see under* fetishism
sexuality
   feminine   6
   fluid   4, 8–9, 12, 15, 30, 39, 41–2, 53,
      62, 73, 76–81, 83–9, 114, 122–8,
      150, 156, 168–70
sexual object   5, 27, 131, 135, 137, 140,
      142, 152, 155, 163–4
   and food   93, 103
Shakespeare, William   2
Shelley, Mary   1, 40, 62, 65, 74, 97
Smith, Zadie   175
sodomy   145–6, 156
Stowers, Cath   100
Stratton, Jon   21
sublimation   134–6
substitution   1–2, 4, 20, 25–7,
      169, 176
   and bodily fetishism   46, 77
   and food fetishism   80–2, 84, 86,
      101–4, 106, 118
   and sexual fetishism   122, 128, 136,
      146–7, 151–3, 162
Sullivan, Nikki   8
symbolic, imaginary and real, *see under*
      Lacan, Jacques
synecdoche   20, 147

taboo   27, 173
   and food   108, 110, 114, 116
   and sex   121, 145, 148, 166
Toulalan, Sarah   83
transgender   16, 40–1, 63, 74, 87, 97–9,
      116, 129, 157–8, 178
transgression
   and body   43, 46–8
   and food   98–9, 113, 117
   and sex   121, 127, 148–9, 153
transhumanism   16, 40–1, 74, 75, 87,
      159, 178
transphobia   118, 133

vegetarianism   98–9, 118
Vermeulen, Timotheus   178
voyeurism   52, 163

Waldby, Catherine   146, 148–9
Wales   75, 133
Winterson, Jeanette
  and the body   29–31
  critical reception   14–19, 100–1, 112, 172
  and food   25–6, 79–82, 110–11
  and language   9–14, 172, 176
  and sex   112, 121–5, 168
  and time   48
  WORKS
    Art & Lies   16, 102, 175
    Art Objects   1, 8–14, 16, 17, 19, 21, 172
    Boating for Beginners   14, 170
      and food fetishism   110–18
      and sexual fetishism   121
    The Daylight Gate   15, 16, 171
      and bodily fetishism   65
      and food fetishism   87, 95
      and sexual fetishism   143–9, 151
    Frankissstein   1, 14, 16
      and bodily fetishism   40–1, 62–3, 65, 74–5
      and food fetishism   87, 97–9, 118
      and sexual fetishism   133–4, 157–9
    The Gap of Time   2, 16
      and sexual fetishism   138
    Gut Symmetries   16, 175
      and bodily fetishism   48
      and food fetishism   107–8
    Lighthousekeeping   15, 114
    Oranges Are Not the Only Fruit   14, 114
      and bodily fetishism   35–7, 48, 73, 76–7
      and sexual fetishism   124, 148
    The Passion   15, 28, 171
      and bodily fetishism   37–40, 45, 58–61, 64–71, 76–7
      and food fetishism   90–7
      and sexual fetishism   127–32, 141–3, 152–7, 161, 166
    The Power Book   16, 24
      and bodily fetishism   30, 41–3, 61–2, 72–4, 77
    Sexing the Cherry   15, 171, 175
      and bodily fetishism   43–5, 48, 72
      and food fetishism   83–9
      and sexual fetishism   147–51
    Why Be Happy When You Could Be Normal?   10–11, 16
    Written on the Body   15, 25, 28, 171
      and bodily fetishism   33–5, 49–58, 71, 76
      and food fetishism   99–107
      and sexual fetishism   124, 132, 135–41, 154–5, 160–6
Winter's Tale, The   2, 12, 16
Woolf, Virginia   17
A Room of One's Own   63
worship   11, 24–5, 170, *see also* religion
  and body   29–31, 34–9, 42, 51, 68–70, 76–7
  and food   108, 110
  and sex   121, 145

Yurchak, Alexei   18

www.ingramcontent.com/pod-product-compliance
Lightning Source LLC
Chambersburg PA
CBHW062225300426
44115CB00012BA/2220